LUDWIG VAN BEETHOVEN

CARL DAHLHAUS

Ludwig van Beethoven
Approaches to his Music

TRANSLATED BY
MARY WHITTALL

CLARENDON PRESS · OXFORD
1991

Oxford University Press, Walton Street, Oxford OX2 6DP
Oxford New York Toronto
Delhi Bombay Calcutta Madras Karachi
Petaling Jaya Singapore Hong Kong Tokyo
Nairobi Dar es Salaam Cape Town
Melbourne Auckland
and associated companies in
Berlin Ibadan

Oxford is a trade mark of Oxford University Press

Published in the United States
by Oxford University Press, New York

German publication © Laaber Verlag 1987
English translation © Oxford University Press 1991

British Library Cataloguing in Publication Data
Dahlhaus, Carl
Ludwig van Beethoven: approaches to his music.
1. German music. Beethoven, Ludwig van, 1770–1827
I. Title
780.92
ISBN 0–19–816148–4

Library of Congress Cataloging in Publication Data
Ludwig van Beethoven: approaches to his music
Carl Dahlhaus; translated by Mary Whittall.
Translation of: Ludwig van Beethoven und seine Zeit.
Includes bibliographical references and indexes.
1. Beethoven, Ludwig van, 1770–1827—Criticism and interpretation.
I. Title.
ML410.B4D213   1991   780'.92—dc20   90–22249
ISBN 0–19–816148–4
72853
Set by Litho Link Limited, Welshpool
Printed in Great Britain by
Courier International Ltd., Tiptree, Essex

Author's Preface

No 'great' biography of Beethoven, fit to stand beside Philipp Spitta's *Bach* and Hermann Abert's *Mozart*, has ever been written. (Thayer's decision not to combine the story of the life with interpretation of the music and portrayal of the musical and historical context disqualified his book, praiseworthy as it was in its way, from inclusion among the 'classic' biographies: those which build up a total picture in which every detail is immersed.) In the study of music, as in the studies of literature and art, the age of the monumental biography came to an end with the First World War, and the book about Beethoven that might have been written around 1900, but was not, will probably never be written now. The result is that the literature about him in smaller formats (smaller both outwardly and inwardly, for the one is more closely associated with the other than the champions of the essay will allow) lacks a centre to which it can refer. To nourish the hope that at some date in the near or distant future a book will be written that will be the summation of the 'contributions' accumulated over decades, and reveal their inner unity, is to dwell in Cloud-cuckoo-land.

But even if it is vain to struggle to extract a meaningful configuration from the steadily growing patchwork that the Beethoven literature presents us with, there is room for a study which, while it does not deny its fragmentary character, sets out positions from which interpretations could take off with the common goal, approached from several different directions, of reconstructing Beethoven's 'musical poetics'. It cannot be a matter of analysing complete works in detail, which would take up more space than is available, but merely of surveying paths capable of leading to an exegesis of the works which is more than merely statistical. The consideration given to the aesthetic theories of the decades on either side of the year 1800, which remain unsurpassed in factual relevance and philosophical insight, is one of the reasons that go some way to justifying the undoubtedly overweening title 'Beethoven and his time'.*

The outlining of possible interpretations—of approaches to individual works or groups of works using both aesthetic and technical commentary—is intended as an attempt to arrive at understanding of Beethoven's musical thinking. It is no exaggeration to say that the metier of composer became, in Beethoven's case, and in a quite special and emphatic sense, a way of thinking about form and structure. The purpose of this book is to clarify the significance of that fact, although the author is conscious that more needs to be written to complete the argument.

The Chronology is not intended as an abbreviated biography but as testimony to the author's conviction, on the one hand, that— whatever the implications of the idea of an imaginary museum of timeless masterpieces—we need a scaffolding of dates and data in order to be able to relate works and events to each other; and on the other hand, that the problems with which the relationship between works of art and biography is fraught are so far from solution that we cannot even venture to say which kinds of facts should be included in a life-story.

It is far from being the author's ambition to compose a 'portrait of Beethoven'. There are certain things that would have to be done first: from analysis of the 'Beethoven myth', which did not come into existence by chance, to precise definition of the relationship between biographical documentation and the reality of the life lived; from investigation of the structural connections between the histories of society, ideas, and music, to clarification of the dialectics of the traditions of musical genres and the character of individual works; and the author does not believe that those conditions could be met by the labour of any one individual.

Translator's note. The translator would like to express her thanks to Stephen Hinton, who was Carl Dahlhaus's associate at the Technische Universität in Berlin for eight years, and has translated some of his work. He has generously shared the fruits of his experience and specialist knowledge.

Even greater thanks are due to Arnold Whittall, who read the draft translation in its entirety, and patiently revised and advised in more instances than can easily be numbered.

---

* The title *Beethoven und seine Zeit* was imposed on the author by the format of the German series in which the book first appeared. When he learned that it was to be translated into English, he expressed the wish for a title on the lines of 'Ludwig van Beethoven: Annäherungen an die musikalischen Werke'. (Translator's note.)

Contents

List of Plates

Between pages 132 and 133

Chronology

1770

17 December: Ludwig van Beethoven baptized in Bonn; the date of his birth was probably 16 December. Until 1790 Beethoven thought he was a year younger than he actually was; later he believed it was two years, and was not easily persuaded of his real age by documentary evidence. It is unclear whether this was due to a mistake or deception on the part of his father, wishing to pass the boy off as a prodigy. His grandfather, also Ludwig van Beethoven (1712–73), was Kapellmeister of the Electoral Court Chapel in Bonn; his father, Johann van Beethoven (c.1740–92), who was Beethoven's first teacher of the violin and piano, was a singer in the Bonn Chapel. Two younger brothers, Caspar Anton Carl and Nikolaus Johann, were born in 1774 and 1776.

The first collected publication of Klopstock's odes. Friedrich Rochlitz recorded a remark of Beethoven's in 1822: 'Are you laughing at something? Aha, at the fact that I have read Klopstock! I carried him about with me for years, on walks and so on.'

1774

Gluck, *Iphigénie en Aulide* (Paris; in Vienna 1808).
Goethe, *Die Leiden des jungen Werthers*.

1776

Declaration of Independence by thirteen North American colonies.

1778

26 March: Beethoven's first public concert.
First edition of Herder's *Volkslieder* (2 vols, 1778–9; the definitive title, *Stimmen der Völker in Liedern*, belongs to the second, posthumous edition of 1807).

1779

Christian Gottlob Neefe arrives in Bonn; his Singspiel *Adelheit von Veltheim* is performed in 1780, and he is appointed organist to the court in 1781. When his tuition of Beethoven began is uncertain.
Gluck, *Iphigénie en Tauride* (Paris).

1781

Reforms introduced by Emperor Joseph II: abolition of serfdom; edict of tolerance towards protestants and Jews; cessation of religious censorship.
Haydn, six String Quartets, Op. 33 (he delivers fair copies on 3 December, having received payment in advance).
Kant, *Kritik der reinen Vernunft*.
Johann Heinrich Voss, German translation of Homer's *Odyssey*. On 8 August 1809 Beethoven wrote to Breitkopf & Härtel, of Goethe and Schiller: 'Those two are my favourite poets, along with Ossian [and] Homer, but the latter two, alas, I can only read in translation.'

1782

Publication of the C minor Variations on a March by Dressler.
Mozart, *Die Entführung aus dem Serail* (Vienna; in Bonn 1783).

1783

Publication of the Piano Sonatas in E flat major, F minor, and D major (the 'Kurfürst' sonatas), composed 1782–3.
Cramer's *Magazin der Musik* for 2 March carries the following announcement by Neefe: 'Louis van Betthoven . . . a lad of 11 years, with a very promising talent. He plays the piano very adeptly and with vigour, reads at sight very well: no more need be said than that above all he plays *Das wohltemperierte Clavier* of Sebastian Bach, at the instigation of Herr Neefe. Those who are acquainted with this collection of preludes and fugues in every key (which might almost be called the *non plus ultra*) will understand what that means. As far as his other activities permit, Herr Neefe has also given him instruction in thoroughbass. At present he is training him in composition, and to encourage him he has had one of his compositions for the piano, 9 variations on a march, engraved in Mannheim. This young genius deserves assistance to allow him to travel. He would certainly become a second Wolfgang Amadeus Mozart, if he progresses as he has begun.'

1784

Grétry, *Richard Coeur-de-Lion* (Paris; in Vienna 1802 and 1810).
Jacques-Louis David, *The Oath of the Horatii*.

1785

Foundation of the University of Bonn, where Beethoven matriculated in 1789.

1786

Antonio Sacchini, *Oedipe à Colone* (Versailles; in Vienna 1802).
Mozart, *Le Nozze di Figaro* (Vienna).

1787

In the spring Beethoven travels to Vienna, and probably meets Mozart; however, he soon has to return to Bonn, as his mother is dying.
Mozart, *Don Giovanni* (Prague).
Antonio Salieri, *Tavare* (Paris; in Vienna 1797).

1788

Count Ferdinand von Waldstein comes to Bonn from Vienna, and makes the acquaintance of Beethoven in the house of the Breuning family. He was later to smooth Beethoven's path in Vienna.
Goethe, *Egmont*.

1789

Fall of the Bastille in Paris. Nothing is known about Beethoven's sympathies for the revolution, although he probably heard the lectures of the revolutionary Eulogius Schneider.
Beethoven, who plays viola in the court orchestra, assumes the role of head of the family because of his father's drunkenness, and collects half of his father's salary in order to support his brothers.

1790

Cantata on the Death of Emperor Joseph II, for soloists, chorus and orchestra; *Cantata on the Elevation of Leopold II to the Imperial Dignity* for soloists, chorus and orchestra.

Mozart, *Così fan tutte* (Vienna).
Johann Georg Albrechtsberger, *Gründliche Anweisung zur Composition*. Albrechtsberger, who handed on the tradition of Fux, taught Beethoven counterpoint 1794–5.
Publication of *Faust, Ein Fragment*, the first form in which Goethe's drama appeared. Beethoven cherished the plan of an opera about Faust for many years.

1791

Mozart, *Die Zauberflöte* (Vienna).
Mozart, Requiem (published 1800).
Luigi Cherubini, *Lodoïska* (Paris; in Vienna 1802). After the death of Haydn, Beethoven considered Cherubini the greatest living composer. He wrote to him in 1823: 'It is with great pleasure that I seize the opportunity to approach you in writing. I have often done so in spirit, for I esteem yours above all other theatrical works. Only, the world of art has good reason to regret that it is a long time since a new theatrical work by you has appeared, at least in our Germany. Highly as true connoisseurs also esteem your other works, it is nevertheless a true loss to art not to possess any new product of your great genius for the theatre.'
Haydn composes his 'London' Symphonies (Nos 93–104) between 1791 and 1795; the first editions, published in Offenbach by André, appeared 1795–1801.

1792

France becomes a republic; some 3,000 royalists perish in the September Massacres.
Franz II succeeds Leopold II as Holy Roman Emperor.
Haydn, stopping in Bonn in July, on his way from London to Vienna, meets Beethoven and accepts him as a pupil. In November Beethoven leaves for Vienna. He never returned to Bonn. In an album of farewell, Count Waldstein writes: 'Through incessant industry, may you receive the spirit of Mozart from the hands of Haydn.'

1793

Execution of Louis XVI and Marie Antoinette.
Six string quartets by Haydn, which really form a single cycle, appear as Opp. 71 and 74.

In 1793–4 Beethoven writes the trios for piano, violin and cello, in E
flat major, G major, and C minor, published as Op. 1 in 1795.
Haydn is said to have advised against the publication of the C minor
trio, and Op. 2, not Op. 1, is dedicated to him.

1794

Robespierre brought down by the 'Thermidoriens'.
Haydn composes the Piano Sonatas in E flat major and C major,
1794–5. Beethoven studies counterpoint with Albrechtsberger during
Haydn's absence on his last visit to London (having already secretly
taken lessons with the Singspiel composer Johann Schenk in 1793, as
he was dissatisfied with Haydn's teaching methods).

1795

29 March: Beethoven probably performs his Second Piano Concerto
in B flat major, Op. 19, at a concert in the Burgtheater.
Chronologically it is his first concerto.
Piano Sonatas in F minor, A major, and C major, Op. 2 (published
1796). They are dedicated to Joseph Haydn.
Schiller, *Briefe über die ästhetische Erziehung des Menschen* and
Über naive und sentimentalische Dichtung.
1795–6: Goethe, *Wilhelm Meisters Lehrjahre*. In 1811 Beethoven
wrote to Therese Malfatti, whom he wanted to marry, and whose
education caused him concern: 'Have you read Goethe's *Wilhelm
Meister*, Schlegel's translation of Shakespeare?'

1796

Concert tour to Prague, Dresden, Leipzig and Berlin. Beethoven
writes the Sonatas in F major and G minor for cello and piano, Op.
5 (published 1797), for Jean Pierre Dupont, cello teacher to King
Friedrich Wilhelm II of Prussia.
Adelaide, Op. 46 (published 1797). The song, or cantata, is dedicated
to its poet, Friedrich von Matthisson, to whom Beethoven wrote on
4 August 1800: 'You should regard the dedication partly as a token of
the pleasure that the composition of your A. gave me, partly as a
token of my gratitude and great respect for the intense pleasure all
your poetry has always given me, and will continue to give me.'
Johann Schenk, *Der Dorfbarbier* (Vienna).
Peter von Winter, *Das unterbrochene Opferfest* (Vienna).
Haydn composes his six late masses between 1796 and 1802.

1797

Peace of Campo Formio between France and Austria. The left bank of the Rhine is ceded to France.
Luigi Cherubini, *Médée* (Paris; in Vienna 1802).
Haydn composes the six String Quartets, Op. 76.

1798

Beethoven starts to use sketchbooks, having previously drafted his music on loose sheets of paper.
1798–9: Piano Sonata in C minor (Sonate pathétique), Op. 13 (published 1799).
1798–1800: String Quartets in F major, G major, D major, C minor, A major, and B flat major, Op. 18 (published 1801). On the basis of the sketches, Gustav Nottebohm reconstructed the order of the composition of four of the works as Nos 3, 1, 2, 5.
The publishers Breitkopf & Härtel launch the *Allgemeine musikalische Zeitung* in Leipzig, with Friedrich Rochlitz as editor. The periodical reviewed Beethoven's work regularly, if not always with approval.

1799

Bonaparte becomes First Consul.
1799–1800: First Symphony in C major, Op. 21 (published 1801).
1799-1800: Septet in E flat major for violin, viola, clarinet, horn, bassoon, cello, and double bass, Op. 20 (published 1802). In a letter to the publisher Franz Anton Hoffmeister of 15 December 1800, Beethoven writes of a 'Septett per il violino, viola, violoncello, contra-Bass, clarinett, corn, fagotto—tutti obligati. (I can't write anything unobbligato, because I came into this world already equipped with an obbligato accompaniment.) This septet has been very well received.'
Étienne Nicolas Méhul, *Ariodant* (Paris; in Vienna, 1804). In 1823 Beethoven wrote to the publisher Moritz Schlesinger: 'Please send me the things by Méhul that you showed me.'
19 March: first performance of Haydn's oratorio *The Creation*, composed 1796–8.
Haydn writes the two String Quartets, Op. 77.

1800

2 April: the First Symphony, Op. 21, and the Septet, Op. 20, receive their first performances at an Academy in the Burgtheater in Vienna. The concert seems to have established Beethoven's reputation with the general public, following his recognition in aristocratic circles.
1800–1: the Sonatas in A minor and F major for piano and violin, Opp. 23 and 24 (first published together in 1801 as Op. 23; the F major Sonata was brought out on its own as Op. 24 only in 1802).
1800–1: music for Salvatore Viganò's ballet *Die Geschöpfe des Prometheus*, Op. 43 (first performance 28 March 1801, in the Burgtheater).
1800–2: Third Piano Concerto in C minor, Op. 37 (published 1804).
Luigi Cherubini, *Les deux journées (Der Wasserträger)* (Paris; in Vienna 1802). According to Julius Benedict, Beethoven's answer to the question 'Which do you think are the best librettos?' was *Les deux journées* and *La vestale*.

1801

The Peace of Lunéville ends the French Revolutionary Wars. France makes a concordat with the Pope.
Beethoven writes of his deafness, the symptoms of which go back three years, in letters to Carl Amenda (1 June) and Franz Gerhard Wegeler (29 June). 'How often I wish that you [Amenda] were with me, for your Beethoven's existence is very unhappy; know that my hearing, the noblest of my faculties, has greatly deteriorated. Already then, when you were still with me, I sensed it and said nothing, now it has just grown worse and worse; whether it can be healed again, still remains to be seen.' 'Sad resignation, in which I must take refuge; I have resolved to rise above it all, but how will that be possible?'
Piano Sonata in C sharp minor (Sonata quasi una fantasia), Op. 27 No. 2 (published 1802). In later years Beethoven said to Carl Czerny: 'People always talk about the C sharp minor Sonata! I have written better things, truly. The F sharp major Sonata is quite a different thing!'
1801–2: the Piano Sonatas in G major, D minor, and E flat major, Op. 31, published in 1803 (Nos 1 and 2) and 1804 (No. 3). With reference to what he intended in Op. 31, Beethoven tells the violinist Wenzel Krumpholz (according to Czerny): 'I am not very satisfied with what I've written to date. From today I intend to enter upon a new path.'
1801–2: Second Symphony, Op. 36 (published 1804).
24 April: first performance of Haydn's oratorio *The Seasons*.

1802

On 6 and 10 October Beethoven writes the so-called Heiligenstadt Testament, in part literally a will in the form of a letter to his brothers, but principally a monologue informed by the most profound melancholy. 'Since the cherished hope—that I brought here with me, of being healed, at least to a certain extent—now must leave me altogether; as the autumn leaves fall, are withered, so—hope too has dried up for me; much as I came here—I leave. —Even the high courage which often cheered me in the fair days of summer—has vanished.—O Providence—let me experience one pure day of joy!'
Fifteen Variations in E flat major with a fugue, for piano, Op. 35 (published 1803). The theme of the variations is one Beethoven used four times: first in No. 7 of the 12 Contredanses for orchestra, then in the Finale of the ballet *Die Geschöpfe des Prometheus*, next in Op. 35, and finally in the last movement of the Third Symphony. He wrote to Breitkopf & Härtel on 18 October 1802, about Opp. 34 and 35: 'I have made two sets of variations, one of which can be reckoned as eight variations, the other thirty. Both of them are worked out in a really wholly new style . . . Each theme is treated individually in them in a manner that is different even from the other set. As a rule I only hear it from others when I have new ideas, and never know it myself. But this time it is I who must assure them that the style in both works is entirely new, and it's mine.'
1802–3: Sonata in A major for piano and violin, Op. 47 (published 1805). It was dedicated to Rodolphe Kreutzer, but he never played it. It was first performed in May 1803 by Beethoven and the violinist George Bridgetower.

1803

Principal Resolution of the Imperial Deputation leads to the secularization of almost all the religious principalities in the 'Holy Roman Empire', and mediatization of over one thousand of the secular ones.
5 April: Academy at which are performed *Christus am Ölberge* (Op. 85, published 1811), the First and Second Symphonies, and the Third Piano Concerto.
August von Kotzebue, *Die deutschen Kleinstädter*, a satirical comedy about small-town snobbery. Shortly after composing his incidental music for Kotzebue's *König Stephan*, Beethoven wrote to him on 28 January 1812: 'I could not suppress the lively wish to have an opera from your unique dramatic genius, whether romantic, wholly

'serious, heroic, comic, sentimental, in short, whatever you cared to write, I would accept it with pleasure. Admittedly, I would prefer most of all a great subject from history, especially from the Dark Ages, e.g. Attila.'

1803–4: Third Symphony in E flat major (Sinfonia eroica), Op. 55 (published 1806).

1803–4: Piano Sonata in C major, Op. 53, dedicated to Count Waldstein (published 1805).

1804

Napoleon crowns himself Emperor of the French in Notre Dame in Paris, in the presence of the Pope.

Ferdinando Paër, *Leonore ossia l'amore coniugale* (Dresden). The opera was not performed in Vienna until 1809, so Beethoven cannot have heard it before he wrote his own *Leonore* (contrary to the anecdote related by Ferdinand Hiller).

1804–5: *Leonore* (first version). The first performance—under the title *Fidelio*, to which Beethoven did not give his approval until 1814—took place on 20 November 1805, shortly after the French occupation of Vienna.

1804–5: Piano Sonata in F minor, Op. 57 (published 1807). The title 'Sonata appassionata' originates with an 1838 edition for piano four hands.

1804–8: Fifth Symphony in C minor, Op. 67 (published 1809).

1805

Admiral Lord Nelson defeats the French fleet at the Battle of Trafalgar. Napoleon wins the Battle of Austerlitz against Austria and Russia. By the Peace of Pressburg Austria loses Venice to the Kingdom of Italy.

1805–6: revision of *Leonore* (first performance 29 March 1806).

1805–6: Fourth Piano Concerto in G major, Op. 58 (published 1808).

1806

Franz II resigns the crown of the Holy Roman Empire.

Fourth Symphony in B flat major, Op. 60 (published 1808).

Violin Concerto in D major, Op. 61 (published 1808).

String Quartets in F major, E minor, and C major, Op. 59 (published 1808).

Luigi Cherubini, *Faniska* (Vienna).
1806–8: publication of *Des Knaben Wunderhorn,* compiled by Achim von Arnim and Clemens Brentano.

1807

Mass in C major for soloists, chorus and orchestra, Op. 86 (published 1812).
Overture to H. J. von Collin's tragedy *Coriolan,* Op. 62 (published 1808).
Étienne Nicolas Méhul, *Joseph* (Paris; in Vienna 1809).
Gaspare Spontini, *La vestale* (Paris; in Vienna 1810). In Beethoven's opinion the text of *La vestale* and that of Cherubini's *Les deux journées* were the two best librettos he knew. In 1825 he told Karl Gottfried Freudenberg: 'Spontini has many good qualities, his understanding of theatrical effect and musical alarums of war is magnificent.'
Hegel, *Phänomenologie des Geistes.*
1807–8: Sixth Symphony in F major (Sinfonia pastorale), Op. 68 (published 1809).
In December Beethoven writes to the management of the Court Theatre in Vienna, offering 'at least one major opera per year', in return for 'a fixed salary of 2,400 florins annually, plus the box-office receipts from the third performance of each such opera'. He appears to have received no reply.

1808

22 December: Concert at which are performed the Fifth and Sixth Symphonies, the Fourth Piano Concerto, sections of the Mass in C major, and the Choral Fantasy, Op. 80; the introduction of this last, for solo piano, was improvised on the night, and not written down until 1809.
Trios in D major and E flat major for piano, violin and cello, Op. 70 (published 1809).
Publication of Part I of Goethe's *Faust.*
1808–9: Francisco Goya, *El Gigante.*
1808–9: Caspar David Friedrich, *Der Mönch am Meer.*

1809

Austrian uprising against Napoleon put down.
Following Beethoven's refusal of the invitation to move to Kassel and

become Kapellmeister to Napoleon's brother Jerome, an agreement dated 1 March guarantees him an annual income of 4,000 florins, to be paid by Archduke Rudolph (fl. 1,500), Prince Lobkowitz (fl. 700) and Prince Kinsky (fl. 1,800). A draft version states: 'It must be the aspiration and goal of every true artist to obtain conditions for himself in which he can be occupied solely with the composition of major works, and is not impeded by other obligations or economic considerations. A composer can therefore have no more lively wish than to devote himself undisturbed to the creation of great works, and then to perform them to the public. In so doing he must also bear his old age in mind, and seek to provide himself with an adequate income.'

Bombardment (11 May) and occupation (from 12 May) of Vienna by the French. Beethoven writes to Breitkopf & Härtel on 26 July: 'What a destructive, barren existence all round me, nothing but drums, cannon, human misery of every kind.'

Fifth Piano Concerto in E flat major, Op. 73 (published 1811).

String Quartet in E flat major, Op. 74 (published 1810).

Joseph Weigl, *Die Schweizerfamilie* (Vienna).

Gaspare Spontini, *Fernand Cortez* (Paris; in Vienna 1812).

1809–10: Piano Sonata in E flat major, Op. 81a ('Das Lebewohl, die Abwesenheit, das Wiedersehn'—'Farewell, Absence, Reunion'). On 9 October 1811 Beethoven wrote to Breitkopf & Härtel: 'I see that you have published some copies with a title in French. Whatever for? "Lebewohl" is something quite different from "les adieux". One says the former from the heart, to one single person, the latter to a whole assembly, whole cities.'

1809–10: Incidental music to Goethe's tragedy *Egmont*, Op. 84. The overture was published 1810, the songs and entr'actes 1812.

1810

String Quartet in F minor, Op. 95 (published 1816).

E. T. A. Hoffmann's review of the Fifth Symphony in the *Allgemeine musikalische Zeitung*.

Johann Friedrich Reichardt's *Vertraute Briefe, geschrieben auf der Reise nach Wien*. Already Reichardt regards the three great classical composers as an entity, and employs a colourful metaphor to characterize them: 'Haydn, who built a summer-house, Mozart, who converted it into a palace, and Beethoven, who erected a high tower on top of it . . .' Beethoven reacts unfavourably: 'What do you say to the scribbling of Reichardt's *Letters*? Of which admittedly I've seen only a few excerpts.'

Zacharias Werner, *Wanda, Königin der Sarmaten*, an early example
of romantic tragedy. Beethoven mentioned that he had seen the play,
in a letter to Archduke Rudolph of 1812, and in 1823 based a plan for
an opera on it.
Germaine de Staël, *De l'Allemagne* (published in German 1814).

1811

The failure of the Austrian State Bank causes a devaluation of the
currency, which leads to a reduction in Beethoven's annual salary
from fl. 4,000 to approximately fl. 1,600. Prince Lobkowitz is
forced to suspend his payments for four years. Moreover, Prince
Kinsky died in 1812; it was only after long negotiations with the
latter's heirs that Beethoven received the sum he thought he was
entitled to.
Trio in B flat major for piano, violin and cello, Op. 97 (published
1816).
1811–12: Seventh Symphony in A major, Op. 92 (published 1816).
Friedrich de la Motte Fouqué, *Undine*. On 6 January 1816 Beethoven
wrote to the singer Anna Milder-Hauptmann: 'If you would ask
Baron de la Motte Fouqué on my behalf to invent a subject for a
large-scale opera, which would also be a suitable vehicle for you, you
would be doing a great service to me and to the theatre of Germany.'

1812

Napoleon's Russian campaign.
6–7 July: Beethoven in Teplitz writes the letter 'to the immortal
beloved', apparently intended for Josephine von Brunswick.
Also in Teplitz, Beethoven meets Goethe, of whom he writes to
Breitkopf & Härtel in a letter of 9 August: 'Goethe enjoys the air at
court too much, more than is proper for a poet. There is not much to
be made of the ways virtuosos make themselves ridiculous here,
when poets, who should be regarded as the first teachers of the
nation, are capable of forgetting everything else for the sake of this
glitter.' On the other hand, he wrote to Goethe in 1823: 'I draw
breath always from your immortal, never ageing works, as from my
youth onwards, and never forget the happy hours spent near you, but
it now comes to pass that I must recall myself to your memory.'
Eighth Symphony in F major, Op. 93 (published 1817).
1812–13: Sonata in G major for piano and violin, Op. 96 (published
1816).

1813

Defeat of Napoleon at the 'Battle of the Nations' outside Leipzig.
Two interpretations have been placed on the fact that the only large-scale work completed by Beethoven in the thirteen months between finishing Op. 96 (autograph dated Feburary 1813) and starting the third version of *Fidelio* (March 1814) was *Wellington's Victory, or The Battle of Vittoria* (Op. 91, published 1816): it has been described as the outcome of a creative block caused by disappointment over the unhappy relationship with 'the immortal beloved', and as marking the end of the 'heroic style' in caricature or petrifaction. But the exegetes cannot make up their minds over whether biographical factors inhibited Beethoven or stimulated him; furthermore, the 'heroic style' reasserted itself triumphantly in 'late' works like the Ninth Symphony, and the C minor Sonata, Op. 111.
8 and 12 December: the Seventh Symphony and *Wellington's Victory* are performed at exceptionally successful academies.
Foundation of the Philharmonic Society in London. Beethoven, who admired England's musical institutions as much as he did her political ones, wrote to Ferdinand Ries in 1822: 'If I was in London, what would I not write for the Philharmonic Society! For Beethoven can write, thank God!—though there's nothing else in the world he can do.'
Gioacchino Rossini, *Tancredi* and *L'Italiana in Algeri* (both Venice; in Vienna 1816 and 1817 respectively).

1814

Congress of Vienna.
Fidelio, Op. 72 (third version). First performance on 23 May.
29 November: Academy in the Redoutensaal, with the Seventh Symphony, *Wellington's Victory*, and *Der glorreiche Augenblick*, Op. 136. A police report of 30 November states: 'Yesterday's event was not such as to increase enthusiasm for the talent of this composer, who has his adherents and his detractors. Against the faction of his admirers, which is led by Rasumowsky, Apponyi, Kraft, etc., who worship Beethoven, there is growing up an overwhelming majority of connoisseurs who unconditionally refuse to listen to his works any more.'
Franz Schubert, *Gretchen am Spinnrade* (published 1821 as Op. 2).
Walter Scott, *Waverley*. Beethoven was an avid reader of Scott.

1815

Napoleon's return from Elba and defeat at Waterloo. Russia, Austria, and Prussia form the 'Holy Alliance'. Venice and Lombardy are returned to Austria.

9 November: Death of Beethoven's brother Caspar Carl, which makes the composer guardian, together with his sister-in-law Johanna, of his nine-year-old nephew Carl. The joint guardianship gives rise to embittered, acrimonious disagreements, leading on several occasions to litigation, and weighing heavily for many years on Beethoven, who looked on himself as his nephew's second father.

Sonatas in C major and D major for piano and cello, Op. 102 (published 1817).

Amadeus Wendt: 'Gedanken über die neuere Tonkunst und van Beethovens Musik, namentlich *Fidelio*', in the *Allgemeine musikalische Zeitung*.

3 December: First concert of the Gesellschaft der Musikfreunde in Vienna. Beethoven's symphonies became virtually regular items in the Gesellschaft's programmes from 1816 onwards.

1816

Song cycle *An die ferne Geliebte*, Op. 98 (published in the same year).

Piano Sonata in A major, Op. 101 (published 1817).

Rossini, *Il barbiere di Siviglia* (Rome), and *Otello* (Naples; both in Vienna 1819). In 1824 Beethoven said to Johann Andreas Stumpff: 'Rossini and his like: those are your heroes now. They want nothing more from me.' A year later he was more restrained in an utterance to Karl Gottlieb Freudenberg: 'Rossini was idolized at that time, and I expected Beethoven to say something derisive about him. Far from it: he said that Rossini was a talented and melodious composer, and his music was attuned to the frivolous, sensuous spirit of the times.'

Cherubini, Requiem in C minor.

E. T. A. Hoffmann, *Undine*, Berlin.

Louis Spohr, *Faust* (Prague; in Vienna 1818). Spohr was Kapellmeister at the Theater an der Wien, 1812–15. According to Freudenberg, Beethoven remarked in 1825 that Spohr was too dissonant, and pleasure in his music was diminished by his chromaticism.

1817

Muzio Clementi, *Gradus ad Parnassum*.
Franz Grillparzer, *Die Ahnfrau*.
1817–18 Piano Sonata in B flat major, Op. 106 (published 1819).
Beethoven wrote to Ferdinand Ries in London on 19 April 1819:
'Should the sonata not be right for London, I could send another, or
you could leave out the Largo and start the last movement directly
with the Fugue, or first movement, Adagio, Scherzo third, and Largo
and Allegro rissoluto. I leave it to you, as you think best. The Sonata
was written under pressure, for it is hard to have to write for one's
bread: that's the position I'm in now!' Beethoven had written no
large-scale works for a year before he started the 'Hammerklavier'
Sonata at the end of 1817, but we cannot speak of an interruption or
period of silence preceding the transition to the late style, treating it
as a dramatic event, because there is no justification for excluding the
Cello Sonatas, Op. 102 (1815), or the Piano Sonata, Op. 101 (1816),
from the category of late works. It is completely wrong to look upon
the four and a half years from February 1813 (date on the autograph
of Op. 96) to the end of 1817 as a 'dead period', separating the
'middle period' from the 'late', and possessing a biographical
foundation, first, in the disturbances of the year 1812, and, later, in
the inner and outer conflicts arising round the composer's nephew.
There were some interruptions, but the years 1814–16 as a whole
were not unproductive.

1818

In February Beethoven begins to keep conversation books, in which
his companions can write down their part of their talk with him.
There were eventually approximately 400 of the books, but about
two-thirds of them were destroyed by Anton Schindler.
Beethoven hails the invention of the metronome by Johann
Nepomuk Mälzel in an enthusiastic public statement, having used the
instrument to fix the tempos of his eight symphonies as early as 1817.
He distinguishes between tempo marks, which can be replaced by
metronome numbers, and descriptive directions, for which he
advocates the continued use of words. He writes to Ignaz von Mosel:
'As for these four principal directions, which are nowhere near as
true or accurate as the four winds, we are glad to be shot of them; the
words signifying the character of the movement are a different

matter, we cannot do without them, as the tempo is really rather like the body, but the latter bear some relation to the spirit of the piece.'
Théodore Géricault, *The Raft of the Medusa*.

1819

Murder of Kotzebue, thought to be a Russian agent. Carlsbad Decrees: tightening of censorship, and of police powers to supervise public life in Austria. Beethoven, who was liable to pass extremist comments in public, is tolerated as an eccentric.
Goethe, *West-östlicher Divan*.
1819–23: *Missa solemnis* in D major, Op. 123 (published 1827). The work was intended for Archduke Rudolph's enthronement as Archbishop of Olomouc, but was not ready in time. It was given at concerts, but as the censors did not permit the performance of the mass in a secular context it was done under the title 'Oratorio' or 'Hymns'.
1819–23: 33 Variations on a Waltz by Anton Diabelli for piano, Op. 120 (published 1823).
1819–23: E. T. A. Hoffmann, *Die Serapionsbrüder*. (This collection of Hoffmann's writings includes a reprint of the review of the Fifth Symphony, but without the analytical section.)

1820

The Vienna Final Acts revoke the promise of a constitution, made in 1815.
Franz Xaver Gebauer establishes the Viennese Concerts spirituels, in which he often included works by Beethoven.
Piano Sonata in E major, Op. 109.

1821

Greek War of Independence against the Turks (till 1829).
1821–2: Piano Sonata in A flat major, Op. 110, and Piano Sonata in C minor, Op. 111 (both published 1822).
Weber, *Der Freischütz* (Berlin; Vienna in the same year). According to Weber's son Max Maria (who is not always reliable), Beethoven commented: 'I would never have thought it of him! Now Weber must write operas, nothing but operas, one after another, without chewing them over too much!'

1822

Grillparzer, *Das goldene Vließ*.

1822–4: Ninth Symphony in D minor, concluding with a choral setting of Schiller's ode *An die Freude*, Op. 125 (published 1826).

1822–5: String Quartet in E flat major, Op. 127 (published 1826). It was probably started in the spring of 1822, but the decisive impulse took the form of a commission from Prince Nikolai Galitzin of St Petersburg, who asked Beethoven for 'one, two or three new quartets' in November.

1823

Weber, *Euryanthe* (Vienna). According to Czerny, Beethoven remarked, after leafing through the score, 'Weber took too much trouble over this.'

Schubert, *Die schöne Müllerin*, Op. 25 (published 1824).

1824

7 May: Academy in the Kärntnertortheater—the first since 1814. The programme includes Op. 124, the Kyrie, Credo, and Agnus Dei from the *Missa solemnis* (under the title 'Hymnen'), and the Ninth Symphony.

Adolf Bernhard Marx, 'Etwas über die Symphonie und Beethovens Leistungen in diesem Fache', in the *Berliner allgemeine musikalische Zeitung*.

1824–8: Carl Friedrich Schinkel builds the Altes Museum in Berlin.

1825

A complete edition of Beethoven's works is planned. He writes to Bernhard Schott on 22 January: 'Schlesinger also proposed to publish all my quartets, and have a new one from me periodically, and pay whatever I wanted. But as this could have damaged my purpose of an edition by me of all my works, I left it unanswered. On this occasion you could well think it over, because it would be better for it to be done by me than after my death.'

String Quartet in A minor, Op. 132 (published 1827).

String Quartet in B flat major, Op. 130 (originally with the *Große Fuge*, Op. 133, as its last movement; the new Finale was composed in 1826; published 1827).

1826

String Quartet in F major, Op. 135 (published 1827).
30 July: Attempted suicide of Beethoven's nephew Carl.
James Fenimore Cooper, *The Last of the Mohicans.*

1827

26 March: Beethoven's death. The funeral on 29 March was a public
event, attended by about 10,000 people. Little as the late works were
understood, Beethoven was a myth in his own lifetime, and his fame
was immense. The funeral oration was written by Grillparzer.

I

Life and Work

1. The Biographical Method

The image of Beethoven that survives in the mind of posterity is a diffuse compilation of impressions emanating from the music and biographical fragments that consist to a great extent of legends and anecdotes. Indeed, the relationship between the works and the life appears all the closer if we place our faith in the revelatory power of anecdotes in which the truth is more symbolic than empirical, instead of relying on documentary testimony that stands up to historical criticism. There is very little documentary evidence for the celebrated scene in Teplitz, in which Beethoven assumes the role of the truculent republican, but any attempt to expunge it from the mind of the concert-going public would be wasted, for it is nothing less than the image that complements the musical gesture of the Fifth Symphony. It persists, in spite of the critical battering it has received, because it testifies to an aesthetic, if not historical, truth.

But the possibility of tangibly linking the work and the life dwindles in direct proportion to the extent to which the impressions based on legend and anecdote are corrected by historical criticism. While the significance of an anecdote lies in the—sometimes deceptive—light it throws on the inner connection between life and work, as a general rule the only role for a confirmed historical fact is to serve as one more component in a biographical narrative that runs along beside the interpretation of the work without making any important intervention in it. Scholarly exactitude, in biography on the one hand and analysis of the music on the other, leads to an almost insuperable separation of the two fields. It is a commonplace, on the face of it, that a composer's biography needs to be written in order to shed light on his work, but it is ceasing to be self-evident.

So it is not by mere chance that the craft of scholarly biography has long been neglected—for so long, in fact, that it is difficult to bring to mind the problems to which it was thought to be the solution, in the days when it was regarded as the most demanding form of writing about the creative arts.

Few would question that a biography as such can be interesting and worth writing, regardless of whether the subject is a composer, a politician, or an explorer, and even of whether the life in question is a remarkable one or not, but that consideration is only peripheral to the problem of biographical method in the scholarly study of the arts and artists. The problem does not touch books written out of a simple interest in a poet or a composer as a person, without any ambition to illuminate the works. Even then, however, it is rare for the author not to indulge in the practice of treating literary or musical works as biographical documents, inferring biographical factors from the works, and, vice versa, discovering in the works reflections of biographical elements that can be confirmed from documentary testimony. If a biographer interprets a work of art as a document — that is, draws biographical conclusions from the ideas and expressive traits that he thinks he finds in it — then he is likely, willy-nilly, to reverse the process and use biographical evidence to 'prove' the ideas and expressive traits in the works: that is, to read into them a programme drawn from the composer's biography.

From the truism that a work of art is a document about a composer, in so far as it tells something about his power of imagination, the biographer proceeds to the questionable hypothesis that the expressive elements contained in it are reflections of the life. And the biography that is written as a result of this is made up of an 'exterior' reconstructed from documents, and an 'interior' discovered in the works.

Undeniably, biographical investigation can be useful and even indispensable to the interpretation of works of art. Some details may simply be incomprehensible without reference to biographical information; some aspects of the genesis of a work frequently turn out to be aesthetically part of the subject-matter of the work itself, and therefore need to be known about. And while the principle that comprehension of a work must be from within has become a commonplace of art history, as a matter of historical fact it has very rarely been postulated that the internal functional coherence of a work must be relentlessly consistent and complete, and still more rarely has the postulate been fulfilled. So there is no justification for bringing a charge of aesthetic dereliction in those cases where it proves impossible to avoid the recourse to biography, or the history of the work's genesis, even if the principle of immanence suffers. The idea of a hermetically insulated, entirely self-referential existence for a work is the basis of the arguments against biographical procedures, but it is only a rule with a limited historical authority, not an immutable natural law of art: the relative legitimacy or illegitimacy of the biographical method depends partly on the nearness or remoteness of a work from classicist aesthetics. Epochs and genres of an 'objective' bent, such as classicism and drama in closed forms, are less accessible to biographical interpretation than those that can be called 'subjective', such as romanticism, and the lyric poetry of personal experience.

The indisputable usefulness that biography can have for casting light on details—such as the title and the dedication of Beethoven's Piano Sonata, Op. 81*a*, 'Les Adieux'—is, however, purely a peripheral factor, and bears only indirectly on the central premisses of a style of biography that can claim to be a scholarly discipline. It is a question of relating the totality of an oeuvre to the totality of a life, not their details alone. The ambitious, monumental style of biography practised in the late nineteenth and early twentieth centuries—from Spitta's *Bach* to Abert's *Mozart*—was based on no less a principle than that a musical oeuvre had to be interpreted as a 'life's work' if it was to be understood from within: as a work, that is, that expressed the substance of the life out of which it had proceeded.

It is uncertain whether it is possible to speak of the totality of an oeuvre at all without relating it to that of a life. It is difficult to make plausible the idea that an oeuvre exists in itself, as a 'whole', independently of its author. As a rule it is the 'minor' works whose position in the total oeuvre is hard to establish without recourse to biography: Beethoven's dances and song arrangements, as well as a large number of the piano variations, drop out of the oeuvre in the emphatic sense of the word, for the conception of that oeuvre is distilled from the symphonies, the string quartets, and the sonatas.

But if the minor works make recourse to biography necessary, and specifically to its empirically understood socio-historical aspects, the acknowledgement of a canon of major works presents the risk of succumbing to the mythologizing style of biography. If we apostrophize the Third, Fifth, Seventh, and Ninth Symphonies as the 'real' or 'essential' expressions of Beethoven's symphonic style, then—without necessarily asserting that the 'Pastoral' Symphony is inferior to the Fifth—we adumbrate a 'myth' of Beethoven as the representative of a 'heroic' style.

The 'life's work' school of biography had an empirical enthusiasm for comprehensiveness that was inspired aesthetically, by the ambition to elucidate and illuminate the work. While on the one hand there was in it an element of Dilthey's '*Lebensphilosophie*' (the hypothesis that a work of art is an expression of an element in the artist's life),[1] on the other hand there is no mistaking its connection with historicism—with the proposition that art is 'historical through and through'. As a sub-species of historical method, biographical method proceeds from the premiss that comprehension from within must always be genetic comprehension: in other words, if we are really to grasp the nature of a thing, we must discover the origins from which it issued. The genetic process sets about the task of uncovering the meaning of a text—whether musical or literary—by re-creating the whole process of the genesis of that text. The conceptual premiss behind it is Aristotle's distinction between *ergon* and *energeia*: interpretation of a work, as Dilthey understands it, consists in translating the *ergon*—the completed object—back into the *energeia* that brought it forth. Recognition—including aesthetic recognition—of the essence of the work is sought in the reconstruction of its genesis, and the genesis is subjected to psychological-cum-biographical interpretation.

There is an obvious objection, namely that a distinction must be made between the genesis of a work, which is amenable to biography, and its aesthetic quality, which is amenable to analysis. The conceptual coherence, the 'objectified spirit' of the work, with which analysis is concerned, does not coincide with the process of the work's genesis. It is the matter of phenomenological, rather than psychological, investigation. And the difference between the conceptual coherence of a work of art and its genesis gains in cogency if it is recognized as being reminiscent of the distinction between the context in which scholarly propositions are discovered, and the context in which they are proved. To the extent that the latter is a construction, so too is aesthetic coherence. Admittedly, for the coherence of a work of art to be testable, it can sustain only so much possible falsification by empirical data—the structural analogy is not perfect. The criterion of the validity of an interpretation consists rather in the degree of consistency that it is able to demonstrate between the elements of a musical work.

Distinguishing between the biographical circumstances of a work's genesis and its aesthetic quality diminishes the pre-eminence of the genetic method, but does not destroy it altogether. It is 'saved' by turning from the biographical subject (the composer as an individual) and focusing on an aesthetic 'subject', discovered in the work itself. The processual element is decisive in the genetic approach, which interprets a musical work as a formal process, 'behind' which an

[1] See C. Dahlhaus, *Grundlagen der Musikgeschichte* (Cologne, 1977), 132 f.; *Foundations of Music History*, trans. J. B. Robinson (Cambridge, 1983), 80 f.

active expressive subject is perceived to stand. Imagined as one who sustains the musical process, this 'subject' forms part of the aesthetic experience, not an extraneous addition to it; it takes the place of the empirical individual—the composer—who can be reconstructed from the biographical documents, and it exists in this one work, this one aesthetic object, and nowhere else.

Some of the objections raised against the psychological-cum-biographical method are so trivial that they do not impinge on the process they are intended to destroy. Accusing biography of the psychological naïvety of interpreting musical expressivity merely as a portrayal of the composer's emotions is a polemical feint. Hardly ever has a biographer worth his salt failed to recognize that a work of art is as likely to serve to mask some biographical element as to be its direct expression, or that it may represent the dream with which the artist held reality at bay, rather than the reality as he experienced it.

It is true that the possibility of alternating between the interpretation of art as 'direct portrayal' and as 'shielding dream' hinders every attempt to disprove psychological-cum-biographical explanations. To speak sometimes of the aesthetic 'reflection' of reality, and sometimes of the delineation of an aesthetic 'alternative world', is comparable, as methodology, to 'immunization strategy'. But immunization against the possibility of refutation effectively disallows an interpretation's claims to 'scholarship' or 'scientific method'—according, at least, to the criteria of Karl Popper.[2]

Moreover, there scarcely seems to be any alternative theoretical foundation for the 'reflection' of a life in musical works other than Georg Lukács's theory of a 'mimesis of mimesis'.[3] According to that, the musical work is an expression of feelings that are for their part a mode of appropriating the substance of events in a given milieu. Admittedly, Lukács underestimates the contribution made by musical modes of thought, the philosophical implications of which establish another kind of contemporaneity than the one illustrated in the fact that Beethoven's 'heroic' works are a manifestation of the spirit of the age of revolution that continued into the Napoleonic age.

The charge of psychological naïvety has been levelled against the entire genre of biography on the strength of a few unsuccessful examples, but it is less powerful as an argument against the biographical-cum-psychological method than the observation that we only start to look for the psychological motivation for a text when direct access to its content of fact and truth is barred—that is, when a passage in the text contradicts the context, the author's supposed

[2] *Logik der Forschung* (Tübingen, [2]1966); *The Logic of Scientific Discovery* (London, [3]1972).
[3] A. Riethmüller, *Die Musik als Abbild der Realität* (Wiesbaden, 1976), 84 ff.

intention, or the reader's unquestioned convictions. The reception of music, too, is affected, though to a somewhat slighter degree, by the everyday experience that it is only when the logic of an argument ceases to be plausible that one feels compelled to search for the psychological reasons why an author expresses himself in an unexpected fashion. August Halm could not understand the reason for the recitative in Beethoven's D minor Sonata, Op. 31 No. 2, and the difficulty made him hesitate in his polemic against Paul Bekker's psychological and programmatic interpretation, lose faith for a moment in his fundamental aesthetic convictions, and experience the temptation to substitute psychology for phenomenology.[4] In other words, psychology is something to fall back on when aesthetic communication fails or is interrupted.

The unexpected—the departure from the customary and the immediately obvious—is, however, precisely an element in the aesthetic substance of techniques that make emphatic aesthetic claims, at any rate in Europe since the Enlightenment and especially in the nineteenth century. To the extent that, as the Russian formalists claim, the function of artistic media is to break down conventions, and 'alienate' and disturb 'automatized perceptions', any irritation in the direct comprehension of a text—any factor, that is, that provokes a search for psychological motives—is adumbrated in the principles of the artistic technique: that is, its motives are in the text and not in the person of the author.

The insertion of a recitative in the recapitulation of the first movement of the D minor Sonata, Op. 31 No. 2, bewildered Halm, and almost drove him to concede something to the 'aesthetics of content', but a formal explanation of the interpolation is perfectly possible if it is accepted that the rupturing of conventions is a structural principle that need not necessarily be motivated by non-musical considerations. The first subject (bar 21) is a variant of the arpeggiated triad, seemingly an introductory flourish, with which the sonata begins (bar 1). The development undergone by the first subject leads, rather uncommonly, to its dissolution: the development (bar 99) reproduces the exposition (bar 21) motivically, but with harmonic changes involving a chromatic sequence; in the recapitulation (bar 159) the chromatic sequence is all that remains of the first subject— the melodic motive has vanished. Logical as the formal process thus appears to be, it is unconventional. But as the first subject dissolves, its precursor, the arpeggiated triad, asserts itself as a theme in its own right; and the problematic recitative (bar 143), which appears to be an

⁴ A. Halm. *Von zwei Kulturen der Musik* (Stuttgart, ³1947), 65.

intruder in the sonata-form structure, is nothing other than an explicit formulation or explication of the fact that the arpeggiated triad represents the first subject in its primary form, and is capable of being 'expressive' in itself, and not merely in the form eventually taken by the 'real' first subject (bar 21). A formal explanation of the recitative does not exclude psychological-cum-biographical exegesis, but it means that it is no longer the only recourse.

One of the justifications for the existence of a biographical literature that addresses itself to the general listening public and aspires to the dissemination of wider musical understanding undoubtedly lies in the impression of foreignness and unapproachability that emanates from esoteric musical works, whether of the present day or of the past. Because the music itself, the coherent organization of pitches, does not yield direct enlightenment, people turn to the composer's biography for information, in the belief that the work contains his 'confession'. Hermeneutical efforts—including the attempt to gain aesthetic access by way of the biographical by-road—begin, as a rule, when what a text expresses is not self-explanatory. (Historians and theorists, unlike the lay public, frequently adopt the sceptical principle that on first acquaintance misunderstanding is what is to be expected, rather than insight, and therefore that even where the layman believes he has grasped something without difficulty there is good reason to suspect that the all too easy assimilation is itself a distortion of meaning.)

Biography transmits a feeling of personal closeness to a creative artist, and that in turn makes an initially recalcitrant work seem more accessible; but the feeling is deceptive. For history as an academic discipline that relies on documented evidence seldom redeems the promise made—explicitly or tacitly—by history as popular literature. A style of writing history that attempts to depict a segment of the past 'as it really was' does not bring people or their works 'closer', as popular literature claims for biography, but quite the reverse: it pushes them further away. In broad terms, the more comprehensive the knowledge of history that one possesses, and the more obstinately one pursues the search for the premises on which the past rested when it was still the present, the harder to understand, and the more foreign it becomes. So the lost immediacy of aesthetic response to music of the past that seems remote is not to be recovered by means of biographical immediacy, for that proves an illusion as soon as one passes from the naïve re-imagination of the past to the writing of authentic history.

A second premiss of biographical interest lies in the inescapable impression that at the heart of musical works—those of the late eighteenth and the nineteenth centuries, at all events—there is a 'subject who speaks', someone analogous to the 'narrator' of a novel or the 'lyrical first person' of a poem. Indeed, purist theories of literature regard a narrator or a lyrical first person as a necessary element in the 'objective' aesthetic substance. The word 'objective' is used in the sense of pertaining to the 'object'—colloquially the 'subject'—of the theorist's study. Yet 'he' is an element in the work itself only in so far as 'he' does *not* coincide with the empirical individual who is the creative artist, the object of biographical interest. That it is wrong to identify the aesthetic 'subject who speaks' in a piece of music, whose expression the musical process purports to be, with the composer, the empirical person amenable to reconstruction from the documentary evidence, has been a commonplace of aesthetic theory for several decades, unquestioned even by those who go directly against it in biographical practice.

On the other hand, it is far from supererogatory to trace the tortuous relationships that exist between the aesthetic 'subject who speaks' in musical works, and the empirical individual who is their author. Necessary as the distinction is, it should not be forced further than it will go. The bald assertion that a biography concerns itself with the empirical individual, and nothing else, falls short of the truth, at all events. At the same time, every attempt to abstract an 'inner biography' from the works runs the risk of the kind of speculation that takes off into the realm of fiction: instead of sticking to the empirical individual who can be reconstructed from the documentary evidence, the biographer will argue that this is the way to do justice to the 'intelligible' person who 'speaks' in the work.

The biographical novel, using intuition to make up for the deficiencies of fact, is a hybrid genre, despised by novelists as much as by scholarly biographers. But in order to understand the success that is achieved time and again by this method of constructing a life-story out of the study of an oeuvre, it is necessary to go beyond the mere demonstration of one's contempt for the general public, and understand that the biographical novel represents the distortion of an ambition that, in itself, deserves to be taken seriously. However wide of the mark the solution it provides may be, it addresses a genuine problem.

The problematic genre rests on the foundation of a depressing experience known to every biographer. This is the recognition that the image of, say, Beethoven that can be pieced together from authentic testimonies that stand up to methodical evaluation of the sources does not suffice even to half-explain the genesis of the oeuvre that has come down to us with Beethoven's name on it. The pale outline of an empirical individual that steps forward from the documents and the 'intelligible speaking subject' that stands 'behind' the musical oeuvre seem to be radically different beings. And as soon as a biographer moves on from the depiction of a man whose life-story and character are outlined in fragmentary testimonies to that of the composer who stands revealed to the listening public as the creator of a monumental oeuvre, he is forced to construct intuitively instead of confining himself to what is transmitted in the attested evidence. It seems, however deceptively, as if the 'essence' will be revealed only in the work of fiction that the scholarly biographer must deny himself.

The reconstruction of a composer from his oeuvre is a fundamentally different business from that of reconstructing John Citizen's life from an archive of documents. Biography that relies on the documentary evidence is subject to laws concerning the evaluation of sources, and those laws are very different from the procedures of interpreting an oeuvre. It is the latter, however, that must govern the reconstruction of an 'inner biography' as soon as it attempts to escape sheer speculation, in which intuitions of the substance and meaning of works transform themselves into fantasies about biographical elements. But aesthetic criticism cannot be regulated as strictly as the historical variety. Instead, in the biography of a composer, the procedure whereby one hopes to reconstruct the 'intelligible speaking subject' is dependent to no small degree on the aesthetic theory the biographer favours. An adherent of the 'aesthetics of content' who regards the works of a composer as 'fragments of a great confession' necessarily inclines towards a different kind of biography from a formalist, whose conception of the genesis of works of art follows the pattern set out in Edgar Allan Poe's *Principles of Criticism*. A formalist scarcely ever comes into conflict with biographical documents, because he starts from the premiss that works of art are generated in a sphere that is psychologically separate from everyday existence. An adherent of the aesthetics of content, on the other hand, is constantly obliged to make biographical interpolations for which there is little support in the purely musical evidence. Yet that should not be allowed to conceal the fact that the former's image of the composer rests every bit as firmly on a construction as the latter's. For one thing, it is impossible as a rule to establish the extent to which elements of real life intrude into the imagination of musical expressive characters. For another thing, the conflict between formalism and the aesthetics of content is primarily a question of principles, not facts, and specifically whether a biographical factor that may impinge on a composer's musical intuition should or should not be regarded aesthetically as 'essential'.

2. Inner form and external intention

The biographer intent on linking a life and an oeuvre will go astray if he does not take to heart the fact that the substance of individual works and elements of the life are not to be coupled together by taking a firm hold on each, and directly aligning them. Both musical texts and biographical documents need interpretation, if the facts that are called 'work' and 'life' respectively are even to become visible. Leger lines and notes no more fully represent the reality of the music than the contents of a deed box do that of the life.

The interpretation of historical evidence resembles a judicial process in which the truth must be deduced from what the witnesses say, according to rules that can sometimes seem artificial in the extreme. The 'facts', strictly speaking, are hypotheses, the empirical material of which forms statements that may be deceptive. In the same way, the aesthetic interpretation of a work of art is 'hypothetical' in a certain sense: the shaping of motives may not be written out 'in the notes', yet the notes do not take on musical meaning unless the shape is assumed; the probability of such an assumption is proved if its consequences for the syntax and the formal processes of the music create functional coherence. (In aesthetics as in textual study the logical soundness of assumptions is an important criterion of their objective sufficiency.)

The attempt to associate specific works with specific, biographically tangible elements of the life shows time and again that a connection that looks plausible as long as it is left to a vague suggestion proves to be dubious and fraught with more guesswork than is desirable as soon as any attempt is made to be precise about it: one of the drawbacks of the biographical method is the fact that the accumulation of detail usually weakens the evidence. Illuminating as it may be in broad terms to declare that Beethoven's works are 'fragments of a great confession' (as Goethe said of his own oeuvre), the objections that appear the moment one begins to decipher the 'encoded message' word by word are virtually insuperable.

The Andante in F major ('Andante favori', WoO 57), originally intended to be the middle movement of the 'Waldstein' Sonata, was secretly dedicated to Josephine von Brunswick, the 'immortal

beloved'. Beethoven sent it to her with the inscription 'Here—
Your—Your—Andante'.[5] The emphasis positively provokes
speculation. Romain Rolland's hypothesis[6] that the movement was
separated from the sonata because of its all too private significance—which no outsider could have suspected, however—is,
methodologically speaking, as problematic as it is typical:
problematic, because the biographical explanation does not hold
water, and because there is a better aesthetic one; typical, because the
involuntary tendency to ascribe a biographical motive to a
compositional decision made it harder, and indeed self-evidently
unnecessary, to search for a reason lying within the music itself—and
yet such a search would not have been fruitless.

Beethoven sent the Andante in F to the printer in 1805, only a year
after the secret dedication, so that it is not plausible to call it a private
document that had to be kept from public gaze because of its personal
significance. In any case, for all its emphasis, the dedication does not
constitute sufficiently certain evidence that the Andante was
composed with Josephine von Brunswick in mind: it may have had
some other private connotation, or—the most banal of the
possibilities—she may simply have had an especial liking for it.
Musically, there is nothing too bizarre about the idea that Beethoven
may have been thinking of her when he wrote the piece: it is a
'character piece' with a high degree of refinement in its
characterization, and as such may very well be interpreted as a
musical portrait—but what is portrayed is a general nobility of
character, not that of one particular person. (The essence of the piece
does not lie in the grazioso theme in isolation, but in the difficulty of
sustaining the grazioso character during the virtuoso progressions of
thirds, sixths, and octaves.)

If the biographical interpretation is thus shown to be too vague, on
the other hand it is interesting to observe that the composer's decision
to replace the 'Andante favori' in the 'Waldstein' Sonata with the
introduction to the Finale can be explained aesthetically, without
recourse to biography. It looks as if Beethoven felt that the
immediate juxtaposition, in the original version of the sonata, of two
rondo movements, both with a lyrical theme, virtuoso pretensions,
and substantial dimensions, was not a very good idea, and therefore
removed the 'Andante favori', which could stand on its own.
Moreover, the slow section he replaced it with develops out of a tonal

    [5] M. E. Tellenbach, *Beethoven und seine 'unsterbliche Geliebte' Josephine Brunswick*
(Zurich, 1983), 207.
    [6] *Beethoven: Les grandes époques créatrices* (Paris, 1966), 133.

construction—the descending chromatic tetrachord—that already provides the foundation of the principal subject of the first movement; this formal idea of linking the new section to the first movement by its musical material, and to the main part of the Finale by its function, was so striking that Beethoven probably needed no further encouragement to jettison the 'Andante favori' in its favour.

The above argument rests on the methodological maxim that in doubtful cases aesthetic motives should be awarded precedence over biographical ones, but it is not an absolute. (Cases where sufficient documentary evidence exists demonstrate that sometimes one element predominates, and sometimes the other.) The tendency of some disciplines to demonstrate 'self-sufficiency' by preferring 'internal' explanations to 'external' ones rests on weak theoretical foundations. Yet it is not purely wilful to assert the primacy of aesthetic considerations. The decision to remove one of the three movements from a cyclic work is a serious one, and refusing to allow such a decision to be dictated by external factors is to some extent a matter of artistic morality. And unless the documentary evidence leaves him with no alternative, a historian does not have any right to assume that a composer has offended against the principle of aesthetic autarky, in a piece that is a 'work' in an emphatic sense and not just a *pièce d'occasion*.

The ideas and the expressive content of a work of art may no more be 'assumed' without aesthetic interpretation than the factual content of a biographical document may be, without historical evaluation and textual analysis. (Evidence that allows the aesthetic or the historical reality to emerge directly is not necessarily ruled out; but it is naïve to predicate it as if it was a rule and not an exception.) But even if 'facts' are always the product of interpretation, there is still not the slightest reason to relax the standards that should always apply to the interpretation of a musical work at a time when the ideas and the expressive content are being discussed with reference to a general historical context, rather than to the work itself in its isolated, aesthetic existence.

It is permissible and even legitimate to use a work of art as a document in the writing of a biography, a history of ideas, or social history, to the extent that every branch of scholarship can act as an ancillary to another. (History frequently serves as an ancillary to textual analysis and vice versa.) But although using a work of art for any of those purposes is not the the same thing as claiming to have explored the aesthetic 'essence' of the work in question, the methodological principles that apply to adequate interpretation of the work are not abrogated. It is never justified to speak of the work's expressive content in a superficial or unconsidered way, on the grounds that it is 'only' a matter of illustrating social history or the history of ideas, not of interpretation of the work. When interpretation of works of art is employed in the role of an ancillary to history or biography, methodological standards remain as relevant as ever.

Historians who regard the *Egmont* Overture as a document with significance in both biography and the history of ideas, generally do so on the grounds that the conclusion, the 'Victory Symphony', is the expression of a 'concrete Utopia' (Ernst Bloch), with which Beethoven identified. But it is too reductionist an interpretation to sustain much weight, and the emphasizing of the end—as if it was an 'outcome'—is a fundamentally inadequate response to the structure of a drama, and to that of a piece of music that holds a mirror up to a drama. The teleological 'temporal form' of the tragedy, hurtling towards its catastrophe, should not be allowed to conceal the fact that—exactly as in Beethoven's overture—the goal-directed process produces a structure with an inner order that is more than merely the logic of the order of events, in which everything is eventually subsumed in something else. Ideas and characters work beside and against each other, and the 'meaning' of this does not consist simply in the resolution of the conflicts that are expounded in the drama. The decisive thing is that the separate standpoints that are expounded and developed relativize each other, so that a paradoxical structure takes shape, coloured by irony and balanced on a knife-edge, a structure in which contradictions are not resolved but grow more profound and more intractable. It is precisely in order to radicalize conflicts—so that 'resolutions' are ruled out—that dramas are written: if not, they would be treatises.

The 'Victory Symphony' at the end of the overture returns on its own at the end of the play, and is an expression of the waking vision with which Egmont goes to the scaffold: a vision of a 'concrete Utopia', as said, but nevertheless a Utopia, the realization of which, whenever it may occur, is subject to the dialectics whereby 'objectification' is simultaneously 'alienation'. Beethoven was painfully conscious of that dialectics: his revolutionary hopes were disappointed, but he nevertheless remained an adherent not only of the idea but also of its realization, however fragmentary that might be. Thus, to regard the 'Victory Symphony' as the 'quintessence' of the overture is to take a distorted view of the dramatic structure, which does not offer an 'outcome', but holds the balance between the reality of power and the ideality of hope, exactly as it does between Egmont's great-souled and light-hearted nobility and William of Orange's cautious *Realpolitik*.

If we admit the high degree of abstraction without which it is impossible to compare literature and music, it is quite reasonable to speak of a structural analogy between Goethe's play and Beethoven's overture: but it is one of form, rather than of content. The 'Victory Symphony', which is 61 bars long, introduces a change from 'allegro' to 'allegro con brio', from 3/4 metre to 4/4, and from minor to major, and it bears no thematic-motivic relationship at all, either evident or latent, to the 'allegro'. It would be wrong to think of it unambiguously either as an appended 'stretta' or as a self-sufficient movement, because ambiguity is its very essence. It is stamped with the paradox of being both—and to the same degree—independent (and hence able to be isolated) and not independent (because dependent on its context); this final section does not stand firmly on its own feet, nor does it have a base in the formal process of the overture. But if form is deciphered as meaning, then this formal ambiguity scarcely permits any interpretation other than the hypothesis that the 'Victory Symphony' is not meant to be the 'outcome' of the drama mirrored in the *Egmont* Overture but merely represents one of the ideas whose interrelationship makes up the structure of the drama. That structure resists summary in a formula, because it is like a continuing process, one that is fundamentally incapable of ever being concluded. In terms of the overture as a 'dramatic' musical structure, the martial sarabande rhythm—a symbol of Spanish domination, heard in the minor in the opening 'sostenuto', and reappearing in the minor in the coda of the 'allegro', after having functioned in the major as the second subject in the 'allegro' itself—is not 'superseded' or 'subsumed' by the 'Victory Symphony'. What remains at the end is not a 'solution' or a 'resolution' but the still undetermined conflict—the 'non-solution' given shape and manifesting itself in shapes.

If we follow Hugo Riemann[7] (though his view was rejected by Arnold Schering)[8] and identify the sarabande rhythm of the opening, changed into a martial form, as a symbol of tyranny, and the sighing figures as an expression of the oppressed people of the Netherlands, a paradox arises: on the one hand, when the major variant of the sarabande appears to form the second subject of the 'allegro', it is inevitable that we will ascribe to it a manifest 'content', which relates

---

[7] In the additional material Riemann contributed to A. W. Thayer, *Ludwig van Beethovens Leben*, iii (Leipzig, ²1911), 240.

[8] *Humor, Heldentum, Tragik bei Beethoven* (Strasbourg, 1955), 43.

as much to the change from minor to major as to the exchange of the primary for the secondary formal position; on the other hand, it is impossible to do so. It is inevitable because a programmatic interpretation cannot simply be abandoned in midstream, and it is impossible because the dramatic process would surely demand that the theme should be neither relaxed, nor lightened, but only intensified.

We have a similar difficulty with the first subject of the 'allegro'. There is no mistaking that it proceeds out of the sighing motive of the 'sostenuto'; Beethoven does not so much 'compose' the theme as allow it to shape itself. If we confined ourselves to the broadest outline, it would not be difficult to give the formal process a programmatic content, to do with Egmont's relationship with the people of the Netherlands. The motivic connections are so complicated, however, that when considered in detail they simply refuse to lend themselves to programmatic interpretation, and the 'surplus' of distinct formal features is aesthetically the determining factor (ignoring them is the false initial premiss of almost all interpretations of 'content'). If the formal process is seen as an aesthetic transformation, then what is perceived to happen, if properly observed, can be understood as the progressive 'assumption' of the content into the form. The formal definition increases in strength as the programmatic content weakens, and the decisive thing is the fact that we are witnessing a process: formal process as formalization. The manifest 'content' elements that are unmistakably present at the beginning, in the 'sostenuto', are drawn to some extent into a development in which abstract musical processes gradually force the programmatic aspect into the background—admittedly without extinguishing it entirely. And it is the transition from the one to the other that must be understood to be the decisive element. The overture is not—from beginning to end—either absolute music or programme music, but is realized aesthetically in the transformation of content into form: the overture itself effects the transformation, instead of merely presenting its outcome.

The admissibility of the 'Victory Symphony' as a document of significance for both biography and the history of ideas obviously diminishes in direct proportion to our degree of allegiance to the high methodological standards that the New Criticism expects of the interpretation of a work of art. One of the underlying premisses of the argument against the biographical method is admittedly not very compelling: the assumption that the 'meaning' based in the dramatic structure of the work is identical with the composer's intention. It would be perfectly reasonable to make a distinction of principle between the 'objectified spirit' of a piece of music, and the composer's subjective intention and opinion (the composer's opinion is quite often a later interpretation, rather than an immediate reflex reaction of the creative impulse). Such a distinction leads to a methodological possibility that should not be rejected as pure speculation: the possibility of taking the 'author's intention', in so far as it is documented or can be reconstructed by indirect means, as a biographical element, without simultaneously asserting that it is wholly identical with the objectified meaning uncovered by interpretation of the work as such. The 'Victory Symphony' could then, on the plane of subjective conviction, represent an entirely Utopian consciousness, and be seen as the 'outcome' of the overture, although there can be no question of a 'quintessence' expressible in words on the plane of the formal structure. (Formal analysis, if it is to be methodologically sound, depends on insight into the fundamental paradoxicality and irony of the drama, and of the music that reflects the drama.)

Thus the biographical interpretation of an individual work is fraught with the difficulty that it is almost impossible to fulfil the methodological requirement to do justice to that aspect of a work which establishes its artistic character, its aesthetically constitutive particularity. On the other hand, it appears less harmful to attempt to relate a caesura in a composer's development to biographical events, in so far as more general elements, when abstracted from the singularity of the works, are as a rule more accessible to a conceptuality introduced 'from outside': biography, the history of ideas, or social history.

A characteristic of the works of the 'second period' or 'new path' beginning in 1802—the 'Eroica' Symphony, for example, or the Piano Sonata, Op. 31 No. 2, or the sets of variations, Opp. 34 and 35—is a change in the relationship between the esoteric and exoteric elements of the musical form: between the outwardly directed expression and the latent structure. The 'heroic style', as Romain Rolland called it, manifests itself in forms in which the thematic material and its 'treatment' evince a new inclination towards the abstract, which looks odd beside the gesture of the composer's addressing himself to all mankind—but, as will emerge, the paradox is understandable looking outwards from within.

The revolutionary stance of the 'Eroica' has never been denied: in the inner chronology of world history, the work cries out to be back-dated to 1789. What Beethoven actually thought about Napoleon— whether he believed he had advanced the revolutionary ideal or, after 1804, betrayed it—is irrelevant to the revolutionary tone of the work.

The spirit of revolution was the spirit of the age that dawned in 1789 and ended in 1814, and was embodied musically by Beethoven's 'heroic style'. But in 1814 it was no longer merely the case that the realization of the ideal was in danger (as it had been at every moment since 1789) because it had been perverted: in 1814 the ideal itself was abandoned, at least for the time being, and the epoch came to an end. *Wellington's Victory* (the 'Battle Symphony') is only a petrifact, a parody of the heroic style established in the 'Eroica'.

The esoteric trait, the complement of the dramatic championing of the cause of mankind, is only perceived when we recognize that (contrary to received wisdom) the thematic material of the first movement of the 'Eroica' is not the arpeggiated triad of bars 3–6 as such, but the relation of the diatonicism to the chromaticism of bars 6–7. The chromaticism, appearing in varying rhythmic patterns, and performing diverse compositional functions, is a counterpart to the arpeggiation; it affects form and the way the music progresses; but it is not a concrete motive, defined by rhythm and interval: it is an abstract structure. Motivicism—the fundamental category of instrumental music in the eighteenth century, as it freed itself from the hegemony of vocal music—is not altogether quashed in the 'Eroica', but it is supplemented by a 'deep structure', the introduction of which signifies a qualitative leap in the evolution of the conception of musical form. The fact that an abstract structure— as in the 'Eroica', but also found in the D minor Sonata, Op. 31 No. 2—is an element in the 'thematic configuration' is, if everything does not deceive, the essential characteristic of the 'new path' (as Beethoven himself called it) that he struck out along in 1802.

Perhaps, however, we can accept that the works composed from 1802 onwards are characterized by a concept of form that mediates between extreme esotericism and extreme exotericism, and between the abstraction of the 'new path' and the revolutionary tone of the 'heroic period'; if we do, it enables us to measure the importance or irrelevance of elements from biography, the history of ideas, or social history, in the evolution of musical history by whether the interventions 'from outside' can be related to the dialectics of the 'new path' and the 'heroic style' or not.

The Heiligenstadt Testament, written on 6 and 10 October 1802, very close, that is, to Beethoven's announcement of his 'new path'— is regularly called in evidence to support the biographical foundation of the 'second period', although it is not obvious at the first glance what the connection between work and life is supposed to be—apart from the coincidence of timing, which carries some weight, but is not decisive in itself. The changes in the relationship between esoteric and exoteric elements of compositional technique and of aesthetic aspirations seem to resist interpretation on biographical lines.

But we might well interpret the growing sophistication of the formal and the aesthetic structure—more precisely, the qualitative leap as which we may regard the idea of a partly abstract thematic structure—as a turn 'inwards'. On the other hand, the simultaneous adoption of the revolutionary stance—the apostrophizing of 'all mankind' in works with the symphonic aspiration characteristic of the 'heroic style' as a whole, even within the chamber music—can be regarded as a turn 'outwards'. This permits a connection to be made between the esoteric trait and the Heiligenstadt Testament, in so far as the melancholy manifest in the Testament can be associated with the brooding trait in the esoteric structures of the 'new path'. (That the melancholy of the Testament should not be regarded as depression merely, but as a 'saturnine' temperament expressing itself in depression, is supported by reference to earlier compositions: the quartet movement 'La malinconia', and the Largo e mesto of the Piano Sonata, Op. 10 No. 3.) The profundity that is manifested in the idea of abstract thematic structures in a sonata-form movement is a sign of *'melancolia illa heroica'*, as it was called by Marsilio Ficino.

There is a connection, however, between the esoteric tendency manifested in the technical compositional innovations of the 'new path' and the ambition to speak to 'all mankind'; without that connection the 'Eroica' could not have been written. The 'saturnine' temperament proves to be a necessary condition of the compositional realization of the 'heroic style'. Psychologically, concern for revolution and the improvement of the human lot may not sort well with *melancolia illa heroica*—which is more likely to choose retreat from the world—but in terms of compositional technique the esotericism of the 'new path' was definitely the fundamental premiss of the 'heroic style', the condition that made possible its realization in the symphonic spirit.

Musical material that could be used in the representation of revolutionary ideas already existed in French music, and was readily accessible. Arnold Schmitz[9] and Claude Palisca[10] have shown the extent to which Beethoven appropriated details of French revolutionary music for his own purposes. From the point of view of the history of composition, however, the decisive factor was not the material, which had long been available, nor the stylistic intention that Beethoven had doubtless been brooding on for years, but the

---

[9] *Das romantische Beethovenbild* (Berlin and Bonn, 1927), 163–76.
[10] 'French Revolutionary Models for Beethoven's Eroica Funeral March', in *Music and Context* (Dept. of Music, Harvard University, 1985), 198–209.

discovery of a formal principle which allowed the material and the intention to be brought to fruition in works of symphonic aspiration—an aspiration that the material appeared to rule out in its original form. The formal principle that laid the foundations for the 'heroic style' was the idea of drawing the 'revolutionary tone' into a complicated formal dialectics, despite the fact that, in the tradition going back to Gluck, the revolutionary ideal had previously been characterized by emphatic simplicity, and by a vigorous cultivation of simplicity and the elemental. As he entered on the 'new path', Beethoven found the way to mediate between concrete and abstract thematic procedures: that is, between apparently simple and latently complex structures. But with that the connection between the growing sophistication of the form and the 'heroic style' becomes apparent: for, in so far as the style is symphonic and not merely martial, it needed the inner complement of a tendency towards the esoteric as part of its means of expression.

3. 'Intitulata Bonaparte'

Beethoven's most famous dedication is the one he deleted: that of the 'Eroica' Symphony to Napoleon. The story told by his pupil and assistant Ferdinand Ries, of how Beethoven tore up the symphony's title-page in republican fury in May 1804, on hearing the news of Napoleon's taking the imperial crown, has all the appearance of credibility, but it is a myth for all that. Actual facts can be converted into myth by being isolated from their historical context and transferred to a symbolical one—and, contrariwise, in order to reconstruct the historical truth (the historian's truth as distinct from that of the myth-maker) it is necessary to play the pedant and tell the story as fully as the documentary evidence permits.

1. In December 1796, during the Franco-Austrian War, Beethoven wrote an *Abschiedsgesang an Wiens Bürger beim Auszug der Fahnendivision des Corps der Wiener Freiwilligen* (Song of Farewell to Vienna's Citizens, on the Departure of the Colour Division of the Viennese Volunteer Corps), WoO 121, and in April 1797 he wrote a *Kriegslied der Österreicher* (War Song of the Austrians), WoO 122. There are no grounds for doubting the sincerity of his patriotic feelings; these two occasional pieces have little aesthetic merit, but their biographical import is incontestable. The patriotism, however, collided with the republicanism that looked to France and that he did not abandon, and this created a conflict of loyalties which he never resolved. Beethoven felt himself to be both an adherent of revolution and a victim of its consequences. (Later in life he tended to associate

republican loyalties with England instead of France.) The political
paradox that the republican ideal in Austria was overwhelmed by
patriotic indignation, at the very moment when the French
revolutionary struggle was transformed into imperialism, was
foreseen by, of all people, Robespierre, the terrorist of virtue. 'Those
who seek to legislate with weapons in their hands will always look
like foreigners and conquerors, especially to those who must be
liberated from their prejudices against the republic and the
philosophy, and led to accept them.'[11] There are accounts of how
patriotic indignation got the upper hand in Beethoven at moments
when his loyalties were in open conflict, and these sources show him
as a Francophobe. If we attempt a general definition of the
relationship between his republicanism and his patriotism, however,
it emerges that the decisive factor in the former was idealistic, and in
the latter it was pragmatic. Austrian or German patriotism, at the
beginning of the nineteenth century, before the wars of liberation,
was not yet 'nationalism' but primarily and in the first instance a
matter of the 'native land', and to only a small degree an ideology.
But precisely because Beethoven's republicanism was idealistic and
even Utopian, by comparison with his patriotism, the former
predominates in the musical works in the 'heroic' style. Faced with
the contradictions in the documentary evidence, it is quite easy to
attach little importance to the effect of Beethoven's republican
sentiments on his life; but there can be no doubt about their
significance in his work, at least if by 'work' we mean the 'Eroica' or
the 'Pathétique' rather than the patriotic songs of 1796–7. The
pragmatic and biographical context, in which the war songs feature
on account of their documentary value rather than for any aesthetic
merits, is contradicted by an ideal context: that of the oeuvre, the
work in the emphatic sense, and the 'inner life' out of which it grew.
In that sphere Beethoven's republican convictions remained
unchallenged.

2. Anton Schindler's tale[12] that the idea of writing a symphony in
honour of Napoleon was first suggested in 1798 by Marshall
Bernadotte, the French ambassador, when Beethoven was,
apparently, a guest at his house, is not very plausible; and it hardly
seems worth the effort to seek a hypothesis to explain the
chronological proximity to the patriotic songs of 1796–7 and the five-
year gap before the 'Eroica' was written. But if the attempt is
nevertheless made, then the awkward relationship to the occasional

[11] Quoted in J. and B. Massin, *Beethoven* (Munich, 1970), 70.
[12] H. Goldschmidt, *Zu Beethoven* (Berlin, 1979), 194 ff.

compositions can itself be seen as an indication that Beethoven's patriotism was more in evidence in wartime, while his higher ideals, including republicanism, came to the fore in times of peace. If we accept that the idea for the 'Eroica' was first suggested by Bernadotte, the length of time that it took to be realized can be explained, as suggested above, by the hypothesis that it was at first impossible to see how the 'tone' of French revolutionary music—representing what was already to hand for a Napoleon symphony—could be linked to a conception worthy of symphonic aspirations. It was only the idea of relating the drama of mankind's struggle and abstract compositional procedures—the exoteric and esoteric elements of the 'new path' of 1802—that made it possible to give the material of the revolutionary music a form that satisfied Beethoven's concept of symphonic style.

3. In 1800–1 Beethoven wrote the music for the ballet *Die Geschöpfe des Prometheus* (The Creatures of Prometheus). The rondo theme in the Finale (No. 16) of that work is the theme of the variations in the last movement of the 'Eroica'. The idea of some association between Napoleon and Prometheus is a persuasive one, and was often adduced by contemporaries, but the significance of the theme is not unambiguous enough to prove it beyond any doubt, especially as rondo form was not taken as seriously at that date as the cycle of variations with fugato interpolations. Little is known of the libretto of the ballet, although it is reasonable to conclude that the Finale would have been the representation of the last sentence in the synopsis on the theatre bill dated 28 March 1801: 'Apollo commands Bacchus to make known to them [mankind] the heroic dance he [Bacchus] has invented.'[13] Thus the heroic character of the dance that is presented as a rondo is associated with Bacchus, not Prometheus.

4. The publisher Franz Anton Hoffmeister had evidently asked Beethoven for a 'revolutionary sonata', probably wanting a companion piece to the 'Pathétique', Op. 13. The composer wrote to him on 8 April 1802:

Does the devil ride you, and my lords too, that you suggest I should write a sonata of that kidney? When revolution was all the rage—that might have been the moment for something of the sort, but now, when everyone and everything is seeking to shuffle back into the old rut, Bonaparte has concluded the concordat with the Pope—a sonata like that now? If it was a *Missa pro sancta Maria à tre voci* or a Vespers etc.—well then I would take my brush in my hand at once and write you a *Credo in unum* with

---

[13] R. Lach, 'Zur Geschichte der Beethovenschen "Prometheus"-Ballettmusik', *Zeitschrift für Musikwissenschaft*, 3 (1920–1), 225 f.

great pound-notes—but in God's name, a sonata like that in these newly burgeoning Christian times—Hoho!—leave me out, nothing will come of it.[14]

This letter is usually interpreted as a refusal to fall in with Hoffmeister's suggestion, but that is by no means self-evident—indeed, it is not very plausible at all. What was the real object of Beethoven's mockery? Was it the fickleness of the 'spirit of the age', which, while he may have abhorred it, he did not set himself up to resist? Or was it the opportunism of those who conformed unresisting? But if Beethoven's scorn was directed at those who denied today what they believed yesterday, then it is entirely conceivable that he entertained the idea of a revolutionary sonata or symphony in direct defiance of the spirit of the age. (The earliest sketches for the 'Eroica' date from 1803, but that does not exclude the possibility that he began to think about it earlier, especially as the problems standing in the way of it were, as already shown, of an abstract musical character.) The significance of the letter to Hoffmeister is, in that case, that Beethoven refused to talk about an idea that attracted him but as yet perhaps took only a vague shape in his mind, because of the technical difficulty of mediating between the exoteric and esoteric elements.

5. On 6 August 1803 Ferdinand Ries wrote to Nikolaus Simrock in Bonn: 'Beethoven will stay here another year and a half at the most. Then he will go to Paris, which makes me extremely sorry.'[15] Both the dedication of the Violin Sonata, Op. 47, to Rodolphe Kreutzer and the intended dedication of the 'Eroica' to Napoleon must certainly be seen in relation to this plan to move. It is impossible to tell whether it was the outbreak of the Franco-Austrian war in 1805, the disillusion with Napoleon, or the thought of the risk involved in exchanging the patronage of the nobility in Vienna for the uncertain existence of an opera composer in Paris, that tipped the balance and made Beethoven give up the plan. (Beethoven must have known that opera was the predominant musical genre in Paris, and he certainly entertained the idea of devoting himself to opera composition at one stage, because in 1807 he proposed to the management of the Burgtheater to write one opera a year in return for a fixed fee of 2,400 florins.)[16]

6. On 22 October 1803 Ries wrote to Simrock again: 'He [Beethoven] has a great desire to dedicate it [the "Eroica"] to Napoleon, but if

[14] L. van Beethoven, *Sämtliche Briefe und Aufzeichnungen*, ed. F. Prelinger (Vienna and Leipzig, 1907–9), i, 91.

[15] M. Solomon, *Beethoven* (New York, 1977), 130.

[16] *Sämtliche Briefe*, i, 167–70.

not—because Lobkowitz wants to have it for a year and will pay 400 gulden for it—then it will be called Bonaparte.'[17] It was a common practice around 1800 for the dedicatee of a piece of music to be allowed to have the exclusive use of it for a fixed period. But it is disconcerting to find Ries treating the profound difference between the symphony's bearing Napoleon's name, and its only being dedicated to him, as if it was merely superficial. A dedication has a solely biographical importance, together with some financial implications; but the title of a work is an aesthetic matter and forms part of the work as an 'aesthetic object'. It is unthinkable that the idea of the aesthetically substantive association that would be expressed by naming the symphony after Napoleon did not enter Beethoven's head until he had realized that it would be financially more prudent to dedicate it to Prince Lobkowitz rather than to Napoleon. The inner, ideal association of the work with Napoleon—and, arising from that, the possibility of naming it after him—must have existed long before the alternatives of dedicating it either to Napoleon or to Lobkowitz were weighed with sober pragmatism.

7. Ries is also the source of the account of a dramatic scene that took place in May 1804, one that became a permanent fixture in the Beethoven myth:

In this symphony Beethoven had thought of Buonaparte, but as he was when still First Consul. Beethoven held him then in extraordinarily high esteem and compared him to the greatest Roman consuls. Both I and many of his close friends saw the symphony, already written out in full score, lying on his table, with the word 'Buonaparte' at the very top of the title-page and 'Luigi van Beethoven' at the very bottom, and nothing more. If, or how, he intended to fill the space, I do not know. I was the first to bring him the news that Buonaparte had proclaimed himself emperor, whereat he fell into a rage and exclaimed: 'Is he too no different from an ordinary man! Now he too will trample all the rights of man beneath his feet, indulge only his ambition; he will set himself higher than all other men now, and become a tyrant!' He went to the table, picked up the title-page lying on the top, tore it across and threw it to the ground.[18]

The story is undoubtedly credible. But Ries did not know when he wrote his memoirs that Beethoven's spontaneous reaction was not his last word. The telling of this tale as if it was all there was to the matter led to its becoming a legend. It got transferred from history to myth, and there it became a symbol.

8. It is true that the words 'Intitulata Bonaparte' are erased from the

[17] G. Kinsky and H. Halm, *Das Werk Beethovens* (Munich and Duisburg, 1955), 131.
[18] F. Wegeler and F. Ries, *Biographische Notizen über Ludwig van Beethoven* (Koblenz, 1838), 78.

title-page of a copy of the score made by a copyist, but four lines below that the words 'Geschrieben auf Bonaparte' ('written in honour of Bonaparte') are added in pencil.

Sinfonia Grande
Intitulata Bonaparte
im August
Del Sigr.
Louis van Beethoven
Geschrieben
auf Bonaparte
Sinfonie 3 Op. 55

9. The pencilled addition (obviously of later date) revoking the erasure is all the more significant in that Beethoven wrote to Breitkopf & Härtel on 26 August 1804—three months after the legendary scene—'The symphony is really entitled Bonaparte'.[19] The adverb 'eigentlich' ('really') can signify only one thing: that Beethoven still acknowledged the work's inner association with Bonaparte—in spite of his anger at the latter's crowning himself emperor—but no longer wished to have it publicly documented. And in any case in 1805, when war broke out again between France and Austria, it became impossible, for reasons of patriotism if no longer for those of disillusioned republicanism, to admit support for Napoleon publicly, whether in the title or the dedication of the piece. But even then Beethoven did not abandon the inner association: it was part of the work and it was ineradicable. It might be objected that a distinction must be made between genesis and statement, between the circumstances in which the work began to be created and the aesthetic meaning of the completed work. (This argument is crucial in the discussion of programme music: programmes that are not revealed can count as part of the aesthetic substance, because they influence the genesis of works; but it is also possible to regard revealed programmes as the only valid ones, because they expound the composer's intention and are part of the works as 'aesthetic objects', regardless of whether they were part of the original conception, or were applied to the works only later. In other words, one refers either to implications of the compositional process or to the composer's documented aesthetic intention.) The remark that the symphony 'is really entitled Bonaparte' is a private, not a public, statement, but it is an expression of an aesthetic intention, and not merely a comment on the process of composition, during which the image of Napoleon was in Beethoven's mind. The title has aesthetic

[19] *Sämtliche Briefe*, iv, 20.

validity, although it was not revealed for reasons both public and private.

10. The title Beethoven eventually gave the work, in the first edition of 1806, is 'Sinfonia Eroica . . . composta per festeggiare il sovvenire di un grand Uomo'. If we take the relationship to Napoleon as aesthetically substantive, then it is difficult to interpret the word 'sovvenire' ('memory'). The theory that Beethoven now regarded the First Consul whom he had admired as belonging to a past that had ceased to be actual and existed only as a 'memory' does not stand up, in so far as it cannot apply to the period during which the work was written. But this makes all the more probable the hypothesis that the word 'memory' signifies the 'mode of being' where the strange paradox of the 'Eroica' is not absurd but means something positive: this is the paradox that the work celebrates both the musical obsequies of the still-living hero whose name it should have borne, and his apotheosis. In an unfinished 'Ode to Napoleon' of 1797, Friedrich Hölderlin wrote:

> Heilige Gefäße sind die Dichter,
> worin des Lebens Wein, der Geist
> der Helden sich aufbewahrt.

('Poets are sacred vessels wherein the wine of life, the spirit of heroes, is preserved.')

And it is as the 'preservation' of 'the spirit of the hero', it seems, that 'memory' is to be understood in the 1806 title of Beethoven's symphony. What the 'Eroica' realizes aesthetically is not the image but the myth of Napoleon, which was associated with the myth of Prometheus. A myth, growing to be larger than reality and receiving, in works of poetry or music, a form in which it will survive, can contain side by side elements that exclude each other in empirical reality. And if the memory that preserves the spirit of the hero portrays for us the image of an entire life, the obsequies and the apotheosis are part of that portrayal—even in the hero's lifetime, once that life moves over into a mythical order of time. It would be mistaken, on the other hand, to take the abstraction so far as to allow the Napoleon connection to shrivel to nothing, by asserting that the work represents nothing more than the idea of the heroic. For Beethoven the 'real' title of the work, although he used it only in private, remained 'Bonaparte', even after the turning-point of May 1804 and the outbreak of war in 1805. In political terms that means that Beethoven needed not only the idea of the heroic, but also—and in equal measure—the realization of that idea, as it had been visible for a moment in history in the person of the First Consul. The inescapable dialectics of revolution and terror, revolutionary war and imperialism, the reign of virtue and tyranny—a dialectics of which Beethoven was undoubtedly as keenly aware as any of the outstanding figures among his contemporaries—did not permit the 'concrete Utopia' to be realized without distortion. But even the distorted version was better than merely abstract ideas, simply because it was a partial reality. In that, Beethoven was of one mind with Hegel: the realized idea, though enmeshed in the dialectics of its realization, is more substantial than the 'pure' idea that remains untouched by reality. And for that reason, like Hegel, he was able to be both for and against Napoleon.

11. Baron de Trémont, a member of the Napoleonic council of state, recorded conversations with Beethoven in Vienna in 1809. 'He was uncommonly preoccupied with Napoleon's greatness and often spoke to me about it. Although he was not well-disposed towards him, I noticed that he admired his rise from such a lowly position. It flattered his democratic ideals.'[20] Although it trivializes the facts, the comment is interesting in so far as it shows that even when Beethoven was filled with patriotic anger against Napoleon he admired his greatness—in the republican, and not merely the martial, sense.

12. On 8 October 1810 Beethoven made a note—for his own eyes alone—concerning the Mass in C major, Op. 86: 'The Mass could perhaps be dedicated to Napoleon.'[21] The note cannot have been meant ironically, for it was not addressed to anyone else, and it looks odd in relation to the letter to Hoffmeister of April 1802, quoted above: what Beethoven mocked then—the willingness to adapt to the opportunistic concordat that Napoleon had concluded with the Pope—now appears to govern his own actions. But if we take the view that dedications are a pragmatic matter, separated from the sphere of aesthetics and ideals by a wide gulf, then the contradiction, if not removed altogether, can nevertheless be seen to be secondary and unimportant.

When an attempt like this is made to gather together in broad outline the documentary evidence that, directly or indirectly, conveys information about the meaning and the implications of Beethoven's dedication of the 'Eroica' to Napoleon, and thus about a paradigmatic example of the relationship between his work and his life, the first impression is that the vacillations and contradictions prevent any consistent interpretation. However, in spite of Beethoven's variations of mood, which were superficial phenomena

[20] F. Kerst, *Die Erinnerungen an Beethoven* (Stuttgart, [2]1925), 139 f.
[21] Solomon, *Beethoven*, 140.

on the whole, some essential factors remain constant over the years: he never lost his admiration for Napoleon's greatness—the greatness that he elevated into the sphere of myth in the 'Eroica' and thereby transferred to a spiritual order where it could become a fit subject for music; never did the republican, who was simultaneously a patriot when pragmatic circumstances demanded it of him, lose the painful awareness of the dialectics of revolution and tyranny, revolutionary war and imperialism; but always, too, he held fast to the primacy of an ideal that had been concretely realized, however unsatisfactorily, over mere abstract principles; and always the work of art signified for him a 'memory' that, in Hölderlin's words, 'preserved the spirit of heroes'.

The musical realization of the governing idea of the 'Eroica' was due to Beethoven's development of the structural principles that allowed him to take the 'tone' that existed already in French music and appropriate it in the symphonic spirit; the outcome was the style that Romain Rolland called 'heroic'.

The thematic material underlying the symphony's Finale is stamped with the same emphatic simplicity that is characteristic of the themes of the first movement: this is the 'noble simplicity' that represented the stylistic ideal of French music of the end of the eighteenth century, which looked back to the tradition of Gluck. The symphonic style to which Beethoven subjects this apparently unpromising material (Ex. 1.1.) manifests itself in a precarious

Ex. 1.1

balance of antithetical formal and structural principles—a balance that is disturbed if any one individual principle is singled out as the 'primary' or 'underlying' one. (Symphonism is manifested differently in the first movement, where the simplicity of the thematic surface is counterbalanced by a tendency towards the abstract.) Undoubtedly, the Finale is the series of variations that it is always described as. But it must be admitted that variations on a double theme ('tema' and 'basso del tema' in the terminology of the 'Eroica' Variations, Op. 35), in which one of the themes is heard alone at the start and the other at the end, can hardly be designated a closed 'cycle' in the usual sense of the word. At all events the shift of focus from one theme to the other requires a formal foundation that cannot lie in the variation principle itself.

The eleven-bar introduction comprises, on the surface, a modulation from G minor to E flat major: V^7 that is, an introduction of the tonality 'from outside'. But essentially ('in the background', as Heinrich Schenker would say) it 'composes out' the note D, so that analogously the first four bars of the bass theme 'compose out' the note E♭, and the 'long breath' that results is a monumental, symphonic trait which differentiates the theme of the 'Eroica' Finale from the 'same' theme in *Die Geschöpfe des Prometheus*. (As the fugatos and the G minor episode show, the substance of the bass theme consists of the first four notes, and it is they that recall the melodic outline of the first subject of the first movement.)

The melodic theme—the 'tema' to the 'basso del tema'—is the third variation on the bass theme on the one hand, and on the other it is an exposition, which should not, however, be mistaken for a statement of the 'real' theme: the terminology of the 'Eroica' Variations is inappropriate to the symphony's Finale, in so far as in the symphony it is the independence and the equality of the bass and the upper part that are decisive, and not the hierarchy of 'tema' and 'basso del tema'.

The exposition of the melodic theme is not followed directly by a variation, but instead by a fugato on the bass theme, with the result that the melodic theme and the bass theme—previously encountered as complementary—now confront each other as contrasting themes. The relationship of simultaneity that they had in their original form in the ballet is expounded here as successive and antithetical. To claim that the thematic contrast introduces the 'spirit of sonata form' into the variation movement, and that the fugato 'results' from the contrast—in accordance with the Romantic conception of fugato as a sonata-form developmental technique—would undoubtedly be to over-interpret (not that over-interpretation should be avoided on principle, but it should be recognized for what it is). But it is hard to deny that the presentation of the counterpoint of the 'tema' and the 'basso del tema' as successive thematic contrast in relation to a fugato that 'results' from it, and is not merely appended to it, represents an element of symphonic style that was alien to the finale of the Prometheus ballet.

The variations of the melodic theme after the fugato are transpositions—without the 'basso del tema'—to C major and to D major (and continuing in sequences until a second fugato). And the transpositions are not so much a means of delineating character (using key-character—as happens in the Variations, Op. 34) as of highlighting the opposition between the harmonic and the contrapuntal principles, as represented by the 'tema' and 'basso del tema'. To some extent the variations act as a counterpart to the intensification of the contrapuntal variations of the bass theme which gave rise to the fugato.

When the recapitulation of the melodic theme in E flat major is reached ('poco andante'), new harmonization leads to the demise of the 'basso del tema'. (It is 'literally' possible to discover fragments of it in the bass-line at cadences but scarcely worth the trouble.) Just as the movement unmistakably rests on a dual structure, therefore, it is equally obvious that the formal development consists in the process of dismantling the formal structure, instead of integrating its component parts ever more closely together. The use of a double theme justifies a double variation in the sense both that the themes are varied alternately, and that the bass theme is heard in isolation at the start and the upper-voice theme is so heard at the end. The alternation of the themes, however, is simultaneously an alternation of principles: contrapuntal variations on the bass theme are confronted by, and contrast with, harmonic and figurative variations on the melodic theme; and the formal process as a whole consists in the overthrow of the polyphonic principle by the homophonic.

It emerges, therefore, that the Finale—superficially a series of variations with interpolated fugatos—rests on a foundation of much abstract formal thought. The slow movement is analogous. One aspect of symphonic style, as Beethoven understood it, is the knotting of a dense network of motivic relationships which form the under-side, as it were, of the heroic, monumental, thematic working on the outside; such a network appears where it might be least expected: in the 'Eroica' symphony's Marcia funebre. Furthermore, the movement is augmented by some elements not normally found in the traditional scheme of a funeral march: a fugato (bars 114–50) and an unusually extensive coda (bars 209–47), which suggests that the one uncommon feature will prove to be a correlative of the other. And indeed, these 'extras' are nexuses of motivic relationships.

The initial motive of the fugato theme is an inversion of the subsidiary motive (bars 17–18), the concluding motive an inversion of the bass figure of the 'maggiore' section (bars 69–73; Ex. 1.2). The

Ex. 1.2

connection is as close as it is significant. It would even be possible to think of the fourth-progressions of the subsidiary theme and of the 'maggiore' section as already related from the outset, even before their relationship is pointed by their being placed side by side in the fugato theme. But it is the immediate juxtapositioning that turns the spotlight on it, and the relationship, moreover, is one that would have no significance in a conventional funeral march but only in a movement with symphonic aspirations; and it is only the fugato that demonstrates those aspirations. (Motivic relationships may be an intrinsic part of the melodic substance, but they remain aesthetically irrelevant if they do not have a formal function.)

In the coda, the other nexus of motivic relationships, there are four significant features. The opening (bars 213–14) is a reminiscence of the 'maggiore' section; the passage developing a sighing motive (bars 217–32) is based on chromatic harmony from the variation of the first subject (bars 31–6); the syncopated motive (bars 232–5) is the outcome of a long-running 'motivic history' (bars 4, 35, and 63); and the breaking-down of the first subject permits a fourth-progression to emerge (bars 241–2) that lay concealed in the first subject—and can be related to the fugato.

In sum, the characteristic feature of the symphonic style in the slow movement of the 'Eroica' is that, as in the first movement, to a very large extent it is the 'elementary' motives—arpeggiated chords and second-progressions—that form the substratum of a network of motivic relationships. It can be said, in general, that symphonism, as Beethoven understood it from 1803 onwards, is characterized by the paradox that differentiation at its most extreme, threatening to lead off towards abstraction, is the correlative of an emphatic monumentalization.

4. The aesthetic subject and the biographical subject

August Wilhelm Ambros expressed the experience and the belief of the entire nineteenth century when he wrote, in *Culturhistorische Bilder aus dem Musikleben der Gegenwart*:

The picture of the mighty inner life of a Titanic soul is unrolled before us— we are no longer interested in the tone poem alone—we are also interested in the tone poet. We already stand, consequently, at almost the same point with Beethoven as we do with Goethe: we survey his works as the commentary on his life—although with both these great men we could also turn that statement round and say with equal accuracy that we survey their lives as the commentary on their works.[22]

[22] Leipzig, ²1865, 9.

Ambros, it appears, started from the premiss that Beethoven's life can be reconstructed from the surviving biographical documents in much the same way, and with much the same degree of certainty, as the aesthetic-cum-psychological substance of his works can be reconstructed from the pages of the scores. It followed that it must be possible to mediate between 'biographical elements' reflected in the historical documentation, and the contents of works, as set out in the scores, without doing interpretative violence to either source.

But the 'subject' whom Ambros imagines standing 'behind' the music of Beethoven and speaking to the listener 'out of' it, is not identical with the empirical person of the composer as that person can be reconstructed—albeit imperfectly—from biographical documents; nor, on the other hand, can 'he' be so strictly distinguished from the empirical person as the adherents of the New Criticism believe. A proper definition of the relationship between the 'aesthetic' subject and the 'biographical' subject—between the hypothetical first person discovered in the scores and the no less hypothetical human being discovered in the documentary evidence—is essential, for without such a definition it is frankly impossible to arrive at a valid interpretation of works such as the Piano Sonata 'Les Adieux', Op. 81a, where some connection with an actual biographical situation is undeniable.

It is by no means always the case that the emotional 'content' of a piece of music appears in the guise of the expression of a 'first person'. An emotion can also be perceived as an objective element, an adjunct of the work (the 'musical object'), without needing to be related to a subject—either the real one (the hearer), or the imaginary one 'behind' the music; the affective character of a funeral march does not need to be personalized to be aesthetically real: the listener perceives the emotion, even if he himself neither feels sorrow nor imagines a sorrowing person, speaking 'out of' the music.

Yet even if subjectivity is not always or necessarily implied by musical expressivity, it is all the more marked as a characteristic of the music of Beethoven, if we accept the validity of the aesthetic experience formulated by Ambros. His work is perceived as 'subjective' to a degree that was unknown to earlier generations. The literature about Beethoven is the prime example of writing where the emotional elements that are adjunct to the 'musical object', the imagined 'aesthetic subject' whose expression they appear to be, and the empirical person of the composer, as reconstructed from the biographical documentation, mingle almost inseparably—and after Beethoven the biographies of 'romantic' composers follow suit.

It is scarcely by chance, on the one hand, that Beethoven's music is especially liable to prompt the equating of one thing with another: questionable though it is, such an equating always seems to be borne out by some element or other of 'the facts'. On the other hand, however, it is equally necessary to try to define the relationship of the aesthetic and the biographical subjects as precisely as possible, and to substitute that for the diffuse identification of the two.

Literary theory distinguishes between the 'lyrical first person' who is aesthetically present in a poem—the 'narrator' of a novel—and the author, who withdraws himself from the aesthetic form his work has assumed at the moment when he finishes it. To the extent that the imaginary 'first person' of the poem is separate from the empirical person of the poet, every poem is a *Rollengedicht*, a 'poem of impersonation' (one that expresses the emotions and thoughts of a generic character: 'the shepherd', 'the lover', etc.).

The 'lyrical first person' and the 'narrator' do not, however, form part of the underlying poietic structure of each and every poem or novel, as some literary theorists of a systematic rather than a historical orientation seem to believe. And it is also uncertain that the gulf between the aesthetic and the biographical subjects was always as deep as theory suggests. (It is undoubtedly right to resist the tastelessness of simple identification, but it is not at all probable that good taste is a reliable guide in the critical attempt to reconstruct a historical, past reality.)

Rather, it would seem that the presence or absence of an aesthetic subject in a work and the identity or non-identity of the empirical and the aesthetic subjects are both liable to vary according to the historical date of a work, and according to the genre as well. In the Classical period, the theory of lyric poetry—the *Erlebnislyrik*, as it was later labelled: poetry of genuine personal experience—required the poet to be aesthetically present; in the same period, however, the theory of drama required the playwright to be absent. Around 1900 the tables were turned, and writers became increasingly present in drama, which tended then towards the 'epic', while poets turned to the greater impersonality of the *Dinggedicht* (the poem [*Gedicht*] that sought to penetrate the essence of an object [*Ding*] in nature). (With the exception of opera, music shared the principle of lyric poetry in both the Classical and the Romantic eras; this is true not only of the song but also of the symphony, in which, indeed, it can be said that an aesthetic subject speaks more directly and personally than in the string quartet, the 'discourse of four reasonable people'.)

The difference between periods becomes particularly clear if the aesthetics of *Empfindsamkeit* are compared with those of the baroque tradition. Carl Philipp Emanuel Bach expressed the essential aesthetic belief of an entire age when he referred to the Horatian maxim that, in order to move others, a poet or a composer must himself be moved.[23] He made no distinction between the author's state of mind, the emotional character adjunct to the musical object, and the affective character of a work. Baroque poetics demanded, on the other hand, that affects should be 'represented'—even, to some extent, 'painted', as a portrait likeness is painted. A distance was maintained between author and work, and between work and public; but that distance was greatly reduced in the age of *Empfindsamkeit*.

While 'self-expression' still reigned almost unbroken in the age of Beethoven (*Empfindsamkeit* and Biedermeier were linked by a tradition that ran parallel to classicism and romanticism), the theory was not so impossible to misunderstand as it appears in its more banal versions. The relationship between the aesthetic and the biographical subjects, which is deceptively represented as simple identity in the writing of C. P. E. Bach or Daniel Schubart, is in fact a complicated one.

The most immediately obvious problem is that the composer cannot always be the interpreter of his own work, while C. P. E. Bach's aesthetic theory, apparently extrapolated from his own piano fantasies, evidently rests on the assumption that he will be. It cannot be expected that other interpreters will identify wholly with the composer. The difference is not so damaging in practice as it might seem at first, because the problem of identification is to some extent cancelled out by another difficulty, which is far more profound, and is rooted in the relationship between aesthetic and psychological subjects. Already in the composer's case, and not just when it comes to the interpreter, 'self-expression' is obviously less a psychological reality than a fiction: aesthetically legitimate, but nevertheless a product of the imagination. The determining factor is not a real emotion, which may or may not be present, moving the composer's heart, but the art to suggest such an emotion. The music of genuine personal experience—an 'Erlebnismusik' to correspond to the *Erlebnislyrik* of the age of Goethe—is thus primarily a stylistic category, rather than a psychological one. The decisive thing is not whether, and to what extent, real emotions form part of the conditions for the composition and interpretation of a piece of music, but the fact that composer, interpreter and audience agree to recognize self-expression—'authenticity', to use the buzz-word of the 'new subjectivity'—as an aesthetic postulate which depends for its fulfilment not on psychological or biographical facts but on aesthetic evidence, acknowledged as an authority in its own right.

[23] See C. Dahlhaus, ' "Si vis me flere . . ." ', *Die Musikforschung*, 25 (1972), 51 f.

The fact that stylistic conventions, including that of 'authenticity', relate ambivalently and uncertainly to the 'inner reality' which, for its part, does not take concrete form until it 'externalizes' itself, is by no means as surprising or alienating as it may appear to the adepts of a banal romanticism. The relationship between aesthetic norms and psychological reality has always been volatile and contradictory. It is true that, in the seventeenth and early eighteenth centuries, the musical representation of an affect was regarded as imitation or portrayal, and not—as in the age of *Empfindsamkeit*—as expression or personal statement: that it was portrayed from without, instead of being brought to light from within the composer's or the interpreter's own heart; but that, too, was a matter of aesthetic consensus, and it did not exclude the possibility of empirical elements—emotions actually experienced by the composer or the interpreter—entering the live performance. The difference was that the share that real emotions might have in the processes of composition and interpretation was regarded as aesthetically neutral, as a private matter that did not concern the audience. The biographical element, if there was one, was 'subsumed' in the aesthetic product. And since the result that was expected of the reception of the piece was the imagination of the affect, and not the re-creation of the direct experience, it is not to be wondered at if artistic imagination, rather than one particular experience, was also regarded as the basis for the composition of the work.

It is obvious that the share of real feelings will be larger when imagination of the psychological reality of the thing represented is the aesthetic norm. But as a matter of principle the stylistic convention requiring either 'portraiture' from a certain distance or 'self-expression' must be distinguished from the actual intervention of 'authentic' emotions in the process of composition and interpretation.

In the case of an oeuvre where the biographical circumstances are, and always have been, well known, the importance of distinguishing between the aesthetic and the biographical subjects increases in direct proportion to the inclination of popular aesthetics to blur the difference. Beethoven's Piano Sonata 'Les Adieux', Op. 81*a*, is dedicated to Archduke Rudolph, and relates to the Archduke's leaving Vienna during the French occupation in 1809. But it would be a mistake to regard the work simply as a document in a case where aesthetic appreciation requires a foundation of biographical knowledge. The audience for which the work was destined when Beethoven published it in 1811 was the anonymous general public, not the intimate circle of friends that C. P. E. Bach had in mind when he said that a composer must be moved himself if he is to move others. And as the intimate circle grew into a 'public', so the aesthetic subject parted company with the biographical subject ever more decisively. The identification of the two was always problematic in itself, and the fact that popular aesthetics nevertheless clung to it, in the circumstances of the nineteenth century, was, generally speaking illegitimate. The image of a group of sympathetic souls was conjured up out of the past, and planted in a present that was already characterized by the alienation of composer and public; real, personal sympathy for the composer was transformed into a fictive sympathy for a legendary biographical subject.

The social-cum-psychological line of argument runs into the sand, however, if there is not a corresponding line in the structure of the composition, which is ultimately what matters. If the aesthetic subject, the 'lyrical first person', of 'Les Adieux' is not to be identified with the biographical subject, it must be demonstrable from the work itself. The possibility of hermeneutical proof consists in understanding the work aesthetically as a process which moves progressively further away from the biographical implications of the thematic material expounded at the start, instead of immersing itself ever deeper into it. 'Developing variation' of the thematic material, which permits its significance to emerge ever more clearly, is a formal process which, rather than elaborating the programmatic element and placing it in the foreground, gradually extinguishes, or at least diminishes it. What the motivic material means is decided by the course the music takes (it is a premiss of the argument that the outcome illuminates the origin and not the other way round), and that course is unmistakably determined by formal considerations, not programmatic ones. (Paul Bekker essayed a programmatic interpretation in his book on Beethoven, but he made the mistake of following his own argument to the end and joining up the elements of content into a connected 'narrative', and thus laid himself open to refutation by August Halm.)[24]

It could be objected that it is anachronistic to expect Beethoven to conform to an aesthetics of which the principles were not formulated until later in the nineteenth century. This is the aesthetics that, in the case of lyric poetry, displaces the colloquial provenance of the words by an emphasis on the aesthetic process within the poem whereby the original meanings of the words increasingly decline in importance or are suspended, while the words weave a net of connotations specific to that one poem.

Undoubtedly the age of Beethoven was unacquainted with what

[24] *Von zwei Kulturen*, 38 ff.

might be called the aesthetics of 'formalization'—if that word is understood to signify a process that takes place in a work of art. In the early nineteenth century people orientated themselves primarily by the thematic material and only secondarily by the way it was formally developed; and they tried to find in the thematic material biographical or programmatic elements to provide a frame of reference for aesthetic appreciation. But to deny the historical reality of the process of formalization in Beethoven, however relevant the argument may be from the standpoint of the history of ideas, is to ignore facts that are present in the work itself. There is no getting away from the fact that thematic development in 'Les Adieux' is determined formally and not programmatically. Quite independently of whether or not Beethoven shared the popular aesthetic beliefs of his time (it is not very probable), the work does not exhaust its meaning—as 'objectified spirit'—in the composer's intentions, and it speaks its own language.

The basic motivic material of the first movement of 'Les Adieux' consists of formulas whose expressive significance would have been unfailingly recognized by audiences of the time. The 'Farewell' motive (bars 1–2) stylizes the descending intonation of the word when spoken (in German: 'Lebewohl', with the stress on the first syllable), and the chromatic progression in the bass (bars 3–4) had been an established, conventional figure of lamentation since the early seventeenth century. Thus the 'subject' (both the expressive subject-matter and the musical theme) is not supplied by the top line alone but by the configuration of the 'Farewell' motive and the chromatic figure together. In turn, the sonata's individuality, which is the basis of its artistic character, arises out of the evolution of the relationships in which the 'Farewell' motive and the chromatic figure are placed. The motivic variations in which the dual subject is developed are, for their part, dependent on the formal functions allotted by tradition to a slow introduction and a sonata-allegro. In other words, the dialectics between the general character of the thematic material and the general character of the form, manifested in the 'developing variation' of the dual subject, gives rise to the individual character of the work.

The dependence on formal conventions is not a simple matter of course, admittedly. Schoenberg, who saw this issue more clearly than anyone else, describes the association between formal functions and motivic relationships, in his essay 'Brahms the Progressive', in a manner that has more to do with his own practice as a composer than with the classic–romantic tradition to which he refers:

I wish to join ideas with ideas. No matter what the purpose or meaning of an idea in the aggregate may be, no matter whether its function be introductory, establishing, varying, preparing, elaborating, deviating, developing, concluding, subdividing, subordinate, or basic, it must be an idea which had to take this place even if it were not to serve for this purpose or meaning or function.[25]

The 'place' of which Schoenberg speaks is the position one variation occupies in a series generated by the process of developing variation. Thus he postulates a primacy of developing variation—a means of creating musical meaning—over formal functions: whether it is direct or indirect, the derivation of the theme should be meaningful and comprehensible, without regard to its 'introductory, establishing [or] concluding' significance.

But it is impossible to establish completely what constitutes the 'logic' of a series of variations without paying some regard to *points d'appui* that lie outside developing variation as a motivic technique. If 'logic' is understood as the principle that allows it to be said why a particular variation comes in one place and not in any other, then in the immediate context the exigency of harmony determines the logic of the series of variations; but in the greater context the functions of the sections of a conventional movement play a part in determining the 'comprehensibility' of the sequence. *Pace* Schoenberg, the decisive factor is not an abstract 'logic' of motivic development (a logic detached from the formal groundplan) but the blending of that logic with the functions and stations of a formal process. (The derivation of a motive from another is always 'abstract' when the variation could be a different one.)

What blending motivic development and formal process means can be illustrated by the first movement of 'Les Adieux'. The introduction, the 'adagio', acts as the exposition, in so far as it sees the establishment of the principal motives—the 'Farewell' motive and the chromatic progression in the bass—which also feature in the 'allegro' section. The confrontation of E flat major (bar 1) and—after an interrupted cadence (V–VI)—C minor (bar 2) is the harmonic correlative to the motivic antithesis and, in its tonal ambivalence, typifies the provisional nature of an introduction. The return to E flat major—now in the upper line—is based on the same chromatic process that, in the beginning, led away from the tonic to the relative minor.

Generally, an introduction has a twofold formal role to play: in terms of harmony and tonality it represents an excursion into

[25] In *Style and Idea* (London, [2]1975), 407.

uncertainty, and thus creates the expectation of a resolution; and thematically it prepares the ground for the main body of the movement. The harmonic excursion (bars 7–12) to C flat major and A flat minor chromaticizes the material of the opening and thus represents a logical advance from the chromatic fourth-progression, and to some extent a transference of the chromaticism to the 'Farewell' motive. Moreover, a chromatic progression (G♭–F–F♭–E♭) forms the framework of the sequential repetition (bars 10–11) that takes the place of the simple repetition heard in the first period (bars 4–5); this sequence is a developmental motive, so that the chromaticization and the development are revealed as two facets of the same process: the chromaticization as motivic 'logic', and the development as formal function.

The 'adagio' is a preparation for the 'allegro' in a number of respects. Firstly, the first subject of the 'allegro' is based on the 'Farewell' motive, even if extended by the addition of semitones, one before the first note and another after the third (bars 17–19). Secondly, the counterpoint to the first subject is a chromatic progression. Thirdly, the reinterpretation of the close of the motive as a suspension (E♭–D) comes about as the result of a reference, in bar 19, back to bar 9 (Ex. 1.3). Fourthly, the modification of the third-

Ex. 1.3

progression by means of the additional semitones reflects the preparation in bars 12–16. That it is a reflection remains recognizable because of the proximity, although, complicatedly enough, it is a matter of a retrograde progression in augmentation (Ex. 1.4). The

Ex. 1.4

chromaticism is strongly marked in this first subject, while the 'Farewell' motive remains latent, but that is understandable when one considers that the relationship between first and second subjects is that of the 'contrasting derivation' (Arnold Schmitz), which is characteristic of Beethoven's movements in sonata form. Since the 'Farewell' motive recurs unchanged and in long note-values in the second subject (bar 50), it had to be significantly modified in the first subject, if there was to be a contrast.

The reason why it is the second subject that presents a quotation of the 'Farewell' motive from the slow introduction is that a second subject was expected to be lyrical. Chromaticism is represented in the second subject in the inner voices in the form of a 'sighing' motive (C♯–D and G♭–F). By contrast, in the development section (bars 77–90)—as in the elaboratory section of the 'adagio'—it is the 'Farewell' motive itself that is chromaticized: as D♭–C, C–C♭, C♭–B♭ it provides the framework of a modulation that fashions the type of 'roving harmony' (in Arnold Schoenberg's phrase) that is characteristic of Beethoven's developmental practice.

If, therefore, the 'adagio' and 'allegro' of Op. 81a are analysed from the standpoint of the relationship between motivic relationships and formal functions, some fundamental correspondences come to light:

1. The same chromatic progression that leads away from E flat major to C minor (bars 2–4) leads, in a different motivic milieu, from C minor back to E flat major (bars 5–7). The developing variation of the motive is the corollary of the tonal disposition.
2. The chromaticism, which is characteristic of the harmonic and tonal instability of an introduction, has a motivic source in the 'lamento' figure in the bass.
3. The first subject's deviations from the 'Farewell' motive provide the foundation of the structural relationship of the 'contrasting derivation' between the first and second subjects. The deviations from the theme of the introduction are prepared, for their part, in the development of the introduction: as anticipation of the suspension E♭–D and as anticipation of the modification of the third-progression in retrograde inversion.

In other words, formal functions like retransition, harmonic excursion, preparation, and 'contrasting derivation' are qualified by motivic relationships—by the developing variation of the 'Farewell' motive and of the 'lamento' bass figure—and, vice versa, motivic relationships are modified by formal functions.

The configuration of the 'Farewell' motive and the chromatic figure represents the true subject of the movement, in terms both of form and of expressive content; and the formal process in the course of which that configuration is progressively elaborated can be interpreted aesthetically as a process in which the music moves steadily further away from its reference to real life. The way the first movement of the sonata develops is determined formally, not programmatically: the biographical element recedes ever further into the background. The sadness at Archduke Rudolph's departure and the joy at his return (a joy which is probably anticipatory, preceding

the actual event) are not by any means made more explicit by the
painting of details during the course of the musical development;
rather, they become more remote as the 'formalization' proceeds. As
the formal elaboration of the motives grows more refined, and the
relationships between them are made increasingly distinct, so the
reference to extraneous reality fades and dissolves. Formal and
programmatic specificity do not match each other, but rather one
waxes as the other wanes.

The 'history' of the thematic configuration turns out, therefore, to
be a process of 'formalization', and not the 'narration' of a
programmatic 'content'; with this, a possible solution begins to take
shape to the problem that was the starting-point of this line of
argument: how to give a more precise definition to the relationship between a biographical subject and an aesthetic subject than is
provided by the all too simple confrontation of fact and fiction. It is
of no importance what share in the genesis of the work is attributed
to 'real' rather than to 'imagined' experience (given the nature of the
relationship between Beethoven and Archduke Rudolph, it is
probably right to think of the expressive character of 'Les Adieux' as
largely a matter of a fictive affect, although the work does not reveal
the slightest trace of distancing irony); but it is obvious that the
aesthetic process that runs its course in the work consists of
movement away from the empirical, biographical subject-matter. The
biographical subject, a distinct presence at the start, merges into the
aesthetic subject, and is finally 'subsumed' in it.

The thematic configuration of 'lamento' bass and 'Farewell' motive
in the sonata is first presented in a conventional formula and is for
that reason accessible to biographical exegesis. The expressive
stereotypes, including relics from the baroque arsenal of musical
rhetorical figures, to some extent form a musical counterpart to
colloquial language. But as the motives enter upon ever more
elaborately refined relationships—in which formal functions play a
co-determining role—so the real-life references of the musical
'words' retreat from the foreground and give way to the coherence
that they work together to form within the piece of music. The
reference point which guarantees cohesion and meaning moves from
a position in the outside world to one in the interior of the work.

The word coherence is used here as a translation of the German
word *Sinnzusammenhang*, a cardinal term in musical analysis, which
is admittedly ambivalent. On the one hand it seems to imply that a
meaning (*Sinn*) is brought into the music 'from outside', and on the
other hand to suggest that musical coherence (*Zusammenhang*) is
already in itself, independently of external factors, a guarantee of

aesthetic meaning. But if musical form is acknowledged to be an aesthetic process, the ambivalence can be resolved: the meaning expressed in 'Les Adieux' does not lie in the extra-musical reality reflected in the work's themes, nor exclusively in the intra-musical structural coherence, but in the transformation of the one into the other. The biographical 'source' becomes, in and through the work, merely the 'starting-point'. Aesthetically, the decisive factor is the outcome of the process that works itself out in the form. At the end of the movement the aggregate image that remains is not an idea of sorrow at the Archduke's departure, defined with ever greater refinement by the music, but the musical impression of progressively more elaborate relationships between the 'Farewell' motive and the chromaticism. This is because the modifications in the mutual relationship of the thematic elements are not guided by any reference to an external object or reality—in other words, a 'story' is not being told—but are the result of the sections of a sonata-form movement functioning conventionally in respect of the process of developing variation. And in the aesthetic process of 'formalization' the work comes into existence as an aesthetic object.

Looking upon Op. 81a as a coded message from Beethoven to Archduke Rudolph is therefore as unreliable a procedure as the converse—shedding the biographical element altogether—is impossible. But if the reference to a 'real' object indicated by the work's title and its dedication is neither simple reality, which the listener need do nothing more than imagine, nor pure fiction, then it can consist only in the transition from one mode to the other.

The aesthetic subject, into which the biographical subject withdraws, as it were, is admittedly not a clearly delineated category with an unequivocal meaning. The aesthetic theory of the *Sturmer und Dränger* Daniel Schubart, which made 'self-expression' the be-all and end-all of music, proved inadequate in so far as it naïvely identified the 'self' that 'expresses itself' with the biographical person of the composer. But the historian cannot simply forget the dialectics of subject and object, as if Hegel or Wilhelm von Humboldt had never formulated it, even though it was still unknown to eighteenth-century thought. Musical aesthetics, too, if it is not to fall back into naïvety, may not ignore the fact that the 'self', of which Schubart speaks as if it was a given fact, does not experience itself until it perceives its reflection: only when it 'externalizes' itself by directing activity on an object, is a light generated which allows it to see its own image. The subject is unable to know itself until it sees itself reflected—refracted—by the object.

If, however, one starts from the position that the 'self' comes into existence only in subject-object relationships, then one has the choice of two things to place in the foreground of compositional activity and treat as the substance of the 'externalization': either the process of work on the piece, or those traces of real-life associations that affect the genesis of the piece. Either way, it is not wrong to regard the aesthetic subject 'behind' a piece primarily as the creative subject, whose activity can be reproduced in an adequate reception of the piece, and only secondarily as the empirical person living in tangible biographical circumstances.

Since the dialectics of subject and object is, in terms of the history of ideas, a discovery of the period around 1800, it is not surprising that the subject that is forever active in musical formal process (and not merely temporarily during the genesis of the piece) does not seem to have found itself until Beethoven. The aesthetic subject is to some extent the subject who composes and continues to exist in the piece, having been written into it as *energeia*. In turn, the sophistication of the process of composition creates the need for an analogous sophistication in the act of listening to music; the process of composition itself cannot be reconstructed, only a reception that reflects it, recognizing the relationship between the musical object and its perception. The aesthetic subject is thus the empirical person of neither the composer nor the listener, but an imaginary subject that combines the creative activity of the former and the re-creative activity of the latter.

The reflecting nature of Beethoven's treatment of sonata form is illustrated in the first movement of the E flat Piano Sonata Op. 31 No. 3.[26] Firstly, the opening of the movement starts by seeming to be an introduction, and only later reveals itself as the main theme. Secondly, the continuation (bar 18), which seems to be a transition (and indeed is such in the recapitulation), loses that role to an evolutionary section (bar 33) which must be regarded as the 'real' transition. By this means Beethoven shows that musical form is something created by the subject. 'Introduction', 'main theme', and 'transition' prove to be categories that are not 'given' as part and parcel of the musical object but are 'brought to' the structure. When the understanding of form is unreflecting, the subject is not conscious of its creative activity; it thinks of itself as the organ for the reception of a clearly defined 'thing' with certain 'characteristics'. It is only on being encouraged to exchange categories for others, that the listener becomes aware of himself as subject, and of his creative role in the formal process.

[26] L. Finscher, 'Beethovens Klaviersonata opus 31, 3', in *Festschrift für Walter Wiora* (Kassel, 1967), 385–96.

2

*Personal Style and the Individuality
of Single Works*

When we speak of individuality in music we are usually, without seeing any problem in it, thinking of a cast of individual character, which is understood as an expression of the composer's individuality. Since, in a purely logical sense, everything that can be perceived as a closed, discrete whole presents an individual character, the specific element that characterizes the individuality of pieces of music is obviously its foundation in the composer's personal style.

The relationship between the individuality of works and their composer's personal style turns out to be delicate in the extreme, however, if we attempt to grasp methodologically how it is actually constituted. A personal style is exactly like a national style, or the style associated with a period or a genre, in that it is a general category, embracing a number of works, which encroaches on the aesthetic integrity of any one single work by abstracting from it the characteristics that recur in other works. To separate the traits of 'personal style' from the context of the whole work is to ignore the individual character of the work. Personal style is something peculiar and unrepeatable in respect of the composer, but it is a generality in respect of any one work. And the configuration of characteristics is differently constructed, categorically, in the concept of personal style from the way it is assembled in the conception of the individual work. Some of the elements which contribute to the individuality of a work are conventions that have no significance for the definition of the composer's personal style, and yet are 'specifics' in the structure of the work, because of the context in which they occur, and the function they perform there; and hence they are characteristics that define the singularity of the particular work.

The practice of pinning a personal style down to detached, isolated details which recur in other works according to a demonstrable, even statistically verifiable pattern is, admittedly, a dubious habit and a matter of methodological convenience. Undoubtedly, in addition to melodic figures or rhythmic patterns, the characteristics in which a personal style manifests itself include the formal conceptions that underlie a work or a movement as a whole. Beethoven's idea of breaking up those features of a formal entity that had 'grown together' by convention, and disposing them differently from what was customary, is quite as significant in terms of his personal style as the individual manner of accentuation within the bar described by Gustav Becking.[1] The formal ideas which can be said to belong to a personal style dwell, in fact, in a curious middle ground which resists easy delineation, between an abstract scheme recurring in the work of several composers, and cited in books on formal theory, and a concrete formal idea realized only in one individual work.

The only statement that can be made about the growth of individuality in music is the unsatisfying chronological generality that it evolved during a process of individualization between the fourteenth and the eighteenth centuries. Obviously it does not consist in the bald ontological fact that—in the language of scholasticism—'individuum', 'ens' and 'unum' are one and the same thing. Rather, it represents an aesthetic idea, behind which there stands the historiographical decision that the features of a work that are to be regarded as making the essential contribution to its artistic character shall not be the general traits that it shares with other works but the particular ones peculiar to itself alone. So long as a work is judged according to general norms, the fulfilling of which is the guarantee of the artistry of a piece of music, its individuality is an ontological fact, but is only secondary in aesthetic importance. Only the notion that the artistic character of a work must have its roots in its originality—in other words, that art must be new to be authentic—makes individuality the dominant criterion.

The statement that every piece of music can be regarded both as an individual work and as an example of a genre will not raise a single eyebrow. Any argument will centre, not on the possibility of looking at it from different standpoints, but on the extent to which the characteristics that legitimize a work's claim to be called a work of art should be sought in what is individual about it, or in what is exemplary.

There is a strong case for regarding the distinction as a historical one. As late as 1725, in Fux's *Gradus ad Parnassum*, the general aspect embodied in the rules of counterpoint is represented as the essential thing, and the particular respect in which one work differs from another as accidental. The norms of strict counterpoint lay down inviolable foundations; only the musical superstructure is subject to historical alterations, which are interpreted as changes in

---

[1] *Studien zu Beethovens Personalstil: Das Scherzothema* (Leipzig, 1921).

fashion; the composer should, of course, conform to fashion, but he should not embrace it so recklessly as to disturb the very basis of composition.

By the late eighteenth century the concept of foundations and superstructure was challenged by the idea that (in a nutshell) art was the expression of genius, and not a matter of conforming to rules. Indeed, the composer's genius is the source of the kind of individuality that first springs to mind when we use the term. However, the statement that, by 1770 at the latest, the concept of art was to some extent transferred from the exemplary aspect of a work to the individual must be qualified, if it is not to be misunderstood. After all, it is by no means established a priori whether the aesthetic importance of the 'Eroica' lies in the abundance and the particular configuration of unique characteristics or in the fact that the symphony represents exemplarily—in its general traits—the symphonic principle.

The genre tradition that is the counterpoise to the individuality of single works was not the same in the nineteenth century as it had been in the seventeenth; changes took place not only in the system of genres but also in the conception of what constituted a genre. Whereas in the seventeenth century the style of a genre was determined essentially by purpose (liturgical, social, or ceremonial), and by the corresponding choice of musical means, in the nineteenth the paradigmatic genres, the symphony and the string quartet, were founded on aesthetic ideas, the realization of which was not linked to a fixed, codifiable store of materials and techniques but, on the contrary, depended for success on constant innovation.

The idea of symphonic style that Beethoven conceived can be described summarily as overpowering monumentality qualified by an utmost refinement, differentiation driven to the verge of abstraction. E. T. A. Hoffmann spoke on the one hand of the 'awe, fear, horror, and pain' that Beethoven arouses, and, on the other, of a half-concealed 'inner structure' that demonstrates 'the master's noble deliberation'.[2] (It is for that reason that Hoffmann's review of the Fifth Symphony begins as dithyramb, and continues as technical analysis.)

An explanation for the aesthetic dualism is to be found in the history of the institution of the symphony concert, without our needing to address the question of whether the institution as such, which is both a form of organization and a state of consciousness,

---

[2] *Schriften zur Musik: Nachlese,* ed. F. Schnack (Munich, 1963), 34–51. (Readers are also referred to E. T. A. Hoffmann, *Musical Writings,* ed. D. Charlton, trans. M. Clarke (Cambridge, 1989).)

should be regarded as the cause or the consequence of the aesthetic idea. While the monumentality is a manifestation of the intention to address both 'humanity' at large and the humanity in the heart of each individual, the differentiation represents the structural justification of an aesthetic aspiration: the aspiration of the symphony to be heard as an autonomous work, for its own sake and in contemplative concentration.

The kind of individualization characteristic of the instrumental music of the eighteenth century—a period that, for the purposes of music history, runs from 1720 to 1814—is generally described primarily in relation to what happens to thematic material. Previously that material was largely determined by standard formulas, so that Gioseffo Zarlino's term 'soggetti' is more appropriate in the sixteenth and seventeenth centuries than the word 'themes'. The 'modern concept of the theme', to use Hugo Riemann's phrase, is the orientation of the composing imagination according to a complex fundamental idea with an unmistakable, individual character, which generates its own development from within itself; while instrumental music worked to free itself from the formulas of vocal music, 'theme' was undoubtedly a fundamental category. But a 'theme', if the term is taken in the original sense of the 'subject' of academic discussion, must be considered in relation to the 'treatise' it underlies; and if the theme constitutes the matter, or substance, of the form that grows from it, it is, conversely, the form that reveals what is in the theme. The individualization of form and that of theme are two aspects of the same process.

To the degree to which concepts of substance were separated from concepts of relation or function, the process of individualization shifted its emphasis from the thematic material—which became merely the starting-point—to the form. Strictly speaking, it is no longer possible to say to what extent the form either reveals the implications of the thematic material, or bestows on the thematic material an abundance of meanings that were only dimly adumbrated in it.

If we recognize, therefore, that, although the individualization of the thematic material is initially something of an unrealizable ambition, in the end it is the form as a whole that decides its fate, we can compare the relationship between the individuality of the work and the formal idea to a problem and its solution. The decisive thing is that we must not unduly simplify the configuration composed of thematic material and form: concrete substance and abstract relation.

The incessantly recurring principal motive in the first movement of the F major Quartet, Op. 18 No. 1, is nothing other than an ornamental figure which does not, however, adorn a melody, but is actually the thematic substratum itself. When the fundamental idea is thus insubstantial, it can only acquire significance from the contexts in which it is placed. In the transition (bar 30) the principal motive, appearing as an ostinato bass, is combined with a phrase from which the rising third and the suspended second subsequently emerge as the two most important components (Ex. 2.1). The simultaneous

Ex. 2.1

association gives rise to a successive one, when the first bar of the counter-phrase is replaced by the principal motive (bar 42; Ex. 2.2);

Ex. 2.2

the motivic combination recalls the consequent clause of the principal motive (bar 17; Ex. 2.3). It would be an exaggeration, however, to

Ex. 2.3

claim that bar 18 is the model for bar 31, even though the rhythmic pattern is identical. Rather, the latent relationship between the bars does not become manifest until the phrase from the transition is combined with the principal motive (bar 42). The rising third and the suspended second return as a cadence in the antecedent clause in the subsidiary theme (bar 60; Ex. 2.4). That there is nothing arbitrary

Ex. 2.4

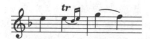

about the separation of the intervals from their context in the transition is demonstrated in the concluding group, in which the element common to the transition and the subsidiary theme appears in isolation (bar 103; Ex. 2.5). We may speak of a network of motivic

Ex. 2.5

relationships that spreads across every area of the exposition, the principal subject-group, the transition, the subsidiary theme and the closing group. Though they are weak in substance to begin with, the motives acquire the distinct character they did not originally possess through the relationships that are established among them. At the same time it would be too much to speak of motivic development: rather, associations that are unrecognized to begin with—between bars 17–18 and 30–1, or between bars 30–1 and 60—are brought to light retrospectively.

From this it emerges that the essential logical determinant of aesthetic individuality—in addition to the singular and unique nature of the individual entity—is the wholeness and integrity of form that was singled out by Karl Philipp Moritz in the 1780s. The significance of this in the theory and history of music does not come to light, admittedly, until we rid ourselves once and for all of the ingrained prejudice, propagated for reasons of pedagogical convenience by theorists of musical form, that form equals 'general' and thematic material equals 'particular'. Once we have recognized that the individuality of the whole entity is the means whereby the thematic material, often a commonplace in its basic form, can become individual in its turn, then we are compelled to pay less heed to the normative discipline that was formal theory in the eighteenth and nineteenth centuries when we analyse individual works. Only then is the way clear to acknowledging that some themes are not already individual entities at the moment of exposition, but only develop as such during the formal process that they unleash in association with other thematic elements.

If formal analysis is the primary means of establishing the individuality of a work, there is a case for applying the converse and taking a psychological approach when we turn to the exploration of personal style, the attributes of which should necessarily be qualified with those that define individual character.

The fact is that if we deny ourselves recourse to psychology and biography it is hard to discover the inner coherence in the agglomeration of musical characteristics that makes up a personal style. It is not surprising, therefore, that investigations of personal musical styles frequently accomplish nothing more than the description of disjunct members: authors produce separate paragraphs about melody, rhythm and harmony without recognizing that they are neglecting the one thing that they claim to be writing about. On the other hand, when Gustav Becking[3] attempted to determine the nature of personal style in music, without seeking the inner associations of the technical elements in a psychological-cum-

---

[3] *Der musikalische Rhythmus als Erkenntnisquelle* (Augsburg, 1928), 23–53.

biographical depiction of the personality of the composer, he found that he had to resort to Wilhelm Dilthey's categories of types of *Weltanschauung*, which represent a kind of transcendence of psychological categories: the finer differentiation of types such as 'naturalism', 'subjective idealism', or 'objective idealism', is supposed to lead to individuality. Indeed, there is no denying that, although this method of approach cannot, as a matter of principle, ever reach the goal, in the hands of an ingenious writer like Becking it does get close to what is implicit in the concept of 'personality'.

It is obvious that Dilthey's types can be given various interpretations, and there is absolutely no compulsion to introduce metaphysics. Metaphysics will support our scholarly conclusions, but need not be hypostasized as a final authority or ultimate premiss underlying every objective insight; we can also think of metaphysics as a heuristic vehicle with the function of providing general categories that can serve as the first stage in the forming of concepts of individualization. Metaphysics represents not a goal but a means of cognition.

In the field of early music, the attempt to use psychology and biography in interpreting the attributes that constitute a personal style comes to nothing because there is so little documentary material. The scarcity is surely not a matter of pure chance. Material relating to the lives of composers takes the form of scraps of data, and scarcely ever that of connected accounts, until the middle of the eighteenth century, for it was only then that people began to think of pieces of music as expressions of individuality: the self-expression of a persona which might be further exposed by psychology and biography. The fact that memoirs then initially showed a preference for anecdote is not necessarily the disadvantage that the historian's rooted prejudice makes it out to be, for although anecdote may be an unreliable witness for the purposes of empirical biography, it can be very illuminating about the form in which the composer as aesthetic subject—the subject manifested in the music—appeared to his contemporaries.

Of course, a historian is not obliged to adopt the criteria of the period he is writing about. The tendency of the late eighteenth and nineteenth centuries towards psychological-cum-biographical interpretation of the composer's individuality need not be respected or imitated by later narrators, even if it was shared by the composers in question, the leading players on the stage of music history. The historian must, admittedly, bear the burden of proof of the validity of his methods, when he deliberately departs from the spirit of the past.

The complications to which this can lead are well demonstrated by the example of the expressive principle in eighteenth-century *Empfindsamkeit*. As mentioned earlier in another context, in 1753 C. P. E. Bach, under the influence of the poetic theory of Johann Jacob Breitinger (and, indirectly, of Horace's *Ars poetica*), declared that, in order to move others, composers and performers must themselves be moved. (Ideally, composer and performer should be one and the same person.) The supposition, however, that every one of the rapidly and abruptly altering emotions expressed by one of C. P. E. Bach's keyboard fantasies was really experienced would be absurd. On the other hand, it cannot at all be ruled out that in the representation of affects in a baroque aria, which was regarded in the aesthetics of the period as the portrayal of an emotion from without, and not as an expression of feeling from within, real emotions felt by the composer or performer were sometimes included. In other words, the empirical psychological reality—the inclusion or not of real feelings—is secondary, if not altogether unimportant. The essential thing is the aesthetic norm: in the Baroque the norm required a distanced representation of affects, in the age of *Empfindsamkeit* it demanded an expression of emotion in a manner that suggested direct experience.

It is possible, then, to interpret the conception of 'personal style' not as a psychological-cum-biographical category but as an aesthetic one with limited historical validity. 'Self-expression' is an aesthetic— by which I mean aesthetically legitimate—fiction, the empirical psychological basis of which is of small importance, certainly not enough to be made the sole basis of interpretation. The matter for historical reconstruction is not the empirical subject, the traces of which can be found in biographical documents, but the aesthetic subject, as which C. P. E. Bach and, later, Beethoven present themselves in their sonatas and fantasies.

The distinction between aesthetic and biographical subjects is an interpretational model from which a historian can start, but it still requires interpretation in its turn. If we understand musical expression as an aesthetic mask depicting a character, as it came to be understood after C. P. E. Bach's pronouncement, then we can meet the objection that it amounts to self-dramatization by viewing the musical 'language of sensibility' as fundamental to the constitution of the subject himself—of his individuality as a feeling being. In other words, the aesthetic subject can be drawn closer to the empirical subject if it is convincingly demonstrated that emotions—the composer's as well as the listener's—are not only expressed by music but also aroused by it, or given form by it. Those emotions cannot simply be dismissed as semblances (it is, after all, virtually impossible to say what a merely 'seeming' emotion might be). The subject does not only 'speak' the language that was called the 'language of sensibility' in the eighteenth century: he is also, in a sense, 'spoken by it' (to borrow from the vocabulary of post-structuralism a curious passive construction that is eminently well-suited to the formulation of a fundamental concept of the philosophy of language that goes back to Wilhelm von Humboldt). The concept of a 'speaking role' mediates, however, between the aesthetic and the empirical subjects, by virtue of the fact that it makes it possible to read the relationship between the real emotions of a composer and the musical language of sensibility as reciprocal, in that he is as much at the service of the language as it is at his.

The formula of 'unity in diversity', which was incessantly invoked in the eighteenth century, is inadequate, because it does not make allowance for the fact that in music, at least, the postulated unity must be established twice: both substantively and functionally. The sonata form of the first movements of the symphonies and string quartets of Haydn and Beethoven achieves thematic-motivic unity through the diversification of melodic-rhythmic material expounded at the outset, and formal unity through the integration of functionally diverse components with names—first-subject group, transition, second-subject group, development, recapitulation—that already indicate the diversity quite as much as they do the cohesion. Ever greater integration is the correlative of ever more abundant diversity; in the organicist theory, which gained ground in aesthetics in the late eighteenth century, and was at the same time implicitly acknowledged in compositional practice, that observation is a commonplace.

If the analysis of a work is not to remain one-sided and fragmentary, a clear distinction must be made between the diversification of the thematic-melodic material on the one hand, and the functional diversification of the formal components, the goal and purpose of which is unity through integration, on the other. In the music of Haydn and Beethoven, new melodic-rhythmic and contrapuntal figures continually issue forth from the basic material by means of what Schoenberg called 'developing variation'; the relationship of this process to the functional diversification of the formal components is by no means unproblematic, and is customarily left in semi-obscurity in analyses that avoid grey areas.

One specific connection between substance and function was designated 'contrasting derivation' by Arnold Schmitz:[4] a first and a second subject have some characteristics—often semi-latent—in

---

[4] *Beethovens 'zwei Prinzipe'* (Berlin and Bonn, 1923).

common; and at the same time, through other attributes, they express on the surface of the music the complementary opposition that is essential to the thematic structure of sonata form. Strictly speaking, however—although Schmitz evidently did not see it—contrasting derivation is nothing more than a special instance of the general relationship between developing variation and functional diversification that underlies all formal entities. Thus, for example, a transition from a first to a second subject can be (as it is in the first movement of Beethoven's Sonata, Op. 2 No. 1) simultaneously an evolution of motives from the first subject and a mediation between the tonic and its relative. It is based, in that case, on motivic derivation under the conditions of a specific formal function; and the function it fulfils determines the kind of developing variation to which the motives are subjected. Similarly, the contrast of first and second subject out of which the contrasting derivation grows is a formal function that regulates the variation process.

Unity in diversity thus has a twofold foundation: once in the thematic substance, the diversification of which by developing variation gives rise to the richness of formal variety in a movement; and once in the form of the whole, which comes about through the integration of components that are functionally different, and related to each other in their differences. And the diversification, especially such as is found in sonata-form movements by Haydn and Beethoven, can indubitably be interpreted as individualization in eighteenth-century terms, although it is necessary to take a roundabout route to prove it.

At first it looks as if musical individualization is fundamentally different from the literary kind that provided Alexander Baumgarten with the exempla for his aesthetic theories.[5] Baumgarten, starting from a theory of poetic metaphor, understood the use of imagery in language as a means of making abstract ideas concrete: the image depicts something real, while what is meant remains abstract, and the logical 'descent' from the general to the particular (which Baumgarten, following Leibniz, regarded as an endless process of convergence that can never reach completion) ought to be recognized as a mode of cognition in its own right, as *cognitio* with specific *perfectio*—the *perfectio sensitiva* which is the foundation of aesthetics. Observation, rather than remaining merely the means to the conceptual end, can itself be an end.

In music, which is a medium for neither the cognition of concepts nor the observation of reality, it is difficult to perceive a relationship

[5] A. Bäumler, *Das Irrationalitätsproblem in der Ästhetik und Logik des 18. Jahrhunderts* (Darmstadt, 1967), 207–31.

between the general and the particular analogous to the one which pertains at least partly in poetry—language that uses metaphor—and can be interpreted as individualization in the sense of the logical 'descent'. It is only possible if the concept of the 'theme' or 'subject' (the fundamental category of emancipated instrumental music) is given a different interpretation from the usual one. The relationship between a first and second subject, or between a subject and a transition, is generally regarded as the transformation of one entity into another, similar entity—in so far as it involves derivation by means of contrast or diversification. But another interpretation is possible, which is particularly appropriate for certain works. This is the view that, instead of a concrete first entity being changed into a concrete second entity, there is an abstract substratum—a purely intervallic construction with variable rhythm, or a melodic shape within which individual pitches may vary—which assumes a variety of concrete forms; furthermore, strictly speaking, it is this abstract substratum that functions as the 'underlying' or 'thematic' element, while the concrete themes, palpable though they may be, are only exterior forms in which the substance manifests itself.

Which of the two interpretations the analyst chooses is not simply a matter of methodological preference alone, but also—and primarily—determined by the nature of the case: there are movements in which the predominant 'thematic' element, ensuring coherence, is an abstract structure, and on the other hand, there are movements which have only themes in the usual, palpable sense of the word. The 'thematic element' in the first movement of Beethoven's 'Eroica' consists of a configuration of an arpeggiated triad and chromaticism, and in Op. 81*a* of the relationship between the third-progression and the 'lamento' bass line; in both these cases it undoubtedly represents a 'general' factor, analogous to Baumgarten's idea of the conceptual in poetry, the specification and individualization of which then leads to the concrete formulations that make up the surface features of a piece of music. The relationship between idea and metaphor, such as Baumgarten described and made the basic model of his general aesthetic theory, recurs in its logical fundamental structure—albeit in that alone—in the relationship between the abstract (the thematic element) and the concrete (the themes and thematic variations).

The 'thematic element' can be understood as the constant factor in the changing pattern of exterior forms, and, hence, as the 'analogue of the ego'—though not by someone who a priori rejects metaphysical interpretations of aesthetic matters as 'unscholarly'. For the conscious awareness of our own selves will always, inevitably, serve as the model of a unity in diversity that manifests itself in abstract, not physical, form: we know that our own selves preserve their identities in changing circumstances, and from that knowledge—from it alone—we know it of other things. To that extent, the identity that we attribute to a piece of music reflects our own identity.

If we feel compelled or challenged by some works to interpret the continual recurrence of a thematic substratum in changed forms not only empirically—as the partial similarity of differing things—but also, above and beyond that, metaphysically—as 'selfhood' manifested in ever new forms—it is obviously due to the fact that, in the case of such concrete manifestations of an abstractly 'thematic' element as are found in Beethoven's late works, the degree of tangible correspondence is too small to make the cohesion of the whole sufficiently comprehensible, while on the other hand the integrity of the work is compellingly clear from the internal evidence; in order to explain it, therefore, we must postulate the existence throughout of an 'underlying' element, which can be defined as the aesthetic subject and its identity.

Interpretation as the 'analogue of the ego' therefore seems to be inseparable from the degree of abstraction in the thematic element— which means the stage reached by the evolution of thematic thought in the late eighteenth century. An abstract thematic substratum linking first and second subjects is more often associated with the notion of an aesthetic subject that maintains its identity than are structures that are varied by means of changes in the compositional context, such as a cantus firmus, an ostinato bass, or a fugue subject. A clearly delineated, palpable musical 'soggetto'—in the terminology of musical theory from the sixteenth to the eighteenth century—does not make an impact that cries out for description as an 'analogue of the ego'. On the other hand, the presence of an aesthetic subject was always felt in Beethoven's works, although to equate it with the empirical subject discoverable in the documentary evidence about his life was to mistake its nature.

Detecting an aesthetic cypher of the awareness of the self in the identity of an abstract thematic substratum is admittedly a hypothesis that cannot be proved from documentary evidence, but one that has a logical basis of some importance in the classical musical aesthetics of the late eighteenth and early nineteenth centuries. In a treatise on the representation of character in music (*Über Charakterdarstellung in der Musik*), published in 1795 in Schiller's periodical *Die Horen*,[6]

---

[6] Repr. in W. Seifert, *Christian Gottfried Körner: Ein Musikästhetiker der deutschen Klassik* (Regensburg, 1960), 147–58.

Christian Gottfried Körner defined 'ethos' as first and foremost rhythm. By 'rhythm' he did not mean the structure of individual note durations as such but an underlying unit of measure—whether the bar, the alternation of systole and diastole, or what Mattheson called the 'musical foot' (*der Klangfuß*): the equivalent of the foot in verse metres. He contrasted 'ethos' (character) with 'pathos' (emotional states), and described it as the means whereby the listener's inner freedom was protected against the power of music to overwhelm and enslave the mind. 'Ethos' was constant, standing its ground in the midst of all the changes of 'passionate states'. Some decades later Hegel, too, identified metre as the fixed and constant element in the ebb and flow of emotions, and, to that extent, the audible symbol of the continuity of self-awareness in the discontinuity of whatever in the way of content is passing through the conscious mind.[7]

It was entirely coincidence that both Körner and Hegel looked for the element of identity in the rhythm, and not in the tonal centre of the harmony or in the thematic substratum of the musical form; and the coincidence seems all the stranger because the concept, at least, of an ethos of tonality—including, *inter alia*, a constant fundamental note amid the fluctuations of the melodic language of sensibility—was foreshadowed in the theories of classical antiquity by which every philosopher was involuntarily influenced in an age when education was still centred on the study of Latin and Greek. But the important thing is not the constraint on the way the fundamental idea was elaborated and exemplified but the decisiveness with which it was grasped in principle.

The fact that it is the more abstract factor that is taken to be the musical sign of identity—especially the abstractly 'thematic' element in the classical sonata, but also rhythm as understood by Körner and Hegel—makes it easier to understand that the path towards abstraction, in the case of Beethoven, did not lead to a loss of individuality, as has sometimes been claimed, but to a more pronounced definition of the individuality of the works. Admittedly, 'abstraction' must be understood as 'composed abstraction'—recognizable as a compositional concept—and it is composed to the extent that it proves to be a unifying element that ensures the inner cohesion of a movement, a work or a group of works. The four-note fundamental motive that recurs in some of the late string quartets is so abstract that it is often no longer possible to trace it in the score, yet no one doubts its aesthetic and actual musical existence, which is proved by its formal function. (The discovery or construction of thematic-motivic relations can be extended *ad infinitum* with very

---

[7] *Ästhetik*, ed. F. Bassenge (Frankfurt am Main, n.d.), ii, 284–6.

little effort, but a limit can be set by making a distinction between what is formally relevant and what is formally irrelevant—and hence has no aesthetic existence.)

The first movement of Beethoven's Piano Sonata in F minor, Op. 2 No. 1, is a paradigmatic example of contrasting derivation, which serves to illustrate certain conditions of musical individualization. The first subject (bars 1–2) recalls the theme of the Finale of Mozart's G minor Symphony, K 550; it is a commonplace, in other words, and one, moreover, that originated in Mannheim. The theme, of the type that Hugo Riemann called the 'Mannheim rocket', is given an element of specificity by the concluding turn in the contrary direction; but the true individualization that blots out (or at least dismisses, as irrelevant) the memory of conventions of the mid-century is not found in the theme itself so much as in the consequences that are drawn from it in the process of developing variation. The transition into the relative major is effected motivically by the use of the first subject in transposition and its second bar in isolation; the second subject is a contrasting variant of the first, sharing its melodic shape and harmonic presentation; but it travels in the opposite direction, the articulation is legato instead of staccato, the tonic triad is replaced by a dominant-seventh chord, and the diatonicism is partly suffused by chromaticism. The structural alterations signify and express a contrast of character that is one of the distinguishing features of sonata form: with all due allowance for the chronic inadequacy of words to describe music, the first subject can be described as rousing and energetic, the second as elegiac and lyrical.

The diversification and integration of the various components have their foundations in both substance and function. The developing variation of the thematic material relates to formal functions. In the exposition, the presentation of the fundamental idea as first subject is followed, in the transition, by motivic segmentation, and its presentation as second subject is followed by a reversal of direction. This cannot be explained in terms of an inner logic of the developing variation, but it is prescribed in the conventions of sonata form: the linking of the transition to another key with the technique of sequential motivic working is a practice in common use since the early eighteenth century. The substantive and the functional interlock: the direction taken by the developing variation—a process that is frequently described in musical analysis as if it was self-reliant—is dependent on the sonata-form schema; vice versa, although developing variation is not the only way to fill the outline of sonata form, in Beethoven's Op. 2 No. 1 it is accomplished by transforming the thematic material step by step. The logical general factor of developing variation and the architectural general factor of sonata form have an effect on each other that leads directly, however, to something specific, and ultimately to something individual; and the fact that the forming of concepts of individualization in musical analysis remains a process of convergence that can never reach completion is less important than the fact that it is nevertheless possible to determine the direction that leads from the general in a work, via the particular, to the individual.

The inner cohesion of Beethoven's sonata exposition is therefore established substantively, by means of the derivation of the components from a fundamental idea, which, as the 'thematic element', links first subject, transition, and second subject; and functionally, by means of the complementary contrast in the tonality and melodic character of the first and second subjects. Additionally, each of these foundations also forms part of the implications of the other: if, on the one hand, the formal functions of the sonata form prescribe the path the developing variation must take, on the other hand, the common thematic source makes the contrast between the first and second subjects recognizable as complementary contrast, rather than as unrelated difference.

The individualization of a work, as exemplified by this sonata of Beethoven's, does not depend on the thematic element alone, therefore, but also on the form that proceeds out of the themes and in turn influences their development. This may run counter to aesthetic ideas that are current as part of the inheritance of both *Empfindsamkeit* and romanticism, but it accords with fundamental premisses of the classical aesthetics of the late eighteenth century.

The demand that a work of art should be a whole, perfect and complete in itself, was placed at the heart of aesthetics and the theory of art by Karl Philipp Moritz in 1785 in his *Versuch einer Vereinigung aller schönen Künste und Wissenschaften unter dem Begriff des in sich Vollendeten* (Essay towards a union of all the arts and branches of learning under the single concept of that which is perfect in itself). The concept of 'that which is perfect in itself' is directly opposed as a principle to the concept of 'exterior purpose'. The work of art that contains its *causa finalis* in itself is a whole in itself, instead of belonging to a larger context in which it fulfils a function: it is autonomous. Moritz is so rigorous in his exclusion of functions that he anticipates Thophile Gautier's aesthetics of 'l'art pour l'art': a musical work, in so far as it makes a serious claim to be a work of art, does not exist for the sake of the hearer, nor does it serve the purpose of communication between the composer and the audience.

In contemplating that which is beautiful I drive the purpose out of myself back into the object itself: I regard it as something complete, not in me, but in itself, therefore as something that amounts to a whole in itself and affords me pleasure for its own sake; I do not relate the beautiful thing to myself so much as, rather, relate myself to it.[8]

In drawing our attention wholly to itself, beauty draws it away from ourselves for a while, and causes us to seem to lose ourselves in the beautiful object: and this very losing and forgetting of ourselves is the highest degree of pure and disinterested pleasure that beauty gives us.[9]

The wholeness, however, that Moritz apostrophizes as the central quality of a work of art is simultaneously the essential attribute of aesthetic individualization, as it was understood in classical theories of art: an individualization that manifests itself primarily in the individuality of the work, and in the formal process that brings it into being, and only secondarily in the composer's personal style and its originality. That something individual—an 'individuum'—must always be a whole is a logical truism, and implicit in the very term. That designation as a whole, as an entity having its purpose and meaning within itself, is a dominant factor in aesthetics, too, is by no means self-evident, however, but is a hallmark of one particular historical period.

The problem that led to reflection on the individuality of a work and personal style seemed at first to be insoluble. On the one hand, in so far as every concrete, self-sufficient, integrated structure is an 'individuum' in a tritely logical sense, the concept of 'aesthetic individuality' must involve something further; and there is a strong case for looking for that specific element in the composer's originality, as expressed in the work. On the other hand, however, from a methodological standpoint at least, personal style as the essence of the common characteristics of divers works by one composer is an abstraction—just like a national style, or the styles associated with periods and genres—that treats the individual work merely as an example, regards it not as a work of interest for its own sake, but as a document of something else, and thus replaces the concept of individuality with that of generality. The personal style that can be discerned in the music is methodologically the product of generalization.

If we start from the fact that in Haydn and Beethoven individuality is based less on the originality of themes than on specific formal concepts—of their contemporaries, only Francesco Galeazzi

[8] K. P. Moritz, *Schriften zur Ästhetik und Poetik*, ed. H. Schrimpf (Tübingen, 1962), 3.
[9] Ibid., 5.

perceived this[10]—it follows that the essential element of personal style must also be sought in formal ideas rather than in prominent details, be they themes, harmonic features or rhythmic surprises. If serious methodological weight is given to the recognition that Haydn and Beethoven were first and foremost geniuses of formal integration, and that it is there that their true originality lies, then the personal style can no longer be defined in terms of a heterogeneous accumulation of outstanding individual traits, but must be understood as a configuration of formal problems and the varying solutions to them. The unity that holds the style together from within is then revealed in the continuity of compositional development, rather than as a complex of characteristics; and the concept of 'personal style' is seen to be a dynamic and genetic category, not a static and systematic one. Its constitution will not be grasped by abstracting the common features from the solutions to various problems, but must be discovered by travelling in precisely the opposite direction, and recognizing that certain formal problems and the ways in which they tend to develop are characteristic of the musical thought of a particular composer. The essential feature that defines Beethoven's personal style is not the fact that he expanded and gave greater prominence to the development section and the coda of the sonata-form movement, but the fact that, having once adopted the principle of conceiving the whole form, and not merely parts of it, as thematic process, he was forced to continue the process beyond the development section; at the same time, however, he had to overcome the impulse to endless development, and bring the movement to an end that was not a stop but a goal: his coda is a paradoxical equipoise of desire to continue and definitive conclusion. But different formal problems were continually being addressed, and different solutions provided; and it is that, rather than any principle able to be formulated in general terms, that generates the individuality of each of the works.

If we concentrate on the problems rather than the solutions, and emphasize what must be reconstructed instead of what is given, the first thing to emerge is that the individuality of the single work—the thing that constitutes its artistic character—remains unaffected, because the very act of getting a problem to assume shape involves more precise and detailed definition (to outline a problem, as will be attempted in respect of the coda, is merely to establish a starting-point). With this greater precision, we necessarily commit ourselves to a concept of diversification and individualization, and thus do not

[10] B. Churgin, 'Francesco Galeazzi's Description (1796) of Sonata Form', *Journal of the American Musicological Society*, 21 (1968), 181.

move further away from the particularity of the single work but, rather, get as close to it as is possible within the limitations implied by the Goethean maxim that the 'individuum' is 'ineffable'. Secondly, one of the logical peculiarities of issues of musical form is that—unlike questions of melody or rhythm—they virtually exclude generalization, except at the cost of losing their substance (as in nineteenth-century textbooks of formal theory). As the studies of Beethoven by Hans Gál[11] and Gustav Becking demonstrate, those characteristics of melody and rhythm which can be attributed to personal style make it possible to focus on a high level of abstraction without the categories becoming starved of substance. Form, on the other hand, seems to offer many fewer opportunities for substantive abstraction, as August Halm[12] and Erwin Ratz[13] discovered when they attempted to expound generalized formal theories, and found themselves increasingly compelled to fall back on analyses that stressed the individual, rather than general, aspects of works. Thirdly, a technical compositional problem can be interpreted in terms of personal style to the extent that with Beethoven the central issue concerning the oeuvre stands in a palpable relation to the biographical facts. The central issue is the idea of mediation between a positively obligatory expression of the sublime style and an equally extreme abstraction, losing itself in esotericism; and this can, for example, be applied to the paradox that a symphony, as 'public' music, tends towards monumentality, while at the same time, as an autonomous work of art, it must justify the aesthetic aspiration to exist for its own sake by technical musical diversification. We can produce totally contrary interpretations, and either say that the central issue propounded above has a psychological and biographical foundation, or take exactly the opposite view and assert that, in the face of a configuration of issues that were 'of the period' in terms of the histories of ideas and of music, 'history'—in the dubious singular of the philosophy of history—surveyed 'the many' whose talent might have justified their choice, and picked out 'the few' who, by character and destiny, belonged to the 'elect'. Whether we are guided by the schematicism of popular biography or by the theological rigour of Holy Writ, one thing is certain: interpreting the history of composition as a history of musical problems creates the hope that it may be possible to arrive by this route—as it is scarcely possible by any other—at a mediation between personal style and the individuality of the single work.

[11] 'Die Stileigentümlichkeiten des jungen Beethoven', *Studien zur Musikwissenschaft*, 4 (1916), 58–115.   [12] *Von zwei Kulturen der Musik* (Stuttgart, ²1947).
[13] *Einführung in die musikalische Formenlehre* (Vienna, 1951).

3

'Ingenium' and 'Witz'*

The word 'Witz' meant approximately the same thing as 'esprit' in the eighteenth century, and the concept was one of the fundamental categories of Enlightenment poetics, applicable to both literature and music; although the meaning changed, its importance carried over into the early Romantic era. *Sturm und Drang*, in very broad terms, contrasted the combinatory facility of 'Witz' with the intuition of genius, and the aesthetics of the Classical era, too, assigned 'Witz' only a peripheral role. And yet, not only in the case of Haydn, where the facts are unmistakable, but also with Beethoven, it is plainly one of those fundamental aesthetic principles that can be established analytically beyond a shred of doubt.

In his *Critische Dichtkunst* (Critical poetics, 1730) J. C. Gottsched wrote:

This 'Witz' is a power of the mind, which easily perceives the similarities between things and is thus able to set up a comparison between them. Its basis is keenness of perception, which is a sign of an ability of the soul to notice much about a thing that another, in possession of a dull perception or slow understanding, would not have observed.[1]

'Keen perception' ('Scharfsinn'—*acumen*), 'wit' ('Witz'—*ingenium*), and 'judgement' ('Urteilskraft'—*iudicium*) are different aspects of the same thing in Gottsched's poetics, which may be regarded as representative of mid-eighteenth-century thinking on the topic.[2] *Acumen* distinguishes between the many characteristics of phenomena; elements observed by *acumen* are related to each other by *ingenium*, on the grounds of their similarities; *iudicium*, finally,

---

* The German word 'Witz' is cognate with the English 'wit' and both have acquired a more humorous connotation in the last two centuries than they used to have ('Witz' commonly means 'joke' today). Carl Dahlhaus's thesis in this chapter is well served by a definition in Locke's *Essay concerning human understanding* (1694): 'Wit [lies] most in the assemblage of ideas, and putting these together with quickness and variety.' (Translator's note.)

[1] (Leipzig, ⁴1751; repr. Darmstadt, 1962), 102.
[2] J. Schmidt, *Die Geschichte des Genie-Gedankens in der deutschen Literatur, Philosophie und Politik 1750–1945* (Darmstadt, 1985), i, 31 ff.

controls *ingenium* by limiting its combinatory facility to what is necessary for the logic and inner cohesion of a work of art.

As a method of creating combinations, wit, yoked with judgement, is directed to the whole of a work of art. The view that it is successful only with regard to details, and exhausts itself in momentary effects, does not do justice to the striving for wholeness which was already a prominent factor in Enlightenment poetics, and did not have to wait for the evolution of aesthetics in the Classical era to be recognized as important.

The exposition of the first subject of the first movement of Beethoven's A major String Quartet, Op. 18 No. 5, is a paradox (Ex. 3.1). After three bars of introduction, the first bar of the theme is

Ex. 3.1

initially stated in a variant form, and the 'original' form is not heard until the consequent phrase (bar 8). The variant in bar 4 mediates between the introduction and the theme. In bar 4 the 'real' beginning is replaced by a combination of the third-progressions from bars 1 and 2.

Clearly, the fundamental categories of Enlightenment poetics can be applied to this, but that does not mean that any sensible major conclusions relating to the history of ideas can be drawn from the observation. Recognition of the comparability of the fifth-progression formed by blending the third-motives of bars 1 and 2 with the fifth-progression of the 'original' start of the theme (though the rhythm of that is different) is an insight in which both keen perception and combinatory facility play a part: qualities that Gottsched approved as 'poetic'; and judgement comes to bear in recognizing that the motivic linking of the introduction to the theme makes sense.

In the Finale of the A major Quartet, the entire movement is governed by a combinatory art which can be interpreted as wit — 'Witz', 'esprit' — in the sense of Enlightenment poetics. The principal motive of the first subject, which is expounded imitatively by all the

Ex. 3.2

instruments, appears in inversion in the consequent phrase (Ex. 3.2).
The three-note up-beat is also present in inversion in bars 3 and 4, but
for the time being that remains latent. In the transition (bars 26–34)
the principal motive initiates a chromatic fourth-progression (Ex.
3.3). In the development section (bars 117–22), on the other hand, the

Ex. 3.3

inversion initiates a variant of the chromatic progression, so that
indirectly, through the interpolation of a third idea, the connection
between the principal motive and the inversion is made more obvious
(Ex. 3.4). The chromatic phrase, which forms a framework for the

Ex. 3.4

sequential repetitions of the principal motive in the development,
appears as the counterpoint to the second subject (bars 36–43), and at
the same time the fourth-leaps of the second subject are prefigured in
the outlining fourths of the principal motive from the first subject.
This produces an indirect relationship between the principal motive
and the second subject, which is reshaped into a direct relationship in
the development: the principal motive generates the sequentially
repeated fourths of the second subject (bars 144–9; Ex. 3.5).

Ex. 3.5

There is nothing arbitrary or perverse about seeing keen perception
and wit at work in the thought of linking two motives, first
indirectly, by the interpolation of a third idea, and then directly, or
in allowing a latent connection to be made manifest through the
analogous functions of different motivic components; and the logic
that underlies the motivic process is calculated, not intuitive. The
chromatic phrase in the transition to some extent anticipates the
second subject, as is appropriate to the function of a transition. And
the principal motive's generation of the second subject is positively
pedantic in its conformity to the textbook rule that the first and
second subjects must be brought into an increasingly close
relationship during the course of the development.

The motivic relationships that exist both within and between the movements of the C minor Piano Trio, Op. 1 No. 3, cannot be approached in the normal manner of musical analysis, with the use of expressions like 'monothematicism' and 'contrasting derivation'. There is an unmistakable similarity between the first subject of the first movement and that of the Finale. Both the 'backward-leaping' third, with which the movements begin, and the arpeggiated 6–4 chord, which governs their continuations, are common features that leave no doubt of the intention of making the cyclic unity of the work apparent in its motivic material (Ex. 3.6). The first and second

Ex. 3.6

subjects are not directly related to each other. This makes their indirect relationship all the more striking, and it can be said without exaggeration that it is accomplished by 'wit', as the Enlightenment understood the word. The counterpoint to the second subject is an inversion—not quite literal, admittedly, but the identical rhythm leaves no doubt about it (Ex. 3.7). The inversion brings to light a

Ex. 3.7

relationship to a component of the first subject, which is not present in the basic form of the second subject (as derived by contrast), but only comes into being indirectly through the contrary-motion imitation of the counterpoint (Ex. 3.8). The counterpoint in turn is

Ex. 3.8

the source from which, as the rhythm is recast, the lyrical continuation of the second subject is derived (Ex. 3.9). Though the expression 'motivic development' can do little to explain the

Ex. 3.9

espressivo

relationship between the themes, they are densely woven together, and there is a strong case for talking of the calculated application of a combinatory facility.

The motivic similarity between the first subjects of the first and last movements is the corollary of an analogy of syntax. Both these subjects are in two parts, with the element of cohesion being as important as that of separation. The first part seems to be introductory but is thematic at the same time, and formal consequences arise from the ambiguity.

In the Finale the transition (bar 35) is a variant of the first subject. Only the first part modulates, however, while the second part remains fixed in the relative major key of E flat for eight bars. This provides some grounds for the erroneous interpretation that this is a second subject of a monothematic sonata form. But the real second subject, also in E flat major, does not appear until bar 69. At this stage, it is now possible to feel that either the separation or the cohesion is the dominant element in the first subject. In the former case, the first and second parts separate, as transition (bar 35) and false second subject; in the latter, the connection between the two indicates that the false second subject is in reality a continuation of the transition.

The observation that the credit for the integrity of the Finale of the C minor Trio, no less than in the case of the A major Quartet, should go to combinatory facility, and not to intuition, appears to contradict Beethoven's poetic creed, as stated in 1823 and recorded for posterity by Louis Schlösser: 'I change some things, discard, and try again until I am satisfied with it; then the elaboration begins in my head: expanding, compressing, raising and deepening; and, as I know what I want, the underlying idea never deserts me.'[3] The context of this statement contains a number of features, as will be demonstrated later, that have a dubious authenticity. The authenticity of the expression 'the underlying idea', however, is beyond suspicion, and what it means is undoubtedly not the theme—that Beethoven kept the first subject in mind all the time while he was composing a movement is scarcely worth saying—but a conception of the form as a whole. If Beethoven's statement is translated into the language of

---

[3] F. Kerst, *Die Erinnerungen an Beethoven* (Stuttgart, ²1925), II, 15.

aesthetics, therefore, the integrity, the formal wholeness which Karl
Philipp Moritz placed at the heart of the Classical theory of art, seems
to be the work of the intuition of genius, where 'genius' is no longer
the rational *ingenium* of Renaissance poetics, manifested in the gift of
invention, but irrational productive power. Instead of the
combinatory facility that progresses from the part to the whole, the
fundamental arbiter is an intuition that imagines the whole in one
flash. And, in spite of Beethoven's practice of noting down isolated
and often quite rudimentary musical ideas in his sketchbooks, there
should be no doubt at all that it was the intuitive conception of the
whole, which then worked back to determine alterations to the
individual details, that was the generative element in the creative
process.

Nevertheless, the significance of the combinatory facility, born of
perception and wit, and regulated by judgement, should not be
underestimated. The fact that two fundamental categories of the
Enlightenment and of *Sturm und Drang*, wit and genius, oppose each
other in direct contradiction, forming an exclusive antithesis in terms
of the history of ideas, is no reason to deny that the two principles
can be united within the poetics of an individual composer, be he
Haydn or Beethoven. Moreover, for Jean Paul and other early
romantic artists, wit and genius—the production of a whole by
combinatory facility and by intuition—interlock in a way that
abrogates the traditional contrast and can be seen to be analogous to
the poetics implied by Beethoven's works, without necessarily
leading to the conclusion that Beethoven was 'really' a romantic.
Inwardly and outwardly, he was a contemporary of both Goethe and
Jean Paul, and how he drew his share of the spirit of an epoch that
cannot be encapsulated in a formula, will not be elucidated by use of
a label that presumes to name the *Zeitgeist* by its name; it will be
worked out only by a 'piecemeal' process, in the sense in which Karl
Popper has used that word.

4

The Symphonic Style

1. The Sublime and the 'Noble Ode'

E. T. A. Hoffmann's review of Beethoven's Fifth Symphony, published in the *Allgemeine musikalische Zeitung* in 1810, has always been regarded both as one of the finest testimonies to an enthusiasm for Beethoven that was informed by thoughtfulness and imagination, and also as a primary document of the musical aesthetics of the Romantic era, and therefore, to that extent, a source of the misunderstandings that were part of the 'romantic picture of Beethoven'.[1] There is no escaping the fact that, in some important features, Hoffmann's musical aesthetics were in direct contradiction to the principles underlying Beethoven's music. When Hoffmann, writing of the 'pure' instrumental music which he calls 'romantic', says that under its influence the listener 'leaves behind all emotions that can be defined by words and concepts, in order to abandon himself to the inexpressible',[2] he is close to Ludwig Tieck's view that symphonies are 'not of this world': 'they reveal the greatest mysteries in mysterious language, they do not depend on rules of probability, they do not need to ally themselves to narrative or character, they abide in a purely poetic world.'[3] Tieck distinguishes between instrumental music, in which art is 'independent and free' and vocal music, which is 'always only a qualified art': 'it is, and will always be, elevated declamation and speech'.[4] Tieck himself was the originator of the aesthetic theory of absolute music, but in ridding it of declamatory and descriptive elements, in order to raise it to a metaphysical plane, Tieck was manifestly at odds with Beethoven, who thought of sonatas and symphonies as 'expressive' art and the 'representation of character' in sound.

On the other hand, for all its tempting simplicity, the notion that Hoffmann subjected the 'classical' symphony to a 'romantic' model

---

[1] A. Schmitz, *Das romantische Beethovenbild* (Berlin and Bonn, 1927), 81.
[2] *Schriften zur Musik: Nachlese*, ed. F Schnapp (Munich, 1963), 34.
[3] W. H. Wackenroder, *Werke und Briefe* (Heidelberg, 1967), 255.
[4] Ibid., 254.

of interpretation is wide, or at least short, of the mark, in so far as some of the essential categories underpinning his review of the Fifth Symphony do not originate in either the romantic musical aesthetics of Tieck and Wackenroder or the rudiments of a classical musical aesthetics that can be found scattered in the writings of Karl Philipp Moritz and Christian Gottfried Körner. Rather, their antecedents lie in a tradition of thought that coexisted alongside classicism and romanticism and, in its relevance to the symphony quite as much as to literature, reached back well into the eighteenth century. This is the tradition manifested in the poetry of Klopstock and Hölderlin, and the novels of Jean Paul. The romanticism of Wackenroder and Tieck—and the *Schwärmerei* of Bettina Brentano—aroused no sympathetic response in Beethoven, whereas the poetics of Klopstock and the group of budding littérateurs who briefly came together in the 1770s as the Göttinger Hainbund (Göttingen League of the Grove) formed an important constituent in the traditions in which he was reared—under the influence of Neefe—and to which he remained loyal all his life. And, as will be seen, those same ideas leave their stamp on Hoffmann's writing about Beethoven.

For a representative view of the ideas associated with instrumental music in the grand style in late eighteenth-century Germany, we can turn to J. A. P. Schulz's article on the symphony, in Johann Georg Sulzer's *Allgemeine Theorie der schönen Künste*. The style that is, or should be, manifested in the symphony, according to Schulz, is the noble or the sublime. 'The symphony is pre-eminently suited to the expression of things grand, solemn, and sublime.'[5] The literary model which Schulz felt the symphony called to mind was the ode. 'An allegro of this nature is in the symphony what a Pindaric ode is in poetry; like the latter, it uplifts and convulses the listener's soul, and it requires the same spirit, the same sublime power of imagination and the same artistic erudition to be happy therein.'[6] According to the eighteenth-century definition, it is characteristic of the ode that it ignores the dichotomy of poetry charged with emotion and poetry charged with thought (*Gefühlslyrik* and *Gedankenlyrik*), and expresses a reflectiveness that is borne up by enthusiasm, or an enthusiasm informed by reflectiveness. Karl Viëtor, in his *Geschichte der deutschen Ode*, defined the style of Hölderlin's odes as the attempt to attain to 'the sublime height of Pindar with deliberation and passion in equal measure'.[7] Passion and deliberation,

[5] *Allgemeine Theorie der Schönen Künste* (Leipzig, ²1794; repr. Hildesheim, 1967), iv. 478.
[6] Ibid., 479.
[7] (Munich, 1923; repr. Darmstadt, 1961), 162.

enthusiasm and reflectiveness are, however, the elements which combine to determine Schulz's theory of the symphony quite as much as Hoffmann's. A symphony's power to 'uplift and convulse the soul' constitutes, for Schulz, the corollary of the 'artistic erudition' that a composer must possess if he is to be 'happy' in the genre. For his part, Hoffmann on the one hand describes the Fifth Symphony in language that strikes the dithyrambic tone of an ode: 'Beethoven's music arouses awe, fear, horror, and pain, and awakens that endless yearning that is the very essence of romanticism.'[8] On the other hand he praises the 'deliberation' revealed in an 'inner structure' of the music, such as could not be achieved without 'prolonged study of the art'.[9]

The multitude, while it does not penetrate Beethoven's depths, does not deny him a high degree of imagination; on the contrary, his works are usually seen as solely the products of a genius who, careless of form and the selection of ideas, has abandoned himself to his ardour and the momentary promptings of his imagination. Nonetheless, in respect of deliberation, he is entirely fit to be set at the side of Haydn and Mozart. He keeps his 'Ego' apart from the inner realm of music and reigns there as absolute lord. Just as the inspectors of aesthetic weights and measures have often complained of the total lack of true unity and inner coherence in Shakespeare, and only a more profound eye sees a beautiful tree, with its buds and leaves, blossom and fruit all growing from a single seed: so too only a very profound penetration into the inner structure of Beethoven's music will unfold the master's noble deliberation, which is inseparable from true genius and nourished by prolonged study of the art.[10]

Thus the underlying categorial model of Hoffmann's critique of Beethoven—a model that is also reflected in the division of the essay into dithyrambic and analytical parts—derives from a tradition of musical aesthetics that exists independently of classicism and romanticism alike, and looks back to the poetics of Klopstock and the Göttinger Hainbund. And the dependence of the aesthetics of the symphony on literary theories of the ode, to which Schulz's article testifies, is borne out even in details of his terminology. 'The allegros of the best chamber symphonies contain great and bold ideas, free handling of the theme, apparent disorder in melody and harmony . . . sudden transitions and digressions from one key to the next, that strike all the more strongly for the weakness that is often found in the connection.'[11] Schulz's use of the expression 'apparent disorder' is a

[8] Hoffmann, *Schriften*, 36.
[9] Ibid., 37.   [10] Ibid., 36 f.
[11] Sulzer, *Allgemeine Theorie*, iv. 479.

direct allusion to the terminology of contemporary writing about the ode. Moses Mendelssohn, for example, wrote of the ode:

The order that is essential to it can be called the order of the enthusiastic imagination. Just as concepts attain, one after another, to the highest degree of liveliness in the enthusiastic imagination, so, and in no other manner, they must succeed one another in the ode . . . The intermediate concepts which link the members to each other but do not themselves possess the highest degree of liveliness are o'erleapt by the poet in the ode; and thence results the apparent disorder that is ascribed to the ode.[12]

And when Schulz singles out the 'expression of the sublime', the 'sublime power of imagination', 'great and bold ideas', and 'sudden transitions' in the symphony, another excursion into literary theory reveals that this entire configuration of concepts, the linking of the unexpected, the apparently unmethodical, and the rhapsodic with the sublime and the enthusiastic, was prefigured in the characterization of the ode set out by Edward Young in 1728, in his discourse *On Lyric Poetry* (published in German in 1759). 'Its thoughts should be uncommon, sublime and moral . . . its conduct should be rapturous, somewhat abrupt, and immethodical to a vulgar eye.'[13]

Thus it was on a tradition in eighteenth-century aesthetic theory that Hoffmann drew in 1810 when he attempted to put into words the overpowering effect of the Fifth Symphony. At the same time the categorial model which underlies that essay is by no means confined to Beethoven in other writings by Hoffmann. In 1821, intervening in Berlin musical politics, he published a panegyric on Gaspare Spontini's opera *Olympia*, in which, referring to the first-act finale, he writes of the 'effect of the aweful' and the 'expression of inner horror' on the one hand, and, on the other, of a development of musical ideas which 'testifies not only to his [Spontini's] genius but also to the deliberation he brings to his mastery of the realm of music'.[14] The association between the emotional convulsion wrought by a work of art and the deliberation with which it was conceived was identical with the association, made in the eighteenth century, between spontaneous outpouring and reflection in the ode. Hoffmann praised the combination in both Spontini and Beethoven. Whether he found it in vocal or instrumental music, it signified the 'grand style' that was his ideal, a style in which monumentality and the art of differentiation were inseparable instead of mutually exclusive.

As a rule Hoffmann is lavish in his use of the word 'romanticism',

[12] G. E. Lessing, M. Mendelssohn, et al., *Literaturbriefe*, no. 275. Quoted in Viëtor, *Geschichte*, 140.
[13] E. Young, *Ocean: An Ode . . . to which is prefix'd, An Ode to the King; and a Discourse on Ode* (London, 1728), 14 ff.   [14] Hoffmann, *Schriften*, 382.

but its only appearance in his essay on Spontini is with reference to Mozart. This suggests that, in the essay on the Fifth Symphony, too, the actual aesthetic discussion of the symphony, centring on the concepts of 'emotional convulsion' and 'deliberation', may not be as closely bound up with the dithyrambs about musical 'romanticism' as it at first appears to be. And if Hoffmann's theory of symphonic style, in some of its fundamental elements, originates in the eighteenth century (a period whose 'aesthetics of genius' should not be equated with 'romanticism'—or not, at all events, when discussing Beethoven, whose proximity to Rousseau is as obvious as his inner distance from Wackenroder and Tieck, Novalis, or Friedrich Schlegel), at the same time his interpretational model was shared by other nineteenth-century writers on music, such as Friedrich Rochlitz, who can scarcely be numbered among the romantics. In other words, although the romantics adopted the idea of developing a theory of the symphony out of the aesthetics of the sublime, and modified it in their own characteristic way, it is by no means their exclusive property.

Rochlitz, it must be admitted, could not accept the contradictions in the concept of the sublime, which, in the language of early nineteenth-century aesthetics, embraced both the vocal style of a Palestrina and the instrumental style of a Beethoven. He made a terminological distinction between the 'sublime', which he found expressed in early sacred music, and the 'grand' or 'great' (*das Große*), as manifested in the contemporary symphony. (In his essay 'Alte und neue Kirchenmusik', 1814,[15] Hoffmann's approach to the issue of mediating between the sublime style in early sacred music and in modern instrumental music related it to more general concerns of the philosophy of history.)

The 'grand', as conceived by Rochlitz, is 'powerful, convulsive'.[16] 'The sense of the grand has—if it is permitted to say so— more of the earthly about it than the sense of the sublime; it has more of violence, affect, rapture.'[17] Even the 'apparent disorder' which figures in writing about the ode crops up again in Rochlitz: 'Music in the grand character demands the press of a multitude of melodies and harmonic turns that at first seem impossible to combine, yet nevertheless come to be united in a melodic and harmonic whole.'[18] And he uses almost the same words as Schulz to describe the surprise—the unexpectedness—of sudden transitions: 'The modulations into remote keys are not rare, or unobtrusive, but

---

[15] *Schriften*, 229.
[16] 'Vom zweckmäßigen Gebrauch der Mittel der Tonkunst', in *Für Freunde der Tonkunst* (Leipzig, ²1830), ii, 166.
[17] Ibid., 167.   [18] Ibid., 169.

striking and rapid.'[19] The idea that a 'whole' can result from things that seem 'impossible to combine'—that, as Hoffmann puts it, the effect of 'the master's noble deliberation' actually overwhelms the listener—was of the essence of the sublime style as it was understood in the eighteenth century. Sulzer expressed it as follows in the article on the sublime in his *Allgemeine Theorie der schönen Künste*: 'When order is created out of disorder and confusion, then, for those who discern in some degree the rightness of it, it is a sublime thought that, out of all the apparent disorder in the physical and moral world, the most beautiful order is achieved in the whole.'[20]

Schulz's article on the symphony, in which he compared an allegro movement to a Pindaric ode, was quoted at length by Heinrich Christoph Koch in 1793, in the third part of his *Versuch einer Anleitung zur Composition*. Koch added a comment on periodic structure which shows how the aesthetic theory applied to compositional technique:

The structure of this period (and of that of the other periods of the symphony) differs from the structure of periods in the sonata and the concerto . . . in that (1) its melodic components are customarily more extended even at their first appearance than in other pieces of music, and, especially, (2) these melodic components usually cohere together better, and flow onwards more strongly, than in the periods of other pieces of music, that is, they are combined in such a manner that their phrase-endings are less conspicuous.[21]

Koch's use of the term 'flow onwards' (*fortströmen*) to describe symphonic forward movement takes up a metaphor frequently used of the ode (Herder called the ode 'a river [*Strom*] that carries away everything movable in its current').[22] It derives ultimately from a poem by Horace, written in praise of Pindar, and warning of the perils of imitating him.

> As when a river, swollen by sudden showers,
> O'er its known banks from some steep mountain pours,
> So in profound, unmeasurable song
> The deep-mouth'd Pindar, foaming, pours along.
> Well he deserves Apollo's laurel'd crown,
> Whether new words he rolls enraptur'd down
> Impetuous through the Dithyrambic strains;
> Free from all laws, but what himself ordains . . .[23]

[19] *Für Freunde der Tonkunst, ii*, 169.   [20] *Allgemeine Theorie*, ii. 99.
[21] (Leipzig, 1793; repr. Hildesheim, 1969), iii. 305.
[22] Quoted in J. Schmidt, *Die Geschichte des Genie-Gedankens in der deutschen Literatur, Philosophie und Politik 1750–1945* (Darmstadt, 1985), i. 182.
[23] *Odes*, iv. 2, trans. P. Francis, *The Works of Horace* (London, 1807).

The general understanding of the Pindaric ode in the eighteenth century was that, firstly, it combined an irresistible and continuous forward motion with a deceptive appearance of rhythmic anarchy ('free from all laws'), and, secondly, it provided a paradigmatic example of the fact that even a 'profound, unmeasurable song', intended to appear 'impetuous' and natural, must rest on a basis of conscious artistic method. It was in that spirit that poets strove to imitate it. Herder, again, wrote of Pindar:

The creativity of his words, and the concatenation of his periods, even unto the rending of the syllables, even unto the overflowing out of the strophe, even unto his manifold number [i.e. the variety of his metres], even unto his apparent fury, is yet (truly!) not the product of wild phrenetis. On the contrary, all requires so much excellent art and selection that, just as the Lyric Speech itself is perhaps the most artistic of all the kinds of poetry, so Pindar, of all the Greeks, in my view, stands on the highest pinnacle of Poetic Art.[24]

The character which Schulz's article gives the symphony seems to anticipate those of Beethoven, among which the earliest musical analogue to the Pindaric ode is not the Third but already the First. The degree of calculation behind the 'onward flow' postulated by Koch can be demonstrated in both the periodic structure and the motivic development (Ex. 4.1). The first subject of the first

Ex. 4.1 Adagio molto   Allègro con brio

movement expounds the motive g–b–c' in three different rhythmic guises. At the same time the chord progressions of bars 12–13 and 18–19, G^7–C and A^7–d (with the chromatic third-progression b–c–c♯–d as upper voice), are prefigured in the slow introduction (bars 1 and 3–4). Consequences are drawn from both these elements. In the transition the quaver version of the first subject and its transposition to D minor are placed directly next to each other (bars 41–2); at the beginning of the second subject the crotchet version appears in a subsidiary part (bars 53–4; it is possible, however, that this is a coincidence, an analogy of the notes but not of the motive); and the closing group quotes both the first subject in its first rhythmic version and the chord-progression from bars 18–19 (bars 88–90, and 93–4).

The metrical and syntactic irregularity that is among the hallmarks of the Pindaric ode, according to Horace, can be observed in the first

[24] Quoted in Schmidt, *Geschichte*, i. 188 f.

subject of the First Symphony, as can a feature mentioned by Koch: the 'melodic components . . . flow onwards more strongly' because 'they are combined in such a manner that their phrase-endings are less conspicuous'. At the beginning of the theme, a five-bar group in the strings and a three-bar group in the woodwind interlock, so that the combination (as Koch would say: *Zusammenziehung*) produces a seven-bar complex that is as irregular as the elements of which it is composed. However, if the first subject is compared with other parts of the exposition in respect of syntactic structure, it is possible to arrive at an interpretation that uncovers a principle at work behind the appearance of anarchy.

The beginning of the transition (bars 33 ff.) is constructed from two four-bar groups, of which the second is a variant of the first. Two bars of tonic harmony alternate with two bars of dominant, and the end of the motive occurs at the beginning of the fifth bar (Ex. 4.2). One hesitates, however, to speak of an overlap between the fifth

Ex. 4.2

bar of one group and the first of the other, partly because it would conflict with the principle of regularity of the four-bar phrase structure (and therefore was not mentioned, even to be denied, by Hugo Riemann), and also because it would make it impossible to avoid the assumption that an analogous interlocking takes place in the third bar also. Thrasybulos Georgiades has borrowed from architecture the analogy of 'skeleton construction' for the succession of harmonically open-ended four-bar groups, the first of which is complemented by the whole of the second—and not by a fifth bar alone that coincides with the first bar of the second group.[25] The harmonic 'skeleton' and the melodic 'cladding'—Georgiades speaks of background and foreground—do not need to conform to each others' outlines: the melodic phrase can extend beyond the framework without its necessarily being an instance of interlocking phrases: an ending is not being reinterpreted as a beginning, but rather the ending and the beginning, appearing simultaneously, belong to different strata of the music.

A framework or skeleton, in the Georgiadesian sense described above, can also be formed from three-bar groups. In the continuation of the second subject (bars 79–87) an oboe phrase, three bars long, is transposed from B flat major to G minor, and closes in G major (Ex. 4.3). To interpret the first bar as an augmentation, and thus reduce

[25] *Schubert: Musik und Lyrik* (Göttingen, 1967), 69 ff.

Ex. 4.3

the three bars to two, would be uncalled-for because the harmony changes. Equally, there is no reason to assume that phrases interlock, because the fourth bar is separated from the third by an abrupt harmonic caesura: the dominants of B flat major and of G minor relate to each other only indirectly. Bar 84 in turn, in spite of the close harmonic connection with bar 85, is primarily an analogue of bar 81; and even bars 85–7—for all the appearance that the elision that Koch called '*Takterstickung*' (the 'stifling' of a bar) takes place in bar 88—can equally well be regarded as 'skeleton' according to the law of inertia.

Against the background of the syntactic structures that can be observed in the transition and in the continuation of the second subject, the first subject can be interpreted as a grouping of 6 + 6 + 6 bars. The three sections (which are harmonically 'open-ended', in the nature of the 'skeleton construction') outline a cadence, I–II–V, in the overall context, (and the concluding first degree is composed out as a cadence in the immediate context), so that it seems justified not only to interpret bar 19 as consequent to 18, and bar 25 as consequent to 24, but also to relate the second six-bar group as a whole to the first, and the third to the second. (The analyst who cannot accept the theory of 'skeleton construction' and would prefer to stay with the idea of phrase-interlock, needs to suppose, at the very least, that the first and the second sections have not one but two bars in common—a hypothesis that may look unusual, but is by no means absurd.)

Regardless of whether we attribute it to the elision of bars, or accept the principle of 'skeleton construction' and admit the distinction between harmonic 'skeleton' and melodic 'cladding', the syntax of the First Symphony, which is representative of Beethoven's symphonic style as a whole, is complex, and wrought with conscious art. The apparent 'anarchy' is as spurious as it is in the Pindaric ode. And it is precisely the apparent irregularity—worked out in advance, but executed freehand, so that it appears spontaneous to that extent— that is the source of the continuity, that 'onward flow' which, according to Koch, is the essential hallmark of the symphony.

2. The Monumental

For the creative musician, the symphony is the means of communicating to a large public, through the vehicle of instrumental music. The thought of this public is with him when he conceives the work, and stays with him as he executes it. Thus he not only composes what can be read plainly in the score, but at the same time he also composes the space and the audience as he imagines them.[26]

Paul Bekker offered this statement as a definition of the symphony, from a sociological rather than a technical postulate. But while he was right to emphasize the effect of performance in an actual space or room, it is a feature that demonstrates how analysis of a score can turn into the discussion of aesthetic issues. The gradual increase in the number of parts at the beginning of Beethoven's Ninth Symphony creates an impression of spatial depth; but at the same time it also serves to introduce the instruments as gradually as the thematic material: the first-subject group in the principal key—a feature that distinguishes a symphony from a string quartet or a sonata—is not only a statement of motives that will provide the movement with its material, but also a presentation of the orchestral apparatus that will be the vehicle of the motivic development. (The definition of the symphony as 'orchestral sonata' is misleading, in so far as it suggests that a symphony is a sonata scored for an orchestra.)

According to Bekker, 'the significance of the Beethovenian symphony'—note the collective singular—is to be found in the fact that 'it organizes the new humanity of the turn of the century as an artistic form'.[27] The humanity to which Beethoven's symphonies address themselves, however, is not just a 'gathering of the people', as Bekker put it, but also the inner humanity of each individual— what Herder had in mind when he spoke of 'an education in humanity'. The idea that the one could not exist without the other, that is, that politics must be based on morals, and morals on politics, was one of the fundamental principles of the idealism to which Beethoven's symphonies give musical expression.

[26] P. Bekker, *Die Sinfonie von Beethoven bis Mahler* (Berlin, 1918), 13.
[27] Ibid., 18.

The monumental style in music, of which Beethoven's Ninth Symphony is the paramount example, is founded—as Arnold Schering propounds[28]—on the aesthetics of the sublime, which was, for J. A. P. Schulz, virtually identical with the aesthetics of the symphony. But Beethoven found his models for the sublime style in Handel's oratorios, rather than in earlier instrumental music. He admired Handel's oratorios above all, it seems, because they embodied in vocal music the monumentality that he sought to achieve in the symphony. One of the essential ingredients of the monumental style is a simplicity that stands up to being stated emphatically, without collapsing in empty rhetoric. The first subject of the first movement of the Ninth Symphony (Ex. 4.4) starts, fortissimo, with

Ex. 4.4

a simple (though rhythmically differentiated and pointed) arpeggiated triad and a cadential figure. This material (the thematic ideas, in the narrower sense) is followed by chords accentuated by sforzatos, which provoke the objection that insignificant material is being manipulated by dynamic means to create an 'event'. But the sforzatos are justified by the irregular syntax: the first motive consists of three bars, and the second of two, the second of which interlocks with the first bar of the continuation; it is this coincidence of end and new beginning that is marked by the first sforzato—from which the others necessarily follow. Thus a reciprocity arises between the syntax, which motivates the accents, and the intention of moulding a monumental style by means of emphatic simplicity; and just as to say that the monumentality is generated by complication of the syntax would tell only half the story, so, too, accentuation that was not justified by the phrase structure would be superficial.

Syntactic irregularity is the exception, however, rather than the rule in the Ninth Symphony. Even the development (bars 160–300), which might be expected to be fissured on the surface, consists almost exclusively of four-bar groups: the originally irregular motives of the first subject are made regular, whereas the usual procedure is for a development section to render the regular irregular. Admittedly

[28] 'Über den Begriff des Monumentalen in der Musik', in his *Von großen Meistern der Musik* (Leipzig, 1940).

the four-bar groups are harmonically open-ended, thus forming a framework, a Georgiadesian 'skeleton': against a harmonic background with regular phrase structure, the foreground fills with melodic motives and phrases that are independent of the framework as a matter of principle, and may keep within its limits or may not.

The third bar of the subject consists of the last note of the first motive and the start of the second; isolating it in this way yields an example of the curious phenomenon that, although motives are habitually compared to words, they can be cut up into syllables, so to speak, and reassembled in new combinations. When it is reworked in the development (bars 192–7), this bar generates a harmonically open-ended group of six bars, based on the chord-scheme I–IV–V (of the subdominant, with scale degree V composed out; Ex. 4.5). The

Ex. 4.5

conventional complement would consist of two bars in the tonic—which allows us to wonder whether the new motivic entry on the tonic of IV (bar 198) should be interpreted as an interlocking phrase encompassing two bars, rather than the usual one bar. (Modifying Hugo Riemann's system, this could be expressed by the formula 7 and 8 = 1 and 2.) But if we admit that phrase-overlap by more than one bar is possible in theory, then the next step could well be to conclude that the 'skeleton construction' understood by Georgiades as the complementation of the first four-bar group by the complete second group—and not as the intersection of individual bars—is in some sense overlapping over a larger span.

Regardless of how the sequence of harmonically open-ended four-bar or six-bar groups is interpreted, it should be beyond question that it is a means of realizing a monumental style, because, alongside the open-ended harmony of the groups of bars, the simplicity of the proportions stands revealed as an example of that 'onward flow' commended by H. C. Koch as a characteristic of a symphonic allegro in the sublime style.

Among the characteristics of monumental style represented in paradigmatic form in the first movement of the Ninth Symphony is a slow, regular harmonic rhythm. It is only a very slight overstatement to claim that a change of harmony every two or four bars is the underlying norm in the development section, in spite of its urgent onward movement. The concept of 'harmonic rhythm', which originates with Jan LaRue,[29] needs to be qualified, however, if a purely mechanical process of counting and measuring is to be avoided. The cadences in bars 196–7 and 214–5 are undoubtedly intended as devices to speed up the slow harmonic rhythm, advancing at two-bar intervals, of the preceding bars. On the one hand, it is not certain whether distinct functional identities are the only elements that may be counted as rhythmic units, or if prolonged harmonies also count; on the other hand, the complete two-bar group can be interpreted as scale degree V, composed out. The change of chord after one crotchet is as real as the change of function after two crotchets and the basic scale degree V, which, by analogy to the preceding degrees I and IV, encompasses two bars. There is no alternative, therefore, but to accept the existence of several strata in the harmonic rhythm, which correspond to the several strata in the metre, in the alternation of heavy and light beats.

Slowness and regularity of harmonic rhythm might both seem out of keeping with fugal style, of which a rapid and irregular change of chord is a standard feature. On the other hand, fugue, or fugato at the least, is virtually a *sine qua non* of monumentality in the music of Beethoven's model, Handel. A fugato duly forms the heart of the development (bars 218–40) of the first movement of the Ninth Symphony. The subject of the fugato is an expanded version of the middle motive of the first subject, and the formal context in which it appears is ambiguous in as much as the fugato is preceded by a variant of the third bar of the first subject, which proves retrospectively to anticipate the first bar of the fugato. As we would expect in Beethoven, the fugato is drawn to some extent into the process of the thematic working.

Strictly speaking, the fugato theme is five bars long, but different methods are employed to ensure that it consists of an even number of bars, as monumental style requires. A modulating introductory bar is attached to it on its first appearance, on the second occasion a harmonic sequence is interpolated, serving the same function of modulation, and on its third entry the end of the subject interlocks with its opening. Thus to some degree the irregular syntax of the fugato covertly reflects the symphonic syntax.

Monumental style and dramatic style would seem to be mutually

[29] 'Harmonischer Rhythmus in Beethovens Symphonien', in *Ludwig van Beethoven*, ed. L. Finscher (Darmstadt, 1983), 181 ff.

exclusive. The sense of pressing onwards to a goal, which lends music the character of dramatic urgency, is in many respects the opposite of the ordered construction on the grand scale, which invites us to pause and reflect. Yet there is no denying the impression that the first movement of the Ninth Symphony is both monumental and dramatic. If we seek an explanation, we can start by acknowledging that the intersection of the opposing elements is prefigured in the first subject, in as much as the arpeggiated triad is a static element, and the accentuation is a dynamic one. But the decisive factor behind the impression of simultaneous stillness and movement towards a goal is the principle of 'skeleton construction' that underlies the development. On the one hand, as already stated, the four-bar groups are harmonically open-ended: the second forms a necessary extension of the first, and the third in turn proceeds out of the second. On the other hand the regular phrase structure, which is in some sense a musical realization of the law of inertia, contains an element of stasis, and the two things seem to exist side by side, instead of developing from each other. But this dichotomous impression is precisely what is characteristic of the monumental style in music, which may be comparable to architecture, but differs from it by reason of a temporal element which always contains a trace— however diffident—of the dramatic.

One of the attributes of the 'noble simplicity' of the monumental style is that it can be seen as a balanced whole. That is ensured in music by the regularity or equality that Eduard Hanslick called 'rhythm over the large span' (*Rhythmus im Großen*). The term means that the relationship of strong to weak beats is reproduced in the dimensions of the bar, the bar-group, the phrase, and the complete period, with the proviso that the limit up to which the principle of complementarity remains effective shall be determined only by the specific circumstances, and not by abstract principle. In the development of the first movement of the Ninth Symphony, which does not contain a single complete period, the complementation does not appear to extend beyond the relative sizes of the four-bar groups. But it is also possible to interpret a succession of four-bar groups, in which the first is neither stronger nor weaker than the second, as 'rhythm over the large span', for simple, undifferentiated succession is—in spite of theorists' prejudices—as much a fundamental form of rhythm as the alternation of strong and weak beats. Perhaps it is a lowlier form, yet even that is open to question if we take into account the fact that the simple equality of elements is one of the characteristics of the monumentality that embodies the sublime or noble style.

3. Temporal Structures

Antoine Reicha, in 1826, compared sonata form to drama, which, according to the laws of classical poetics, consists of an exposition—the 'tying of the knot', and a dénouement—the 'untying' of the knot. And there can be scarcely any doubt that, after years spent close to Beethoven, in Bonn and later in Vienna, Reicha based his interpretation of sonata form on Beethoven's works, above all the symphonies.

If Reicha's comparison is to be anything more than an association of passing interest, we must distinguish between 'drama' as a genre and 'dramatic' as a stylistic concept. A novella can be 'dramatic', and a theatre piece can be 'epic' or 'lyric'. What Reicha thought he recognized in Beethoven's symphonies was not the pragmatic category of the drama as an action involving characters, but the aesthetic concept of dramatic process. It is not that the themes of sonata-form movements represent protagonists and antagonists, acting together or against each other; rather, the temporal structure of the symphonic allegro is equivalent to that of dramatic style, which was characterized by Emil Staiger as '*reißende Zeit*' (a term which represents time as something in motion that snatches up and bears away whatever lies in its path, like a river in spate).

If we translate this metaphor into a language appropriate to musical matters, the temporal quality manifested in Beethoven's symphonies can well be described as teleological: the symphonic allegro seems to strive inexorably towards an end that is both a goal and a result; and the individual musical moment, rather than being self-sufficient, demands to be understood as the consequence of what has gone before it, and the premiss of what comes next. The substance of the present consists in the past from which it has emerged, and in the future to which it beckons. (The terms 'present' and 'moment' are used to mean a present time as understood in the psychology of perception, and not the punctuality of the 'now' (*das Jetzt*), from which Hegel developed a theory of rhythm in his *Ästhetik*.)

The fact that the symphonic allegro is goal-directed means that the time to which it belongs is not merely a medium in which it moves but is itself sensed as a forward movement that the music makes palpable and perceptible. Music enables time to be experienced as a process. Processuality is embodied in a particularly emphatic and extreme form in Beethoven's symphonies, where it manifests itself in the development of a theme or that of the interaction of themes. The 'modern concept of the theme', as Hugo Riemann called it, was one of the fundamental categories of eighteenth-century instrumental music, alongside harmonic tonality and the principle of rhythmic-syntactic complementarity. Hitherto instrumental music had been subject to the models provided by vocal genres, and conditioned by the extra-musical functions it fulfilled in association with dance and ceremonial; but emancipation dawned when it achieved aesthetic independence in the allegro, for one thing, as a demonstration of the 'musical logic' of thematic development, and in the adagio, for another, as the melodic utterance of the 'language of emotions'. Initially, in the process of emancipation, the emotionally charged adagio was regarded as the most important movement in a symphony, to which the lively allegro served merely as an introduction; the fact that the allegro later came to be regarded as more important is one of the differences between the ages of *Empfindsamkeit* and classicism.

Interpretation of the temporal structure that underlies thematic process is never independent of the metaphor used to describe the process. H. C. Koch thought of the totality of the themes in a work as the plan or disposition (*Anlage*), the actual substance of which was worked out in the later sections of the composition by means of 'dissection' (*Zergliederung*), complementation, and elaboration. He started, that is, as an unwitting Aristotelian, from the premiss that the thematic material is an epitome of possibilities that are turned into actualities by the formal process.

August Halm described sonata form as the 'history of a theme'; evidently the analogy he had in mind was the *Bildungsroman*, in which, by virtue of the situations he encounters, a character progresses from a condition of diffuse uncertainty to one of understanding and confidence. For Halm, sonata form was less a function of the theme than the reverse: the theme was a function—a dependent variable—of the form.

Another option is to regard the theme as a text, and the formal process as one of exegesis. Some theories of form adopt the biological model, which achieved a dominant position in aesthetic theory in the late eighteenth century; from that standpoint, musical formal process is seen as an organic development which allows something to become manifest that was present in the theme but concealed at first.

In textual exegesis—and hence in musical formal process, if that is understood as exegesis—the starting-point around which commentary and elaboration circle, as it were, is usually more important than it is when the development of a theme is regarded as a 'history' that not only brings its latent meaning to light, but also draws conclusions from the given premisses which go beyond what was in the theme as originally laid out. Verbal models never fit musical works perfectly, however, and it is by no means altogether certain whether the process is one of 'explication'—literally 'unfolding' to reveal what is hidden in the 'folds'—or of the concatenation of inferences that lead on into the unforeseeable. However, in Beethoven, as a general rule, the feebler the substance of the initial theme is, the more urgent the development seems to be; and that observation permits the conclusion that forward motion stimulated by the poverty of a theme, rather than by any richness, is particularly teleological in nature, and creates a strong impression of a series of consequences, in which each present moment grows out of the immediate past, and simultaneously puts forth the shoots of the future.

The word 'development', which we regularly use without giving it a second thought, is like most familiar expressions, admittedly, in that it is full of implications that cause musicological havoc if they are ignored. The notions that the latent substance of a theme gradually rises to the surface, that a thematic germ swells and grows into a form, or that a theme is the epitome of possibilities that are gradually made into actualities, all remain vague as long as we fail to remember that, in Aristotelian philosophy, the term 'motion' refers not only to change of place, but also to qualitative change, and that this dual meaning applies conceptually to the way time manifests itself in music.

The association of a musical process with a change of place (an association that is physically expressed in the horizontal spread of the notation) is probably impossible to undo now, in spite of the argument of Bergsonians in favour of the definition of 'motion' as articulated by individual beats in the bar, and their relative strength or weakness. As a convention in the reception of music, it has so long a history that it is almost possible to call it a natural attribute, and it may legitimately be regarded as a fact that can be said to be built into the foundations, at least, of European music.

If we adopt the Aristotelian definition of time as the 'measurement of a motion, taking "before" and "after" into account', then we can apply the concept of motion to qualitative changes of thematic material, as well as to rhythmic structure articulated by bar-divisions; the 'measurement' of the motion is time manifesting itself in the music. And it is only by having recourse to qualitative changes that we can obtain a definition of time that is uniquely descriptive of music. Music, on the one hand, must be localized in time—in unrepeatable 'real' time—and, on the other hand, it encompasses or fills a given (repeatable) period of time: this is fundamental, yet it is still unspecific in that it also applies to other processes which have nothing to do with music. Again, the phenomenon of 'experienced' time—the observation that objectively equal periods of time are experienced as longer or shorter, according to their content, and/or the mood in which they are perceived—is not confined to music. By contrast, a theme as the substratum of a 'motion'—the thing that underlies the formal musical process—is a specifically musical phenomenon: the decisive element is the fact that what underlies the qualitative changes is produced from within the music itself. However, if music on the one hand invokes the association of a change of place, and on the other hand consists of qualitative changes, the substratum of which is contained in the music itself, then it follows that it not only proceeds in the medium of time, but is also, in an emphatic sense, 'composed time': 'time' understood as 'measurement of a motion', and doubly defined as an imaginary change of place, and as the qualitative change of its own substratum; the double definition is also that which characterizes the Aristotelian concept of motion, preformed in the Greek language.

That the qualitative changes of a theme, usually called motivic working and development, represent a 'motion' that corresponds to a specific temporal structure, does not amount to a definition of all music, but only of music in 'the age of thematic processes' (K. H. Wörner). It has always been acknowledged that the temporal quality of music is at its most pronounced in Beethoven's symphonic style, which is regarded as the quintessence of a processuality launched by thematic material, so that the metaphysical speculation—as so often—finds a foothold in everyday experience, and serves as its explication.

The most prominent syntactic characteristic of a symphonic style that is perceived to be dramatic is that its parts lack independence: tension is created because the individual element is not self-sufficient but demands a complement, and thus points the way to something else beyond itself. Admittedly, in order to furnish an adequate description of the symphonic allegro as distinct from the adagio— thematic form as opposed to melodic—we must distinguish between simple and problematic (or disrupted) complementarity. In the dramatic symphonic style, the decisive factor is not so much the correspondence as such, but rather, so to speak, the imperfection of the correspondence: a balance should be perceptible, certainly, but so should a compulsion to continue.

In the first movement of the Eighth Symphony the tempo seems more relaxed than the direction 'allegro vivace e con brio' suggests, because the dotted minim can be sensed as a secondary pulse, alongside the crotchet. The categories of 'antecedent' and 'consequent' clauses do in fact hold good in the bar-groupings of the first subject, not as a significant structure in itself, however, but as the means of achieving the opposite to the usual function of an integrated period: a process of continuous forward motion from one bar-group to the next. The ambiguity manifested in turning the consequent phrase into an antecedent cuts across the syntactic solidity that we expect from a theme (Ex. 4.6). The first eight bars can

Ex. 4.6

be interpreted as antecedent and consequent. The harmonic succession I–V is reversed to give V–I (bars 7 and 8 compose out scale degree I); and the beginning of the consequent corresponds rhythmically to that of the antecedent. Thus the conditions of a period—motivic analogy and harmonic complementation—are met. But the ending reached in bar 8 is not a strict periodic full close, and therefore bars 9–12 act not as the repetition of bars 5–8 but as their consequent. Thus, since bars 5–8 form both a consequent phrase and an antecedent, bars 1–12 are an entity in the sense of the 'onward flow' of symphonic music advocated by H. C. Koch. Bar 12, however, is simultaneously the start of a transition, in line with the principle of 'skeleton construction'. True, bar 12 is the conclusion of the first subject motivically, while bars 13 and 14 belong together motivically (as do bars 15–16 and 17–18). But harmonically, and structurally, bars 12–19—and not bars 13–20—form an integrated block, based on the scale progression I–IV–IV$^5_6$–V; according to Thrasybulos Georgiades, when a bar-group is harmonically open-ended, the whole bar-group following represents a complement. Thus by a variety of means—reinterpreting a consequent phrase to make it an antecedent, making an ending and a new beginning interlock, and realigning the phases of harmonic and compositional skeleton and motivic cladding—continuity is achieved; and in spite of the fact that the syntactic construction started out on the basis of regular phrase structures, that continuity is founded on precisely calculated disruptions of the equilibrium.

Joining elements together by always leaving an unresolved remnant which forces a continuation is an alternative to Hanslick's 'rhythm over the large span'; this, too, establishes syntactic continuity, but by means that are different in principle. The first syntactic unit—a single beat, a bar, a phrase, a partial or a complete period—is followed by a second such, which acts as the necessary complement. The question as to whether the second unit is strong or weak is irrelevant, in so far as a dominant on the up-beat leading to a tonic on the down-beat may be perceived as strong, if it is informed by a propulsive intensity, or weak, if the premiss merely yields to the outcome. The decisive factor is that there is a steady increase in the order of magnitude, so long as complementarity between first and second units is the rule: we relate the second bar to the first, the second pair of bars to the first pair, a four-bar consequent to a four-bar antecedent, and finally the second period to the first.

The Larghetto of the Second Symphony is a sonata-form movement, and the development, the material of which consists essentially of the opening bars of the first subject, is by no means as rudimentary as we normally expect in a lyrical slow movement. Yet, except in the development, the dominating principle is not that of thematic contrast and development, but that of melodic parataxis. The continuation of the first sixteen bars is not subordinate, but a formal element of equal importance, and even the transition (bar 33) is melodically independent.

The first eight bars form a period with a half-close on the dominant, and a full close in the key of the dominant; motivically, it is true, the consequent does not relate to the beginning of the antecedent, but it follows on from its conclusion. The second period reproduces the first, but the richer orchestration lends it the character of a complement, and the juxtaposition of two things that are otherwise the same is enhanced. The continuation is syntactically an eight-bar 'period', put together from a sequence of 2 + 2 bars and a cadential consequent. Since the beginning recalls bars 1–2 motivically and the close is in the principal key, it is reasonable to regard the first subject (which closes in the key of the dominant, as mentioned) and the continuation as being in the relationship of a period 'over the large span' (16 + 16). The continuation is repeated, like the first subject, with the weak cadence in bar 24 matched by a stronger one in bar 32. Moreover, again as with the first subject, richer instrumentation suggests complementarity rather than mere repetition. Thus, without interpretational wilfulness, we can speak of a realization of the periodic principle in three orders of magnitude: in the ratios of 4 : 4, 8 : 8, and 16 : 16. The differentiation of half and full closes, the alternation of cadences in the dominant and the tonic, the motivic associations, and the richer orchestration, all serve the purpose of making the 'rhythm over the large span' perceptible as a hierarchic principle.

The procedure whereby ever larger elements occupy the forefront of attention, while the correspondences of smaller details continue to be noticed, of course—the establishment, in other words, of a balance of corresponding segments in regularly increasing dimensions—is the opposite of a goal-directed process, without necessarily excluding teleological elements in details. We may speak, with Jacques Handschin, of 'architectonic' form, as distinct from 'logical' form. The three-dimensional metaphor suggests that the music to some extent obstructs the passing of the period of time to which it belongs, instead of yielding to it, or representing it, as Beethoven does in his allegro movements, so emphatically that it seems that it would not exist if the music did not make it.

It is wrong to assume that 'rhythm over the large span' requires strict equality in the dimensions of the corresponding units: the 'Quadratur' mocked by Wagner. A relationship that we perceive as one of balance and complementarity can perfectly well exist between bar-groups of differing lengths. It is not unreasonable to interpret a group five, six, or seven bars long, which forms the consequent to a four-bar antecedent, as a variant of a latent, underlying regularity of phrase structure—an extension by means of interpolation, augmentation, or addition. Hugo Riemann's method of deriving irregular bar-groups from the 'normative base scheme', without exception and as a matter of principle, has admittedly attracted frequent and outspoken criticism, but his mistake was not the procedure itself but its wholesale application. The fact that there undoubtedly exist three-bar and five-bar groups that cannot be reduced, whatever Riemann may have thought, is no reason for drawing the conclusion that reduction is fundamentally wrong: the sensible antithesis to rigidity of dogma is not rigid repudiation of dogma, but making finer distinctions and differentiations therein. And whether deriving a three-bar or five-bar group from a regular four-bar structure answers the purpose or not depends, among other things, on whether the principle underlying the syntax is that of 'rhythm over the large span', or that of complementarity with 'unresolved remnants'. If the balance of the elements overall is form-building, then it is not unreasonable to leave the question of how best to reduce irregular bar-groups unresolved.

The temporal structure in a piece of music is generally interpreted as the placing and layering of accents in the relation of the present to the past on the one hand, and to the future on the other hand (as above, in this context the word 'present' is understood in the sense that it has in the psychology of perception, and does not mean an abstract 'now', a point in time).

The statement that the principle of 'rhythm over the large span' is a means of establishing a relationship of complementarity between ever larger formal elements—from bars to bar-groups, and so on, up to periods and on to period-groups—also implies that the aesthetic present bears on its back an ever-growing burden of the past, which the listener must keep in mind. Conversely, the principle of looking upon each element of the form as a problem whose solution lies in the next element—which will prove to be a problem in its turn, also demanding a solution—gives rise to a process in which the present is, to use Hegel's terms, not so much 'at itself' (*bei sich*) as 'beyond itself' (*außer sich*) in the future towards which it strives.

In a movement where the form is built by means of 'rhythm over the large span', the past is present as a 'first rhythmic element', which demands to be augmented and complemented by a 'second rhythmic element'. The overall form is the outcome of the fact that, as each new element presents itself, we do not experience it as an arbitrary addition, but expect it to prove to be the complement to the earlier elements, in ever-increasing orders of magnitude; while an ever larger past must remain aesthetically present.

On the other hand, in movements where the present's relationship to the future predominates, the significance of the past is problematical. The various interpretations of Beethovenian sonata form that were outlined near the beginning of this section can all be understood—without this being what the authors necessarily had in mind—as answers to the problem of how to interpret the temporal structure of a form that is both theme-dependent and teleological, and is therefore accented simultaneously by its beginning and its end.

The deficiencies of the metaphors used in the attempt to describe the relationship between the starting-point and the end, understood as a goal, are so obvious that it would be supererogatory to make a polemical issue of them. A drama in which the catastrophe—literally the 'turn for the worse'—meant the return of the initial situation would be, strictly speaking, nonsense. And the idea that the possibilities in thematic material are rendered actualities through transformation of the themes or thematic fragments is an unsound metaphysical interpretation of the simple empirical facts of variation technique: it represents an attempt to mediate between the fact of the transformation of something that was given at the start, and the impression of goal-directedness.

One answer to the difficulty of establishing a correlation between theme-dependent and teleological—that is, backward-looking and forward-looking—identity, is to choose thematic material with an aptitude not so much to generate the form from within itself, as to be, on the contrary, a function of the form, as August Halm put it. The goal-directed urge that is unceasingly at work in Beethoven's symphonies is then not the outcome of the material, but something that takes possession of the material.

Thematic material that is 'in the service of the form' is almost always melodically rudimentary, which August Halm lamented as a deficiency, although he recognized the necessity for it. As a result it provides less a constant point of reference and more the mere starting-point of the development. But in Beethoven's case the functionally determined poverty of the material is not infrequently linked to the formal concept of transferring the 'real' thematic material from the surface of actual melody and rhythm to a lower 'submotivic' stratum, consisting of more abstract structures. (If what we understand by a motive is a concrete melodic and rhythmic construct, then an intervallic configuration without a fixed, constant rhythmic identity represents a more abstract structure that belongs to a 'submotivic' region.) Nothing could be more abstract than the arpeggiated triad in the first movement of the D minor Piano Sonata, Op. 31 No. 2, which serves, without rhythmic specificity, to link the preliminary form of the theme (bar 1) with its more substantial manifestation (bar 21): the latter modulates, however, so that the preliminary form is endowed retrospectively with the function of an exposition in the tonic.

If we allow that melodic poverty and abstraction can be proper attributes of thematic material, the whole purpose of which is to be the function of a goal-directed formal process, we can also, conversely, see a relationship between melodically richer material and a passage of time that is more like a circling motion than a teleological process. In a form which is not, or is less emphatically, goal-directed, the development of motivic fragments of the theme is comparable to exegesis in a verbal medium, as an alternative to drama. (Schubert provides examples which must be regarded as a valid alternative to the Beethovenian type, rather than as something that suffers from the comparison.)

The idea of a circling motion, showing a theme or its elements from a succession of different aspects, and serving to establish a specific temporal structure of the music, provokes the objection that it is impermissible to project characteristics of a process that takes place in time on to time itself. In the face of the problematical relationship between theme-dependent and teleological identity, different emphases are possible: an elaborative, backward-looking orientation consequent upon richly differentiated thematic material on the one hand, and, on the other, the effectuation of an urgently forward-moving formal process; but these are, however, processes in which time not only represents a medium but is also, to some extent, 'composed'. In a Schubertian development, the first-subject material is constantly present in the mind as the object of exegesis, and in this aesthetic present time it wears the colour of the past; the 'past-ness'—the conception of the time that extends between the development and the exposition—is, however, one of the aesthetic facts of the music. But if the past is 'subsumed' in the present, as an aesthetic fact of a goal-directed process that leaves the past behind, circular motion around the thematic material is like a memory in which the past reaches out into the present.

5

Issues in Sonata Form

1. Motivic Relationships

One of the preconceptions that do more harm than good in musical analysis is the belief that it is a triumph of methodology if it can be shown that the entire motivic and thematic substance of a movement—and even the non-thematic components—derive from the same motivic 'cell', just one interval-succession.[1]

It is, for one thing, unsound to start from configurations of notes or intervals alone, and to ignore rhythm, as if the latter did not belong to the musical 'idea' but only to its 'presentation' (to use Schoenberg's terms). The thesis that the identity of a note is 'central' and its duration 'peripheral'[2] may be illuminating in theory, but in analytical practice—including the analysis of twelve-note music—it proves deficient. Separating the parameters or characteristics of notes, and following up intervallic associations without reference to rhythm, or rhythmic associations without reference to interval-succesions, is appropriate and useful in many contexts; but it never implies that rhythm is intrinsically less, or more, important than the intervallic aspect.

Secondly, the method employed to deduce the evolution of a whole movement from a handful of notes or intervals is clumsy, in as much as, for the sake of the omnipresence of the 'cell', the analyst must accept so great a number of transformational possibilities that virtually everything can be derived from everything else. There is a beguiling simplicity about the idea of having the principle of the inner unity of a movement set out before one's gaze in a tangible substratum; but there appears to be no escape from the unhappy alternatives that either the scope of the analysis must be restricted to a few sections, or the number of types of variation to which the intervallic substance can be subjected will grow to an unmanageable total.

[1] R. Réti, *The Thematic Process in Music* (London, ³1961).
[2] J. Handschin, *Der Toncharakter* (Zurich, 1948), 388 ff.

Thirdly, the process of finding the whole of a movement or a work preformed in a single intervallic 'cell' is linked to a debatable conception of development. The interpretation is influenced by a model adopted from organic life, which encourages thinking of intervallic substrata as if they were seeds in which the growth of the form is already determined, although empirically there is nothing to be observed other than that certain characteristics of a structure recur in the variants, and others are changed. The conception of 'development' is a metaphor which is unexceptionable so long as it means nothing more than that the alteration of characteristics is a process in time; but it becomes questionable if it is made the basis for the metaphysical conclusion that an intervallic configuration is a 'cell', from which growth proceeds according to a musical law of nature which a composer must obey, rather than make the law himself.

The truth is that a musical formal process does not issue from any one single origin, but requires a number of different, linked or overlapping, initial starting points and associations; and there will be differences in the attributes of the notes in which these manifest themselves, in the degrees of abstraction underlying them, and the extent of their range. A configuration which serves to build form can be abstract or concrete, essentially intervallic or rhythmic, and possess local or wider significance.

The first subject of the first movement of the A major Piano Sonata, Op. 2 No. 2, is rich in internal relationships, which we can usually—but not always—describe as motivic (Ex. 5.1). The rising

Ex. 5.1

fourth-progression in bar 10 recurs in bars 11–12 in a different metrical position, and this repositioning within the bar is a change as significant as setting the original rhythm aside would be. The motivic forms in bars 12–13 and bars 13–14 can be interpreted as analogous to a tonal statement and answer; the recourse to fugal technique includes, admittedly, a measure of reflection such as is not found in the usual forms of motivic variation. The sequence of the motives in bars 12–14 is then (with the tonal answer no longer recognizable) presented in diminished form in the transition (bar 32), and the fourth-progression from which the development started is quoted in inversion (bar 33).

Metrical repositioning is also instrumental in the transition to the second subject (Ex. 5.2). The changing-note figure in bar 48 is not

Ex. 5.2

only inverted in the next bar, but also differently accented. And the start of the second subject is then formed by presenting the interval-succession of the first version in the metre of the second. It is therefore not exaggerating to speak of a high degree of abstraction.

It is scarcely possible to dismiss the associations as fictive, but they are impossible to describe unless we adopt criteria which allow for changing parameters. Inversion is a purely intervallic phenomenon, tonal answer one of fugal technique, diminution one of rhythm, and repositioning in the bar one of metre: and none of these can be ignored in the attempt to reconstruct the network of motivic relationships to which the exposition of the A major Sonata owes its continuity and its integrity. (It would be dangerous to speak of total comprehensiveness, for the ambition to expound the derivation of each and every note could become an obsession.) It might be objected that—except in the case of a tonal answer—we could set rhythm and metre aside and still discover the same associations: in other words, that the interval-succession alone provides the substratum of the inner unity. But the intervallic structure is not the only essential feature of the motivic references in bars 48–9 and 59: the dialectics of melody and metre also plays a vital part, and that dialectics is processual and not, like intervallic derivation, to some extent independent of time.

In the discussion of musical aesthetics the idea of likening musical structures to verbal ones—that is, comparing a period to a sentence, and a motive to a word—is a commonplace that goes back to the Middle Ages. But the delimitation of motives, unlike that of words, is frequently uncertain or ambiguous. Hugo Riemann invariably began a phrase at an up-beat, as a matter of principle, but it sometimes led to absurd consequences, and was only possible because the uncertainty leaves room for dogmatism.

The articulation of a theme according to its motives is not always

clear-cut, with the result that it can vary. Repositioning the caesura—
a phenomenon that occurs frequently in Beethoven—is not a form of
distortion, whereby the composer abuses his own ideas, but the
exploitation of an ambiguity that is present in the theme from the
first.

The first subject of the first movement of the Ninth Symphony is
syntactically irregular in so far as the first motive comprises three
bars, and the second two; furthermore, the end of the second motive
interlocks with the beginning of the third (Ex. 5.3). In the

Ex. 5.3

development bar 3 is isolated for repetition and sequential treatment
(Ex. 5.4). It is unlikely that, in the exposition, the D in bar 3 is meant

Ex. 5.4

to be understood not only as the close of the first motive, but also as
the start of the second, producing an interlocking like that in bar 5:
unlikely, because the leap of a tenth, which is modified to one of a
third in the development, marks a caesura. But reluctance to abandon
the belief that the subject is distorted in the development leaves no
alternative but to accept the existence of an ambiguity which goes one
way in the exposition and the other way in the development.

Systematic investigation is scarcely possible without going into
much greater detail, but it can at least be said that the ambiguity of
articulation which invalidates the word/motive analogy is one of
the characteristic ploys of Beethoven's syntax. The first subject of the
first movement of the 'Pastoral' Symphony begins with a phrase, the
articulation of which is interpreted in a number of different ways in
the course of the movement (Ex. 5.5). Reading the first note of the

Ex. 5.5

second bar as both the last note of the first motive and the first of the
second seems to offer a way out of the problem that the theme can be
dissected or segmented in a number of different ways; but, strictly
speaking, it is not so much a solution to the problem as merely a way
of expressing it. Bar 2 is isolated in the development, and repeated

wellnigh obsessively to provide the motivic substratum for extended passages of music. Bars 5–7 of the exposition, however, display the contrary articulation, reaching not from the first quaver to the fourth but across the barline, from the second to the first; and the same articulation forms the basis of bars 16–29. Thus the theme implies the possibility of a twofold articulation, but nothing would be gained by regarding one variant as the fundamental form and the other as merely a sub-form.

This changeableness is not a lack of clarity—although it can manifest itself as uncertainty—but a means of varying a theme or a motive, like a change of rhythm. At the same time it means that when we are reconstructing the motivic relationships on which the inner unity of a movement is based, we need not shrink from accepting a relationship as still valid, even when there has been a change of articulation. In so far as differentiation of the articulation is one of the techniques of thematic-motivic working, it is also one of the premisses from which the discovery of motivic relationships can begin.

The first subject of the first movement of the D major Piano Sonata, Op. 10 No. 3, is unmistakably articulated as 4 + 4 + 6 notes (Ex. 5.6). (The consequent clause begins with sequential treatment of

Ex. 5.6

the first motive, which leaves the articulation in no doubt.) The second motive is an inversion of the first, with the further change that the stepwise progression is replaced by an arpeggiated triad; and the third motive represents a middle course, in so far as it fills in the triad with seconds.

Unambiguous as it is, the articulation of the first subject does not prevent the reduction of the second motive to a three-note group, by the subtraction of the last note. If we accept this reduction as a comprehensible variant (although it causes the motivic relationships within the first subject described above to go into abeyance), we can then see a relationship between the first subjects of the first and last movements which would remain fictive if we insisted on the motive's having four notes (Ex. 5.7). If therefore, on the one hand, the

Ex. 5.7

discovery of motivic relationships depends on the extent to which we are prepared to accept variant forms as aesthetically real, so, conversely, the formal range of a motivic relationship can be a reason for not dismissing a hypothetical relationship as merely a fiction.

It seems doubtful whether the second subject of the D major Sonata can be derived partly from the first (Ex. 5.8). The notion that

 Ex. 5.8

the quavers at the beginning of the second subject decorate the note a′, thus creating a framework that represents an inversion of the second motive of the first subject, is not very plausible at first sight. However, the reality of motivic relationships depends to some extent, as has been said, on the formal functions they fulfil. If we accept that there is an association between the first and second subjects, then we have a case of the phenomenon Arnold Schmitz called 'contrasting derivation'.[3] But a link which simultaneously creates antithesis remains necessarily latent; and the possibility of ascribing an aesthetic reality to the hypothetical relationship rests on two things: firstly, that latency is one of the generic characteristics of 'contrasting derivation', and secondly that, as Schmitz demonstrated, 'contrasting derivation' is a positively stereotypical Beethovenian procedure, which experienced listeners can detect, so long as they expect it, in even its more remote manifestations. Furthermore, the second subject is followed by a continuation, the material of which is the opening motive of the first subject, so that the context in which the second subject is placed confirms the association with the first subject: the association manifests itself with progressively greater clarity, in the overt presentation of an initially latent motivic relationship.

2. Models of Sonata Exposition

The scheme known as sonata form was first drawn up in the early nineteenth century, on the basis of the works of Beethoven, especially the piano sonatas.[4] It was not intended primarily as an analytical tool, but as an aid in teaching the rudiments of

---

[3] *Beethovens 'Zwei Prinzipe'* (Berlin and Bonn, 1923).

[4] F. Ritzel, *Die Entwicklung der 'Sonatenform' im musiktheoretischen Schrifttum des 18. und 19. Jahrhunderts* (Wiesbaden, 1968).

composition. The over-simplification with which it has been charged was therefore a consequence of the purpose it had to serve.

As formal theory was subsumed in analysis, the scheme was not so much revised as subjected to a change of function. It no longer has the status of a norm regulating the outlines of a sonata movement, but it serves as a heuristic model, providing the starting-point for an analysis, and supplying the categories with which the analyst seeks to pinpoint the particularity of the individual work, on the grounds of differentiation or emendation. In theory the sonata-form scheme has been discredited; in the practice of analysis, however, it seems to be indispensable even now, and we continue to use the traditional nomenclature in the consciousness that it would be equally difficult either to replace it or to give a serious justification of it.

The idea that the scheme and departures from it relate to each other like the general and the particular is attractive but deficient. The differences between the model and the reality of Beethoven's piano sonatas constitute in part not the particular traits of individual works, but characteristics that, while not actually generic, occur so frequently that it is possible for us to speak of modifications occupying a position midway between generalities and particulars. A presentation that summarizes and draws general conclusions is therefore valuable, without it being necessary to decide whether there are sufficient departures from the textbook scheme to make revision of the scheme essential. (The decision is unnecessary in so far as the modifications, together with the general attributes, constitute the premisses which must underlie the analysis of the particular and the individual.)

No one who brings an open mind to the analysis of Beethoven's piano sonatas will deny that sometimes, between the transition and the second subject, there occurs a melodic idea which is self-sufficient and pregnant, but—inasmuch as it modulates—cannot rank as the first of two second subjects; or that the section that follows the second subject is too long, as a rule, to be regarded as the mere customary appendix; or that the final group is frequently no mere epilogue, but achieves thematic self-sufficiency and even represents the countersubject in monothematic movements (which therefore, strictly speaking, are not monothematic at all).

The facts outlined here are so patent that the habit of not taking any notice of them must be rooted in the intuition that we would get into insoluble theoretical difficulties if we did. That is not to say that there is no argument about the model of sonata form: but controversy over the question of whether the dualism of an exposition is primarily thematic or tonal in origin does not touch the essentials of the scheme—the tripartite framework that would be affected by consideration of the modifications mentioned above. The old dogma that thematic contrast is the decisive attribute of a sonata exposition, which goes back to the nineteenth century, has been revised in the last half-century by theorists and historians like Leonard Ratner[5] and Jens Peter Larsen,[6] who in part invoke theories of the eighteenth century, and propose the alternative view that tonal antithesis is the crucial characteristic. The tendency towards monothematicism which is prevalent in Haydn's works of the 1780s is easily explained if we refer to contemporary formal theory: in so far as the marking of the dominant or relative major by a theme— which, does not matter—is the decisive element, a second subject still fulfils its primary function even if it corresponds in part or *in toto* to the first subject, instead of contrasting with it.

If we claim to proceed descriptively and not normatively, we should admittedly take care not to hypostasize the primacy of tonal antithesis as an attribute of sonata form—sonata form, that is, as a collective term for a prescriptive form which does not exist. During the nineteenth century, thematic structure gradually usurped the pre-eminence of tonal structure—although Beethoven's works formed the exemplar for A. B. Marx,[7] his theory of sonata form reflects this development to some extent; then in the twentieth century, with Schoenberg, the ultimate consequence of the primacy of thematicism proved to be the paradox of atonal sonata form. In Beethoven, by comparison, the significance of tonal structure is still paramount; form, as August Halm recognized,[8] is less a function of thematicism than the reverse: thematicism is a function of form. The reciprocation between thematic and tonal structure is so subtle, however, that it is impossible to make any pronouncements of general principle about the forms it takes, or the degrees of emphasis on the two parties; it can be discussed only by reference to specific cases.

The debate about the primacy of the thematic and the tonal, which should really be an argument about differences of degree and the course of their evolution, does not touch on one of the essential premisses of traditional sonata-form theory: that certain correlations between tonal and thematic elements are constitutive in sonata form. We expect a transition to be both tonally open-ended and non-thematic, whereas in the case of a second group we expect exactly the

---

[5] 'Harmonic Aspects of Classic Form', *Journal of the American Musicological Society*, 2 (1949), 159–68.
[6] 'Sonatenform-Probleme', in *Festschrift Friedrich Blume* (Kassel, 1963), 221–30.
[7] *Die Lehre von der musikalischen Komposition*, iii (Leipzig, ³1857), 281 f.
[8] *Von zwei Kulturen der Musik* (Stuttgart, ³1947).

opposite, namely that it will be tonally closed and melodically substantial; furthermore, as stated above, the decisive factor will not be the novelty of the theme but the fact that the entry of the opposing tonality will be marked by a theme—even if it is only a variant of the first subject. The prominence given to the entry of the contrasting key is the decisive new factor by comparison with the unobtrusive introduction of the dominant or relative major in suite-movement form: it becomes an 'event', as August Halm put it. (Halm was wrong to accuse suite-movement form of a lack of clear articulation, however; the error arose because he thought normatively rather than historically.)

Using the term 'non-thematic' of a transition is not a crude simplification. Rather, it rests on the terminology coined by Hugo Riemann, which seems at first more bizarre than plausible. According to Riemann,[9] only the first statement—and any subsequent restatements—of a pregnant and complex musical idea can be described as thematic, not the working of it. Transitions and developments therefore count as non-thematic sections, even when they work motives from the first subject—and thus rest on the principle that Riemann himself called thematic-motivic working. The terminology may seem self-contradictory, but it is useful in formulating the correlations that underlie the conventional theory of sonata-form exposition; and it is not impossible that that was the very purpose Riemann pursued with his eccentric use of words.

The simple formula whereby the tonally closed sections in a sonata exposition—regardless of whether they are in the tonic or the dominant—are simultaneously thematic and, vice versa, the tonally open-ended sections are simultaneously non-thematic, represents the premiss for the sake of which the three-part scheme (made up of first subject, transition, and second subject, with the closing group merely an appendix) became entrenched in formal theory, although in practice certain deviations are not only obvious but also widespread. The correlations between the thematic and the tonally closed on the one hand, and the non-thematic and the modulatory on the other, are deeply rooted in the tradition of independent instrumental music; and it is no exaggeration to say that they are among the fundamental preconditions of formal thinking in the instrumental music of the eighteenth century. The linking of these defining attributes lived on in the practice and the theory of sonata form, but in the early eighteenth century it was an essential trait common both to the concerto and to the fugue, which could not have been a form at all in the narrower sense without it. The ritornello and the episode in a

[9] *Große Kompositionslehre*, i (Leipzig, 1902), 426 f.

concerto, like the development and the episode in a fugue, relate to each other as tonally closed and open-ended sections on the one hand, and as thematic and non-thematic sections on the other.

The fact that this correlation was one of the traditional features that had made possible the evolution of an independent instrumental music, emancipated from vocal music and operating with its own formal categories, explains the reserve shown towards phenomena that deviated from the conceptual stereotype: the melodically pregnant, independent, but modulating musical idea intervening between transition and second subject; the expansive continuation of the second subject, which threatens the relative proportions of first and second groups; the closing group invested with thematic interest, with motivic material that frequently underlies substantial sections of the development. (Convention has it that the closing group did not become a 'third subject' until Bruckner, with whom its dimensions grew so large—in proportion with the other sections—that it was no longer possible to speak of a secondary formal section, but that is a *fable convenue*.)

There were probably two reasons justifying the view that thematic dualism was the fundamental attribute of a sonata exposition—apart from a general liking for dichotomies: one was the fact that the second subject, as distinct from the closing group, introduces a contrasting tonality; the other was the preconception that the drama, which, ever since Reicha, had been regarded as the principal characteristic of sonata form, must be based on the conflict between a protagonist and an antagonist. The inconvenient fact that the second subject is frequently of minor importance in the actual battleground—the development—or even fails to turn up there at all, was quietly ignored.

The investing of the closing group with thematic interest is not a norm in Beethoven's piano sonatas, but it occurs frequently enough to permit us—bearing in mind the questionableness of the normative pretensions of sonata-form theory—to call it an attribute with scarcely less general validity than the standard scheme itself. In the A major Sonata, Op. 2 No. 2, the closing group (bar 104) has a hymnic quality which distinguishes it from both the first and second subjects. In the F major Sonata, Op. 10 No. 2, the closing group (bar 56) acts as a scherzando foil to the lyrical second subject (bar 19), and the resulting character contrast is positively a stereotype, found in sonata expositions as early as Haydn. The closing group (bar 106) of the D major Sonata, Op. 10 No. 3, also strikes a hymnic note; the fact that it has been anticipated in the continuation of the second subject (bar 87) does not affect its thematic independence. In the E major Sonata,

Op. 14 No. 1, the closing group (bar 47) is everything that Hugo Riemann required the first subject of a sonata to be: a complex structure containing contrasts within itself. In the G major Sonata, Op. 14 No. 2, it consists of particles from the first and second subjects (bars 49–50 = bar 33, and bars 52–3 = bar 1). And in the D major Sonata, Op. 28, it is another scherzando (bar 136).

This rapid survey of Beethoven's piano sonatas of the 'first period' suffices perhaps to show that it is not a lack of melodic independence but the fact that the closing group does not have a new key of its own that is the reason why it has been denied recognition as a 'third subject'. The concept of thematic dualism does not tolerate a 'third subject', but although it represents the aesthetic 'idea' of sonata form its structural foundation is shaky. The second subject owes its status to the fact that it marks a change of key—which is an element that belongs to the tonal, not the thematic, structure of sonata form; and although it is true that the tonal structure is the dominant one in Beethoven, it leads by so short a head that it was possible for A. B. Marx to adopt the mistaken view that the thematicism was the decisive factor. But at the very moment when theorists chose to emphasize the thematic structure, they ought really to have abandoned the dualism thesis in the interests of which they made the choice, because the only justification for denying the closing group the status of 'third subject' lay in the tonal structure which gave the second subject its importance.

The closing group is not the only section of a sonata movement to be undervalued in the theory of 'classical' sonata form—which is in fact an epigonal theory. The second subject is usually followed by quite a long, non-thematic section, the self-sufficiency of which is denied in sonata-form theory by means of a terminological feint: the expression 'second group'—in place of 'second subject'—is justified in so far as it acknowledges the separation of the tonal and the thematic elements, but it also serves to play down the non-thematic continuation of the second subject, as a mere prolongation of little or no functional significance. Only in descriptions of solo concertos did it acquire a name of its own, where the difference between the lyrical second subject and the virtuoso 'display episode' was impossible to overlook.[10] But there are obstacles to the adoption of 'display episode' as an expression for general use: it is appropriate in the cases of Op. 2 No. 2 (bar 84), Op. 2 No. 3 (bar 61), Op. 10 No. 2 (bar 38), Op. 13 (bar 89), and Op. 22 (bar 44). On the other hand, in Op. 10 No. 3, the continuation of the second subject (bar 67) is a

[10] H. Engel, *Die Entwicklung des deutschen Klavierkonzertes von Mozart bis Liszt* (Leipzig, 1927), 124.

development of the opening motive from the first subject; in Op. 14 No. 1 (bar 39), it has the scherzando character which is normally an attribute of closing groups.

The difficulty of discovering a suitable term is doubtless one of the reasons for the reluctance to do theoretical justice to the relative self-sufficiency of the continuation of the second subject. Admittedly, the decisive factor must have been that there is no proper place for a non-thematic and non-modulating episode in a formal specification that depends on the distinction between thematic and non-modulating sections on the one hand, and non-thematic and modulating sections on the other, even when it is hard to deny that the episode in question is at least as independent as the transition.

It is not easy to decide whether the relative self-sufficiency of the second subject's continuation and the thematic pregnancy of the closing group are sufficient reasons to speak of a five-part model of sonata exposition—replacing, or at least offering an alternative to, the three-part model of first subject, transition and second subject. There are too many instances of the need to expand the customary scheme to allow us to speak of a mere variant, lacking an independent status. On the other hand, 'display episodes' and closing groups invested with thematic interest do not occur as regularly as the other formal sections, so that one hesitates to propose a root-and-branch revision of the scheme. Furthermore, to the extent that the textbook scheme no longer represents a norm, only secondary importance now attaches to the question of whether, in the case of the models—the five-part and the three-part—on which an analysis can be based, the possibilities deserve to be regarded as equally valid or not.

The most bewildering problem in the way of constructing a theory of sonata exposition to do justice to the reality of Beethoven's sonatas is neither the continuation of the second subject, nor the closing group, but the odd phenomenon of a section that is melodically pregnant, sometimes even lyrical, but also tonally open-ended, and comes between the transition and the second subject. There can be no question of a mere continuation and extension, which can be lumped together with the transition because it duplicates its function. On the contrary, the interpolated episode, which lacks a name, is quite distinct from the transition, and in some sonatas it gets under way after preparatory and delaying figuration of the kind that is characteristic of the situation immediately before a second subject. Furthermore, the concept of the 'lyrical transition'—a transition that, for lyricism's own sake, to begin with at least has a key of its own, albeit often a remote one—is a paradox: a self-contradiction which, while not impossible aesthetically, is so uncommon that its recurrence in several sonatas has an alienating effect. On the other hand, it would be unsound to speak of the first of two second subjects, for this interpolation does not fulfil the primary function of a second subject, which is to confirm the harmonic integrity of the whole movement by using the dominant or the relative major.

The inner contradiction of a formal section which combines the modulating function of a transition with the lyricism of a second subject can be regarded as a particular manifestation of a general principle which is among Beethoven's most significant formal ideas. In late eighteenth-century sonata form—both in the state that became codified as the theoretical model and in other states—the sections of the exposition are characterized by the fact that formal functions, tonal structures, and aesthetic characters have to some extent grown together: a transition is tonally open-ended and melodically unspecific, a second subject, by contrast, is tonally closed and lyrical. Beethoven, however, tends to take the complex apart, and put its separate components together again in an assemblage other than the usual one: a transition takes on lyrical traits, although it modulates, and a second subject, although tonally closed as one would expect, motivically resembles a 'display episode'. Naturally the departures from the standard model of sonata exposition presuppose that the listener is acquainted with it, and will make comparisons with it; and it could well be said that structures that have come to be regarded as quasi-natural phenomena ('second nature' in the sense used in the Russian theory of formalism) represent a form of that lightening, even dissolving, of mass that is sometimes known as 'durchbrochene Arbeit'. The modified form, which to some extent represents the common form at two removes, is based on a process of reflection which can be reproduced by the understanding listener—or what we might call the 'implicit' or 'implied' listener, to employ another term from literary theory.[11]

In the exposition of the A major Sonata, Op. 2 No. 2, the transition (bar 32) leads in orthodox fashion to the dominant of the dominant, but thereafter two melodic ideas confront each other; it is hard to decide which of them is the 'real' second subject, because of the way the mix of attributes is shared between them. It cannot be ruled out that the intended meaning of the formal structure is the ambiguity, rather than either one of the alternatives. (It is sometimes virtually impossible to arrive at an interpretation that transcends banality, without running the risk of inadmissible 'modernization'.) The first melodic idea (bar 59) provides a lyrical contrast to the first subject, begins in the dominant minor (E minor), and returns to it at

[11] W. Iser, *Der implizite Leser* (Munich, 1972).

the end, but is characterized by continuous modulation and sequential process in between. The second idea (bar 84) is tonally closed, and employs the orthodox dominant key, but its motivic material is that of a 'display episode'. Furthermore, it is followed after a few bars by a return to the transition (bar 92) in analogous rhythm, so that it is not unwarranted to regard bars 84–103 as a whole as an interpolated episode mediating between second subject and closing group. However, as suggested above, arriving at a clear-cut description is probably less to the point than understanding the ambiguity—the interchange and redistribution of attributes between the formal sections—as a formal idea in its own right.

The exposition of the C major Sonata, Op. 2 No. 3, consists of no fewer than six sections that can be provisionally designated first subject, transition (bar 13), lyrical episode (bar 27), second subject (bar 47), 'display episode' (bar 61), and closing group (bar 78). As in the A major Sonata, the lyrical episode begins and ends in the dominant minor, but is essentially modulatory. However, the next section differs from its counterpart in Op. 2 No. 2, in that it is not a 'display episode' but an orthodox lyrical second subject in the dominant. If one is inclined to regard the lyrical episode in the dominant minor as the 'real' second subject in the case of the A major Sonata, here in the C major Sonata, with its largely analogous structure, the opposite view is more attractive. But the fact that the difference supporting these two responses to the ambiguity is so slight indicates that the paradox of the structure in each case represents its aesthetically decisive attribute.

With the exposition of the E flat major Sonata, Op. 7, the impulse to speak of two second subjects is very strong, because the first of the episodes in question (bar 41) is already in the dominant, and tonally closed. On the other hand it is scherzando in character, and the second of the two (bar 60) appears to be the 'real' second subject on the grounds of its lyricism. If the extra episode (to which it is so hard to give a name, because it is defined by the redistribution of attributes instead of by those it possesses) is lyrical but modulatory in the Op. 2 sonatas, in Op. 7 it is tonally closed without being lyrical.

In the D major Sonata, Op. 10 No. 3, the harmony in the transition (bar 17) does not involve modulation but a barely discernible disturbance of the tonic. Only the episode (bar 23) brings a decisive modulation into the dominant, yet its lyrical character resists denomination as transition. The formal function and the aesthetic character contradict each other.

In the exposition of the 'Pathétique', the C minor Sonata, Op. 13, the middle sections—from the transition, with its modulation and sequential working (bar 36), to the closing group, which is at first cadential and then reverts to the first subject (bar 114)—are formally ambiguous. Bars 51–88, which modulate from the mediant minor, E flat minor, to the relative major, E flat major, can be interpreted as either a lyrical episode or the second subject; and bars 89–113, while they are a tonally closed passage in the relative major, present themselves motivically as a 'display episode' of an emotionally charged character. It could be argued that the E flat minor episode is the second subject, because, although it modulates, at least it returns to the initial key towards the end (bars 76–9); and if it is not the second subject, then the movement lacks the continuation of the second subject which is one of the normal components of a Beethovenian five-part exposition. But it cannot be denied that arguments directed towards the goal of formal consistency lead into a labyrinth, because the redistribution of attributes is governed by an aesthetic concept that was known to baroque poetic theory—which experienced a revival of interest among the early romantics—as 'beautiful confusion'. The listener should reflect, but his reflections should lead him to a point at which reasons and contrary reasons cancel each other out. Sometimes Beethoven lets us feel that he was a contemporary of Jean Paul, but the relationship registers as no more than the occasional flash of lightning, and it would be a mistake to think of it as an established factor in terms of the history of ideas.

3. Introduction and Coda

To find a beginning that produces a continuation from within itself, and an ending that comes to a conclusion rather than a halt, is almost as difficult in music as in a play, which must have a pre-history integrated into it, and a catastrophe that ideally leaves no loose ends. There is good reason, therefore, for Peter Gülke to speak of the introduction as a 'contradiction in the system',[12] and for Joseph Kerman to assert that 'sonata-form theory breaks down completely at the coda'.[13]

A comparison of the openings of the Cello Sonatas, Op. 5 Nos 1 and 2, shows that the F major Sonata has unmistakably a slow introduction, whereas in the case of the G minor Sonata it is possible to be in doubt as to whether the 'adagio sostenuto ed espressivo' is an introduction or a separate movement. The attributes we can point to

[12] 'Introduktion als Widerspruch im System', *Deutsches Jahrbuch der Musikwissenschaft für 1969* (Leipzig, 1970), 5–40.
[13] 'Notes on Beethoven's Codas', in *Beethoven Studies 3*, ed. A. Tyson (Cambridge, 1982), 141–59.

in support of either view are more or less equally balanced, so that a decision in favour of one to the exclusion of the other might be thought arbitrary. But if, for that reason, we look upon this 'adagio' as an intermediate, or mediating, form, we will discover that it presents a particularly drastic statement of the structural problem of an introduction: the instability of an introduction is not rhapsodic but congruent with its function of leading towards the goal of what follows it. The longer this intrinsic provisional state lasts, the greater the problem grows: and the G minor Sonata is an extreme case. The difference between the openings of Op. 5 No. 1 and Op. 5 No. 2 is therefore qualitative as well as quantitative.

In the F major Sonata the impression of provisionalness is undoubtably achieved in the 34-bar introduction, in spite of the presence of well-rounded melodic features, because of the way harmonic and metrical means undermine the scheme of a closed syntax. Both bars 1–7 and bars 7–14 would be regular periods with complex motivic substance, were it not for the disruption of the syntactic norm by the elision of bars—(4) = (1) and (8) = (1)—in the first instance, and the interrupted cadence on the subdominant minor in the second.

The progression from subdominant minor to dominant seventh, which leads from the cadential bar 14 to bar 15, and bridges over the caesura, also plays a determining role in what follows: while the subdominant minor is emphasized on its next appearance, with its own secondary dominant (bars 20–1), it is merely an interpolation later (bar 28), as the dominant-seventh chord spreads itself over an area of no less than eleven bars. And to some extent the variability in the presentation of the subdominant minor forms to some extent an aesthetic 'condition of possibility' for the permanence of the dominant seventh, which for its part is instrumental in producing the impression of provisionalness.

If the postponement of the goal in the F major Sonata is therefore based on metre at first and harmony later, in the G minor Sonata, in which the introduction comprises 44 bars in an even slower tempo, it has an additional foundation in the thematic-motivic structure. The first group is a 'period' of six bars with model (2), tonal sequence (2), and fragmentation (1 + 1), the second a passage of sequences modulating from G minor to E flat major (2 + 2), and the third a four-bar melodic idea in the cello, imitated by the piano a bar behind (bars 11–15). The motive presented at the start of the movement subsequently appears as the material of an extended cadence (bars 16–18) and of a first section of a development (bars 19–27), the second section of which consists of a version of the lyrical phrase first stated in bars 7–10 (bars 28–37): the quavers in bars 35–7 can be read as the diminution of the crotchets in bars 30–4.

The opening of the movement is thus thematic, and the motivic complexes it expounds are developed regularly. The second melodic idea, however, which has a potential for well-roundedness, is absorbed into modulating sequences; and the development is followed, not by a recapitulation but by the 'allegro', the goal of the introduction: the teleological character of the development is to some extent made to serve the function of introduction. As a radical modification of sonata form, though it allows the fundamental pattern to show through, the slow introduction achieves a provisional character, which is appropriate to its formal function. On the other hand it is self-sufficient enough to count as representing or standing-in for the slow movement which the work would otherwise lack. The sonata is simultaneously in two and three movements.

The thought of an introduction which is less an entity in its own right, and more a means of leading to the goal of the main part of a movement, suggests that it will prove a particularly striking example of the processual character of music. Yet musical experience paradoxically contradicts this expectation. It is as rare for a slow introduction to spread itself in the 'pure present'—as some independent slow movements do—as it is for it to be goal-directed in the sense that Beethovenian developments usually are (Op. 5 No. 2 is an exception). There is no getting away from the impression of 'provisionalness'; what may be expected to issue from it remains indeterminate for the time being. Because an introduction—unlike a development—lacks a thematic starting-point, it also lacks a thematic goal.

The framework of the introduction to the first movement of the Seventh Symphony is provided by a chromatic progression in the bass, first descending (bars 1–8 and 15–22) and later rising (bars 29–41). Its appearing in the form of a fourth-progression is a commonplace, and hence a guarantee of comprehension, and it ensures that the harmony appears consistent in itself, even though there is no functional foundation for it: the bass formula acts as a substitute for functional logic, and historical precedent replaces system. But the way the harmony roams from A major via D major to C major—together with the irregularity of the harmonic rhythm—creates the impression of a state of suspension, in which there is no discernible direction to the harmonic and motivic changes.

The chromatic progressions are interrupted by a woodwind episode (bars 23–33 in C major and bars 42–52 in F major) that it is mistaken to interpret as the 'theme' forming the point of reference of the introduction. Firstly, the keys—C major and F major—do not permit interpretation as the thematic centre. Secondly, the provisional character that clings to the introduction as a whole is not revoked during the episode, which, in spite of the simple cadential harmony, makes a curiously 'unfounded' impression, as if the tonic triad was a 6–4 chord. And thirdly, the episode is linked to the chromatic progressions by the fact that the bass-line of the episode can be said to 'grow into' the chromaticism.

The episode conveys a state of expectancy, but that is not the same thing as the urgent processuality characteristic of Beethoven's developments. While provisionalness may be a trait common to introductions and developments, yet, as stated above, their temporal structures differ in so far as the relationship to the thematic material is fundamentally different: a development refers back to a theme already stated, and an introduction moves forwards towards the goal of a theme that has yet to be stated.

The harmony is 'roving' without being complicated: the C major— later F major—of the episode is not the outcome of a modulation that 'leads' to that tonality, but arises from a pause on one of the steps reached by the chromatic progression in the bass—a progression that is a properly formed construction in itself, and one with a long prehistory, but not the manifestation of progress in the emphatic sense that the category assumed in Beethoven.

The introduction to the Seventh Symphony is comparable to that to Florestan's aria in Act II of *Fidelio*, in so far as both these exceptionally long preludes rest on the foundation of a chromatic fourth-progression. In the case of the aria, moreover, the 'lamento' motive is even thematic, in the sense that it forms a point of reference for developmental work—for subdivision, variation and augmentation. The diatonic–chromatic fourth-progression (F–E–E♭– D♭–C) expounded at the start in the bass is both symbolic and expressive (bars 1–8), and out of it come the semitones D♭–C and F– E as a melodic 'sigh' (bars 11–12); semitone motives, creating a dense network of relationships, permeate the whole texture. It is true that it is only by their continuing reference back to the chromatic progression, which represents a common centre, that the semitone motives knit together to form a close association—which they would not constitute on their own account as semitones in different rhythmic patterns that do not derive from one another.

The rising chromatic progression in the bass at the end of the recitative (bars 49–50; B–C–D♭–D–E♭, a positively baroque figure for the expression of suffering) should be seen, given the background of the motivic development of which it is the conclusion, as a compressed fourth-progression, the abbreviation of which—viewed technically—results from the enharmonic reinterpretation of the second chord.

The construction of motivic relationships is almost always a partly hypothetical process, and it is left to one's sense of the fitting, or the just-about-permissible, to make a specifically humanistic intervention in the methodology of scholarship, and judge 'how far one may go too far', as Karl Kraus puts it. But there is nothing wrong, all the same, with talking about an extension of the semitone motive, which prefigures the shape of the fourth-progression (bars 11–12 and bar 34), by means of a further semitone, Gb–F (bars 6–7, bar 14, and bar 35). The diminished fifth which results from the extension then presents itself in isolation as a timpani motive (bars 14–16), the rhythm of which is given in turn to a semitone motive (bars 31–2). (There is nothing in the least unusual about the intermingling of a rhythmic structure and an intervallic structure of different origins in bars 31–2: the 'poco allegro' bars 44–5 present a rhythmic variant of the syncopated motive from bars 21, 23, and 41–2.)

The orchestral motives of the accompanied recitative are therefore not pieced together at random, but in part related to one another within the recitative. Another part of the relationship between them is discernible, however, only against the background, and through the mediation, of the introduction. If, therefore, the apparently rhapsodic writing of the recitative shares in the network of associations in the introduction, on the other hand the recitative sheds light back on to the expressive character of the introduction. Not that there is anything vague semantically about the introduction as such: the 'lamento' bass is an expressive figure with a tradition as well established as the 'sigh', or the timpani motive's diminished fifth, which, in combination with the string tremolo, and even without any text, depicts a 'quiet' that somehow suggests horrors. Musical 'words', however, like verbal ones, gain precision from the context in which they are placed. And that a context may be formed by the introduction and the recitative together is one of the possibilities inherent in the function of the slow introduction.

Put in very broad terms, the problem that has to be solved in that part of a musical form to which we give the inadequate name 'coda' consists in how to shape a second development which, however, is actually a goal—in contrast to the first, which leads towards a goal.

The coda of the first movement of the 'Eroica' can be regarded as a second development in so far as it is a contracted reproduction of the first. It is not a priori certain, however, whether the function that a reproduction fulfils is analogous to that of the original or—precisely because it is a reproduction—directly contrary to it.

The coda begins with the transposition of the first subject from E flat major to D flat major and C major, which is an analogue of the modulation from C minor via C sharp minor to D minor in the development. (Admittedly, in the coda the move is merely a feint: within a space that allows it to be detected, D flat major proves to be VI of F minor, and F minor in turn proves to be II of E flat major.) The new subject of the development, complementing the exposition, is first stated in E minor and E flat minor, whereas in the coda it appears in F minor and E flat minor, and is hence more closely related to E flat major; in the development it alternates with evolutionary forms of the first subject, and thus appears in the context of a 'thematic treatment', whereas in the coda it stands on its own feet, in isolation, as in a recapitulation. The retransition in the coda differs from the development in that, while it retains the motives in the bass, it does not feature the fragmentation of the first subject in the higher parts. And the first subject presents itself in a different form in the coda, and by means of mere repetitions, instead of the sequences of the development.

It emerges, then, that the concern of the coda is not the evolutionary development of the first subject, but the dismantling of that evolution; it is recognizable as such because of the structural similarity of development section and coda, which causes us involuntarily to remember the first when we hear the second. The transposition of the first subject, the harmonic presentation of the new subject from the development, the retransition, and the last presentation of the first subject are all less elaborately differentiated, harmonically and motivically, in the coda. Yet the dismantling is the corollary of a bid to surpass, and the essence of the coda consists in the combination of these two factors: conclusion and culmination. Just as it is impossible to say of the last guise adopted by the first subject that it is the 'true' form of the theme—as if it was the hero of a *Bildungsroman*, who reaches the best of which he is capable at the end—so it is equally impossible to deny that it is a culmination, and that this is the case not in spite of, but because of the simplification, which gives it a monumental quality. But if we understand the conclusion of the movement as simultaneously and jointly a reduction and a process of monumentalization, then it is easier to understand why it can fulfil, in a paradoxical combination, the twin functions of a coda: that of surpassing the development and that of concluding the recapitulation.

The recall and monumental simplification of something from the

past is an especially plausible solution to the problem of fittingly
representing the passage of time (it is 'composed out' by the changes
made to the musical substance), while at the same time not allowing
the recall to be sensed as an encouragement to further evolution—as
in the development—but as a mode of justified closing: a closing that,
in a 'backward look', lets the music come to rest after its goal-
directed striving .

In its basic elements, the coda of the first movement of the Fifth
Symphony resembles the coda of the 'Eroica', which can be regarded
as the prototype of a 'second development'. The harmony—restricted
in any case to the degrees of C minor, so that the tonal unity is never
at risk for a moment—grows steadily more stark as the coda
progresses, and finally shrinks to an obsessively repeated alternation
of dominant and tonic. And the motive from bars 6-9 is repeated in
the tonic at the end of the coda, instead of being 'answered' in the
dominant. It is true that the motivic evolution in the development
continues to some extent in the coda: the last variant in which the
principal motive appears in the development—the thirds of the first
subject assume the rhythm of the fifths of the second subject—forms
the launchpad of a motivic evolution in the coda. But the rhythmic
element, not the intervallic, is the one that performs the essential
function of determining the outcome. The minims of the second
subject are reduced to crotchets, wherein the important thing is not
the melodic material but the crotchets themselves, because the
sustaining of the regular crotchet movement over quite a long period
forms the precondition, and the contrasting foil, for the sense that
when the 'motto' returns, modified and fortissimo—but not, as in the
'Eroica', transformed by variation processes into a triumphal
statement it is a final, overwhelming culmination.

If the motivic (melodic) element is stressed, the association with
the development—the quality, that is, of a 'second development'—is
what determines the outcome. If the rhythmic element is
emphasized, then its function, which is to provide the background
for the monumentalization of the 'motto', without which the final
culmination would remain mere repetition, is seen to be an essential
characteristic, corresponding to the formal meaning of a coda.

When a movement is not a sonata allegro, the coda can take on one
of the functions of the development in a sonata-form movement: that
of establishing associations from within between contrasting themes.
So far as mediation between things that differ has the character of a
result, it is perfectly logical to carry it out in a section which
represents the goal of a formal process—although, in these
circumstances, the word 'coda' is inadequate.

The 17-bar 'coda' of the slow movement of the E flat major Piano Sonata, Op. 7 (Largo, con gran espressione) seems disproportionately long, in relation to the ternary movement in 'song form' (A¹ B A² : 26 + 26 + 23 bars) that it concludes. The unusual length is a compelling consequence, however, of its formal function, which is to mediate between the 'A' section and the contrasting—or deviating—'B' section, and establish a synthesis that has been prepared well in advance.

The 'coda' ends with a chromatic progression in the bass, stretching ostentatiously over three bars. And the chromaticism that takes the centre of the stage at the end—like a kind of summing-up—is the 'motive of change' in both the 'A' and 'B' sections: the compositional element by means of which subjects are modified when they recur or return.

The opening (bars 1–2) of the 'A' section appears in bars 15–24 in what Schenker calls a 'prolongation', which 'grows' out of the rising semitone B–C of the bass in bar 2; it takes the form of a chromatic formula, C♯–D–E–F–F♯–G, which is the underlying common element of a motivic development that first elaborates the opening of the movement (bars 17–19), and then goes off at an abrupt tangent (bars 21–3).

The chromatic formula appears at first to have only a 'local' significance, but then consequences are drawn from it which spread themselves over the entire movement; in the 'coda', untransposed, it forms the skeleton of a variant of the thematic material of the 'B' section (bars 76–8, in an inner part).

The transference from the 'A' to the 'B' section is preceded in the 'B' section itself by a kind of 'prehistory': the subject of the middle section contains a semitone step (bar 27: A–B♭), out of which, when the theme is repeated in transposition, a chromatic third-progression develops sequentially (bars 35–6: D–E♭–E–F). The chromatic formula C♯–D–E–F–F♯–G is thus not only transferred from the 'A' to the 'B' section, but at the same time forms the last step in a development within the 'B' section itself.

The chromatic synthesizing of the two sections in the 'coda' is also associated with a motivic synthesis. The subject of the 'B' section is made, in bar 76, to differ from the original form in bar 27 by a leap of a third (Ex. 5.9). The same third appears three bars later—again as

Ex. 5.9

a modification—in a motive (bars 79–80) that unmistakably assumes the position of the opening of the principal subject (Ex. 5.10). The Ex. 5.10

chromatic formula's mediation between the 'A' and 'B' sections in bar 76 is thus the correlative of a parallel motivic move. And it is not an exaggeration to say that in bar 76 the formal idea of the movement is to some extent summed up in an emblematic figure, of which it can be read as the resolution. The inappositely named 'coda' proves to be a 'synthesis'.

4. Form as Transformation[14]

The argument about 'visual' and 'aural' methods of analysis has been conducted essentially as a debate about the perceptibility of motivic relationships that analysts have read in the score. No end to the controversy is in sight, for firstly it is not certain whose perception shall serve as the standard for perceptibility, secondly the hearing even of abstruse constructions can be learnt, and thirdly it ought not to be categorically ruled out that hearing augmented by score-reading is an aesthetically legitimate approach to some forms of music.

The dispute about perceptibility has become inseparable from issues surrounding the reception of new music, and this has given it that particular edge characteristic of arguments in the frontier region between scholarship and ideology. Another outcome is that the question of the structure of musical hearing, understood as process and completion, has been pushed into the background. No one denies the commonplace that musical form represents a process. But it seems as if some of the consequences of its processual character have not been drawn by analysts in either theory or practice, because music is thought of as a linear course of events, moving towards the outcome of a complete view of the work. What is written down in the spatial dimension of the score grows through performance— extension in the temporal dimension—to what might be called a 'second spatial dimension'. After the total sound structure has been successively dissected, the musical imagination understands it in a kind of imaginary simultaneity, in which music as form comes into its own.

[14] This section was first published, with the title 'Musikalische Form als Transformation: Bemerkungen zur Beethoven-Interpretation', in *Beethoven-Jahrbuch* IX (1973–7; Bonn, 1977). Reprinted with kind permission.

But while the imaginary simultaneity and its aesthetic significance for the present-day cultivation of the musical 'work' cannot reasonably be denied, on the other hand distinguishing between process and outcome is questionable. To regard musical perception exclusively as a path towards a goal is to mistake how it works. Rather, the process is itself—paradoxically—the result. Inasmuch as it alters as it is perceived, music is, strictly speaking, not an object of perception at all. And it positively challenges the listener who plays an active part in re-creating it as a coherent unity, instead of allowing it to roll past him like an acoustic movie, to be conscious of his activity, and of the conditions in which he is doing it—that is, to turn away reflexively from the object of his perception to the process whereby music comes into existence.

The attempt to indicate some of the consequences that abandoning 'teleological prejudgement' will have for analytical method will be confined to a phenomenological outline, in which it will not be necessary to decide whether the description can exist on its own terms, or is of interest only as a heuristic outline that might be worth investigating by the light of experimental psychology. The objection that the reactions depicted are those of one single listener can be met, perhaps, with the argument that the decisive thing is not the details of the analysis, which may bear individual colouring, but the fundamental structures which can be agreed as established within the bounds of certain historical, ethnic and regional, and social traditions.

The exposition of the C major tonic at the beginning of Beethoven's Op. 53, the 'Waldstein' Sonata, is more like a hypothesis than a statement. The involuntary assumption that the chord of C major in bar 1 represents the tonic is contradicted in bars 2–4 by a cadence in which C major fulfils the function of G major's subdominant. The apparently strong outline of the G major cadence becomes shadowy when it is abruptly confronted in bars 5–8 with a cadence in F major/minor. The listener who starts from the assumption that, at the beginning of a movement in sonata form, he can expect stable rather than 'roving' harmony may well infer a centre of C major from the juxtaposition of G major and F major. The darkening to C minor of the C major that might be expected in bars 9–13 is foreshadowed in the stepwise descent of a fourth: C–B–Bb–A–Ab–G. The significance of this progression for the inner coherence of bars 1–13 must be stressed, all the more so because it recurs in the sonata's slow movement (bars 1–6), transposed to F major. The last note of the progression, G, is pronounced enough to assert itself as a latent tonic in bar 12, and make the arpeggiated C minor chord seem to be a 6–4 chord that is absorbed into the dominant harmony of bar 13. C major is not reached until bar 14, and there, as in bar 1, it remains provisional, and reinterpreted as the subdominant of G major, although that reinterpretation does not erase the distinction that in bar 14 the tonic is the goal and the result of a cadence, whereas in bar 1 it was only a premiss and a hypothesis. The tonic in bar 14 is the same as, and yet different from, the tonic in bar 1.

Sketchy as it is, the above suffices to demonstrate that it is not enough to define the harmonic-cum-tonal meaning of the opening of the 'Waldstein' Sonata by the simple formula (S D) D (S D) S D T. There is nothing wrong with the formula as such, but it reflects, strictly speaking, only a single moment in the musical experience— namely the situation in bar 14, where it is possible to look back and summarize the way the tonic has been presented. The stations that the musical perception has passed through have not by any means been obliterated, however, at the point reached in bar 14. There is no basis for the assumption that the different aspects in which the original C major has been seen from the perspectives of bars 1, 3, and 14 can be levelled down to a single 'final' and 'definitive' meaning. In other words, the harmonic-cum-tonal sense of the opening of the movement is not fully represented by the suggested cadential formula, but by the total course of assumptions, denials, reinterpretations, and contradictions that the musical consciousness has travelled along. The meaning is not something fixed and given, to which the listener drives a path through a series of obstacles; rather, it lies in the musical perception, as the activity the music itself prompts; it is in the dialectics of assertion and retraction, confrontation and mediation. What is crucial in the harmonic structure of the first subject of the 'Waldstein' Sonata is not so much the goal, the establishing of the tonic by means of a perfect cadence, as the action which the listener feels compelled to take when he tries to discover in the opening of the movement the tonal coherence that his knowledge of the tradition of the genre leads him to expect. The result reached (and immediately relativized) in bar 14, expressed in the formula (S D) D (S D) S D T, is one element in the process of constant transformation: the process is not merely the means whereby the result is achieved.

That a piece of music is not a box containing a ready-made meaning, but, rather, represents a challenge to pursue an activity, the total—sometimes tortuous—course of which makes up the meaning of the work, is perhaps more obvious in the case of the 'Waldstein' Sonata, whose harmonic-cum-tonal structure aims to draw the listener into a dialectic process, than with simpler forms, whose sense seems to be clear from the start. And yet Moritz Hauptmann demonstrated as long ago as 1853, in *Die Natur der Harmonik und der Metrik*, that even the cadence I–IV–I–V–I includes a process of transformation (though it remains latent in such a well-worn formula). Chord I is tonic to begin with, on its own; then it becomes a dominant to IV and subdominant to V; finally, through a transformation of 'being dominant' into 'having dominant', it is restored as the tonic (with subordinate IV and V). We may come upon a phrase or a period where the harmonic-cum-tonal sense is never in doubt for a moment, but these are borderline cases which do not justify talk of a paradigm: that is, the assumption that there is a model in which meanings are given, and to which the listener needs only to find the means of access. Rather, the path is itself the goal: the path as the totality of the stations that the musical consciousness passes through, and at each of which each previous one is revealed in yet another new light.

At the same time it cannot be denied that the transformational and processual character of musical structures—and that includes the need to stress the subject, which 'provides' the meaning, instead of the object, which 'has' meaning—emerges with differing degrees of clarity. And it is undoubtedly characteristic of the special nature of the works of Beethoven's 'middle period' that musical form presents itself emphatically as the process of coming into existence, and not as 'static' existence, unfolded in time but not produced in it. Yet while Beethoven's conception of form from Op. 31 onwards facilitates the discovery of transformational processes in the musical consciousness—in the perception as it categorially shapes the acoustic substratum, that fact does not mean that insight into the structure of hearing must be restricted in its range of operation to Beethoven's works. If we have once appropriated the shift of accent from *ergon* to *energeia*, as Wilhelm Humboldt would say, and made it one of our means of musical perception, we recognize that a meaning which is certain from the first is a merely borderline instance of transformation; and we can also see that the possible alternative—that transformation is a detour made by the subjective consciousness on the way to an objectively certain meaning—is not the case.

For decades the thematic structure of the first movement of Beethoven's D minor Sonata, Op. 31 No. 2, has been the topic of controversy, and will continue to be so for as long as the disputants go on suppressing the contradictions between motivicism, syntax, and harmony by insisting on a distinction between 'essential' and 'accidental' attributes—that is, by stressing one element at the expense of another. They would do better to understand these 'antitheses' as the vehicle of a dialectics, by means of which the form of the movement comes into being as a musically perceived transformational process.

The beginning of the sonata is motivically loosely constructed, and both harmonically and syntactically open-ended, so that at first it seems to be an introduction, not the exposition of a theme. The formal section that begins in bar 21 distinguishes itself by a stronger melodic outline and more regular syntax, and at the same time it receives emphasis from the fact that bar 21 presents itself as the goal and the outcome of a harmonic development that has moved towards the delayed tonic. (In bars 3–4 the tonic is provisional and not fixed.) Admittedly, a modulatory process begins in bar 31, which leads to the dominant, so that by tonal criteria bars 21–40 present a transition.

The motivic dependence of bars 21–2 on bars 1–2 is ambiguous. It remains open whether bar 1 is an anticipation of the theme in bar 21 or, vice versa, bar 21 is a secondary variant of bar 1; whether, that is, bar 1 should be regarded as an introduction, or bar 21 as a developmental section which in tonal terms mediates the transition to the dominant. To plump for either of these alternatives would not do justice to the formal idea of the work. We discover, to be sure, that bar 1 first presents itself as a prelude lacking in thematic significance, later (when viewed in retrospect from bar 21) as the anticipation of the theme, and finally (after it has emerged that bars 21–40 are a modulating developmental passage) as the actual exposition, but this discovery should not be greeted as an irritating uncertainty, from which we attempt to extricate ourselves by imperfectly founded hypotheses about 'what is really meant'. Rather, it ought to be seen as providing access to a paradoxical structure that gives the form its artistic character by virtue of its very contradictions. Bars 1–2 'are' not either prelude, or anticipation, or thematic exposition; they fulfil the function of prompting an activity and setting in motion a dialectic process, in which earlier meanings continue to coexist on an equal footing with later ones. If the listener takes the right approach to the work, he does not arrive gradually, and only after overcoming obstacles, at the recognition that the unremarkable arpeggiated triad that he took at first for an introduction was in fact the theme itself; instead he actively follows the process of transformation, in which the terms 'prelude', 'anticipation', and 'exposition' can be said to pile up above one another, without any one of them being squeezed out by any other.

It might be objected that the processual character of musical form—represented in Op. 31 No. 2 by the fact that the arpeggiated triad in bar 1 is 'not yet', and in bar 21 is 'no longer' the exposition of the theme—is an attribute peculiar to some of Beethoven's works, and that no general principle can be derived from it about the perceived structural processes. But this argument does not reach far enough. Even in works in which there can be no dispute about the functions of the sections, the formal meaning is not exhausted in the sense of completeness that remains with the listener at the end of the process of perception in an imaginary simultaneity of the successive events. The formal sense of a work is not constituted by the final shape alone, in which all the events have conjoined: the totality of the provisional structures—as they have been suggested and revoked, have complemented or contradicted each other—is also part of it.

The fact that musical form consists in the process of coming into being, as well as in the result that is seen at the end of the process, is of course particularly obvious in works like the D minor Sonata, in which it is scarcely possible to say that those formal functions that are recognized later outrank those that are assumed at first. But in the case of other works, too, where the different perspectives in which a formal section is seen are not equal, but observe a hierarchy, none of the formal functions can be wholly suppressed without sacrificing the artistic character revealed in the alternation of perspectives, for the sake of a logic that clings to schemata. Just as there is more to poetry than the amount of information that can be extracted from it if one prosaically puts one's mind to it, so musical form is not subsumed in the lucidity that it finally reaches, or appears to reach. Rather, the 'real' meaning that emerges at the end is—to express it in a paradox— only part of an overall sense which exceeds that and includes the provisional meanings that the consciousness has left behind but not forgotten. The path, not its end, is the goal.

The question that analysis customarily seeks to answer concerns the harmonic or syntactic sense of a musical phrase. The method outlined here substitutes the different question, of how the phrase comes into being within a listener's consciousness. The subject under investigation is not what music 'is' but what it 'does'. And yet strictly speaking, surprising as the process may seem, it is nothing other than the matter of drawing certain compelling consequences from an undeniable fact: namely, that the successive apprehension of the parts goes into the understanding of a whole. Naturally, the listening process must be slowed down and dismantled in the intellectual process of reconstruction, in order to allow analysis access to events that would otherwise go unnoticed. It is only in the imagination that it is possible to extend the time by slowing it, and yet retain in the memory the tempo that is part of the musical character of a work; it would scarcely be feasible to do so in an actual psychological experiment. For that reason it would be laborious, if not actually impossible, to devise a practicable experimental procedure based on the phenomenological method outlined in the last few pages. The technical difficulties in the way of an experimental investigation should not, however, create the suspicion that the phenomena that reveal themselves to introspection when time is extended are merely fictitious.

The central section of the Largo e mesto of Beethoven's D major Sonata, Op. 10 No. 3, a movement which depicts the 'state of a melancholy person's soul', begins with a lyrical passage in F major that appears as a fleeting moment of reconciliation and relief from depression (Ex. 5.11). For orientation purposes, the five bars (30–4)

Ex. 5.11

can be subdivided into 2½ + 2½. The metrical relationship between the two parts is contradictory, however: the antecedent extends from the second half of a bar to the first half of another, while the consequent extends from a first half to another first half, if we accept that the similarity of the motivic endings in bars 32 and 34 is stronger than the tendency (founded in a metrical law of inertia) to count the second half of bar 34 as an appendix to the consequent, for the sake of regular phrase structures, instead of thinking of it as an interpolation between two periods.

The reconstruction carried out by introspection reveals that the actual process of hearing is more complicated than is allowed for by the assigning of certain metrical functions in advance. The first half of bar 30 appears at first to be a constituent part of the metrical unit (and the absence of a change of harmony causes a state of metrical suspension to survive in bar 31). It is only later, at the end of the consequent in bar 32, that it emerges that the beginning of bar 30 does not belong in the regular phrase structure, but is 'extra-territorial', metrically speaking. Conversely the second half of bar 32 is at first perceived as an interpolation, like the first half of bar 30. However, the end of the motive in bar 34 turns out to correspond to bar 32, so that the motivic content of the consequent seems to be compressed; and if the regular phrase structure is to be preserved in spite of that, the second half of bar 32 must be perceived retrospectively as analogous to the second half of bar 30, not the first: that is, as a constituent part of the metrical unit and not as an extra-territorial interpolation. (The analysis rests on a premiss which would require considerable space to expound fully. It is the assumption that the similarity of the motivic endings is stronger than the tendency towards regular phrase structure, but that the tendency asserts itself in the metrically neutral, melody-less half-bars.)

The secondary meaning of bars 30 and 32 does not suppress the primary meaning, but overlays it. Metrical lucidity was clearly not Beethoven's objective. Rather, the method of conjuring uncertainty serves as the means of lending the cantilena a hovering quality.

To start by asking what a formulation 'causes to happen' in a listener is to infer the composer's intentions from reactions, instead of seeking them 'behind' the text as something given but concealed. It is to focus one's attention on the 'surface structure' of a piece of music, in the terminology of transformational grammar. The analyst who adopts this course does not aim—or not exclusively—to reconstruct a 'deep structure' as the 'real' meaning, which manifests itself only inexactly, in clouded and distorted form, in the 'surface structures' that successively take shape in the musical consciousness. On the contrary, he is guided by the expectation that the listening process, as it feels its way along the 'surface structures', will reveal a richness of meaning that would be diminished if he assumed that there could only be one meaning, hidden like a kernel in a shell. The meaning consists in the circuitous paths that lead to its discovery.

6

Theme and Character

1. The Dual Concept of 'Theme' in the Eighteenth Century

Theories of musical form, the origins of which lie in the eighteenth century, depended for their terminology on the theory of affects on the one hand, and on rhetoric on the other. It remains impossible to understand the use of an apparently unambiguous word like 'theme'—one of the central concepts of instrumental music in its striving for independent status—so long as we disregard the fact that, with varying degrees of emphasis, it represents an aesthetic category as well as a technical compositional one. It would be a mistake to attempt to expunge the ambiguity, because its very ambivalence raises issues, the reconstruction of which provides access to the epoch's thinking on musical form.

H. C. Koch, in his *Musikalisches Lexikon* (1802), defined the word in aesthetic terms first: 'Principal subject [*Hauptsatz*] or theme is that melodic component of a piece of music which denotes the chief character thereof, or presents the emotion that is to be expressed therein in a comprehensible picture or image.' This emphasis on content as the factor which defines a theme is drawn from the theory of affects, but Koch then adds a formal definition which derives from rhetoric:

Just as in a speech the principal idea, or theme, provides the essential content of the same, and must contain the material for the development of principal and subsidiary ideas, so it is in music, with respect to the modifying of an emotion that is possible through the principal subject, and just as an orator moves on from his principal subject to subsidiary subjects, antitheses, dissections etc., and employs rhetorical figures which all serve to give more strength to his principal subject, so the composer will act in the same manner in the treatment of a principal subject.[1]

What Koch understands by 'theme' is thus not only a formulation which provides the starting-point for development, but also the affect or character that it expresses musically. The musical formulation and

[1] *Musikalisches Lexikon* (Frankfurt, 1802; repr. Hildesheim, 1964), 745 f.

what it expresses are compressed into the same concept, which comprises the 'material' of the musical presentation as much as its sounding 'form'.

The aesthetic postulate of the unity of affect or character and the technical compositional principle of monothematicism appear in Koch's writings as two facets of the same thing as they do in eighteenth-century formal theory as a whole. Unity of theme, understood as unity of emotion, was admittedly by no means interpreted rigorously in an age whose pre-eminent aesthetic maxim was the commonplace one of unity in diversity, or diversity in unity. The fact that a specific affect or character—one to which a name could be given—was depicted did not rule out the deployment of subsidiary ideas, which qualified or modified it, or even antitheses, against which it stood out in effective relief. A contrast that was dismissed—the *confutatio* of rhetoric—did not detract from the effect of unity but enhanced it. Thus, whether we underpin the analysis of a musical form with the principle of monothematicism or the principle of thematic dialectic does not depend on technical compositional facts alone, which can be read in the score, but also on aesthetic aspects, which have to be reconstructed from the literary testimonies of the age. In some works it is possible to interpret a second theme, according to technical compositional criteria, either as a contrasting idea, betraying a dualistic formal conception, or as a mere subsidiary idea that serves as a foil to the principal idea: in such a case the authority for an aesthetic decision must be sought outside the pages of the score.

In the second of Beethoven's 'Kurfürst' sonatas (WoO 47), in F minor, the three movements are linked by motivic associations, the purpose of which is to suggest a unity of character that embraces the entire work. The beginning of the Andante derives from the second subject of the Allegro assai (bars 20–1); and the fundamental idea of the Presto, which is heard in the minor as the first subject and in the major as the second subject, recalls a phrase from the first subject of the first movement (bar 13). The overall tendency towards monothematicism justifies regarding the two themes of the Allegro assai as variants of each other, although superficially they are contrasted (Ex. 6.1). There is no mistaking the rhythmic analogy, but

Ex. 6.1

there is not the slightest connection in purely intervallic terms. If we remember, however, that the tendency to emphasize the intervallic is a twentieth-century bias, and that eighteenth-century theorists like Koch did exactly the opposite, and regarded rhythmic correspondences as the decisive factor, then it is surely not inappropriate to speak of a similarity of the themes which is merely inflected by their differences.

To the extent that the expression 'theme' relates primarily to affect or character and not to the sounding formulation, it is possible in principle to leave open the question as to the compositional parameters within which the postulated unity of the 'theme' manifests itself musically. Not only the fully rounded melodic shapes that first come to mind when we encounter the term, but also recurrent rhythmic and harmonic attributes, which are not integrated in a specific melodic figure, can be thematic and support the inner coherence of a movement. Under the double headword *'Leidenschaft* [passion], *Affect'*, Koch describes melodic, harmonic, rhythmic, and metrical means 'whereby the material of music, or the notes placed in a certain coherent relation, become capable of expressing such different passions'.[2] The individual affects or characters—the two terms were used as synonyms in the middle of the century, but towards its end C. G. Körner differentiated between them—demand means of representation which are different not only in themselves but also in their formal functions. The fact that some emotions are most aptly expressed by melodies or motivic complexes does not rule out others being more readily manifested in a configuration of compositional elements such as chromatic harmony, dissonance, and syncopations; consequently, the inner coherence that exists between the sections of a movement can consist in the developing variation of melodic elements or motives, but it can also take the form of the recurrence and transformation of harmonic and rhythmic attributes, which, in accordance with the premiss that an affect or character forms the 'real' theme, are every bit as thematic as a melodic figure, but in a different way.

The first of the 'Kurfürst' sonatas, in E flat major, is even more consistently monothematic than the second. The second subject of the Allegro cantabile (bar 11) quotes a particle of the first subject (bar 3) literally, but the use of quotation, of which this remains an isolated example, is less significant than the rhythmic similarity. It permeates the entire first movement, and goes on to establish associations with the Andante, the sections of which are linked by means of a rhythmic pattern originating in the first movement. While there is no question

---

[2] *Musikalisches Lexikon*, 896 ff.

of the recurrence of themes with literal similarities of both melody and rhythm, there is an abstract rhythm, dissociated from any melody, which decisively governs both the Allegro cantabile and the Andante (and which we may unhesitatingly call thematic because it expresses the character, the 'aesthetic theme', of the movements). The fact that the rhythmic pattern is one of the essential features of the themes could justify explaining all its forms of manifestation as the results of thematic-motivic working. But it makes better sense to start from the idea of an abstract rhythm which has a decisive influence on the themes, among other things.

In step with the tendency to emphasize the character that a musical formulation embodied rather than the melodic shape, when the concept of 'theme' was under examination, the possibility increased of discovering the postulated unity of the theme in places where the melodic sections of a movement may appear heterogeneous on the surface but are inwardly united by recurrent structural features, in which a specific, identifiable character is expressed. There are countless late eighteenth-century works for which the principle of melodic monothematicism is no more satisfactory an interpretative key than the idea of thematic dialectic; in view of that, to start from the notion of a unity of character manifested in recurrent structural features, rather than in a melodically rounded thematic shape, is an analytical procedure which deserves consideration.

2. Formal and Aesthetic Themes

Specifying the expressive character of individual musical themes and motives is generally not particularly contentious, if we admit variants into the formulation; it is, at any rate, no more so than describing syntactic and formal structures. (There is no justification for expecting a degree of intersubjectivity that even formal analyses do not achieve.) The difficulties only begin to accumulate when we try to draw consequences from the maxim that the overall structure has priority over the parts, and start to give consideration, when interpreting expressive character, not only to individual themes and motives, but also to configurations of them and their various developments. (Innumerable analyses have implied that a theme has a specific content, while the development is 'merely formal', but the tacit acceptance of this principle should not be allowed to disguise the fact that it is absurd.)

The fact that 'theme', in the late eighteenth century and into the nineteenth as well, was a dual concept denoting both the 'content'— the affect or character—of a movement and the musical formulation

of the 'content' in a melodic opening statement, supports the
assumption that a simple correspondence will exist between the
developments of content and form, and, hence, that the motivic
working of the 'formal theme' will have a correlative in a growing
elaboration of the 'aesthetic theme'.

The aesthetic theme of the Largo e mesto of the D major Piano
Sonata, Op. 10 No. 3, is the 'state of a melancholy person's soul' —
whether or not we choose to accept Schindler's testimony to one of
Beethoven's remarks. The musical features — the minor key, the slow
tempo, the chromaticism in the motives and in the compositional
structures, the harsh dissonances, and the presence of the musical
'sigh' — speak so plainly that, in the climate of the period around
1800, the expressive content of the movement was unequivocal. The
association between the aesthetic and formal structures is crucial, but
it does not come to light until we recognize that both are irregular,
and that the irregularities constitute one of the premisses of the
specific mediation between aesthetic and formal elements that is
characteristic of the movement.

The exposition (bars 1–29) and recapitulation (bars 44–64) define
the outline of the sonata form (first subject, bars 1–9; transition, bars
10–17; second subject in the dominant minor, bars 17–26; closing
group with references back to the transition, bars 26–9). In
accordance with the principle of 'contrasting derivation' (sometimes
modified to 'differing' derivation), the second subject is a variant and
elaboration of bar 3 of the first (Ex. 6.2). Even without the formal

Ex. 6.2

derivation, the expressive character of the second subject is
unmistakable; but it is affected by the association with the first
subject, although there is no need to search for words to describe the
effect of the rhythmic and harmonic differences.

The middle section is partly developmental in character (bars 35–
43: a two-bar model is repeated sequentially with the progressive
hiving-off of small elements), but the link with the thematic material
of the exposition is only vaguely associative: the development model
remotely recalls the continuation of the second theme (bars 23–4) in
a fortissimo diminished seventh chord, with the seventh resolving on
to a 'sigh'.

The cantilena at the beginning of the middle section introduces an
elegiac tone, or, to put it another way, the elegiac tone calls for
lyricism, so that developmental technique must for once be kept at

bay. On the other hand, in that part which is developmental, the melancholy intensifies to despair or contrition. Thus the idea of depicting the 'state of a melancholy person's soul' in some extreme modifications of that state—now moderated to sadness, now driven to despair—imposes certain formal features upon the middle section: the regular, 'quadratic' syntax of the cantilena, and the developmental sequences, which are employed as a means of intensification, in accordance with rhetorical tradition.

The recapitulation and the coda differ from the exposition in some features which, if they are considered in their totality, can be interpreted as a modification of the melancholy to the 'saturnine temperament', as it was termed from the fifteenth century onwards. Imitation between the top line and the bass, which, in combination with chromatic harmony and strong dissonances, represents the kind of musical profundity often ascribed to Bach (bars 46–7); development of the principal motive from bar 1 above a chromatic, palindromic bass-line—that is, one that to some extent circles meditatively within itself (bars 49–52: G–G♭–F–F♯–G); the chromatic octave movement of the bass, which never seems to find a way to end (bars 68–72); the E♭–D–C♯ motive (bar 81) that retrospectively integrates the development model of the middle section into the thematic material of the exposition: all these deviations from the exposition express a brooding intellectuality such as distinguishes the essence of heroic melancholy—'*melancolia illa heroica*' (Marsilio Ficino)—from the more commonplace feeling of depression.

The important thing is that these are all unusual incursions in the structure of the movement, not common features of variation technique in a recapitulation; and the structural irregularities constitute the technical correlative of an aesthetic transformation that can be defined as a reinterpretation of melancholy as 'saturnine temperament', instead of the sensibility that the word 'melancholy' would initially have suggested around the year 1800.

If, in the second half of the movement, the melancholy does indeed take on attributes of the 'saturnine temperament' that were latent at the start, then it is a process that both modifies the content and is intimately connected with the formal process, as an example of Hegel's 'conversion of form into content and content into form'; specifically, it is linked to those structural elements that were not prescribed in the traditional scheme of sonata form. The development of 'content' that is executed in the movement is as specific as the formal development to which it is joined by reciprocity.

It is by no means always the case that the underlying mood of a movement can be given a verbal label; such defining by words and concepts is the exception rather than the rule in Beethoven. Quite apart from that, the fact that it is possible in the case of the Largo e mesto should not mislead us into regarding the label, or the paraphrase of the content, as the 'real' meaning of the music, reduced to a verbal concept; we ought not, that is, to confuse the hermeneutical attempt to approach something by means of words with the 'essential form' that underlies the sounding 'phenomenal form'. The fact that we are so ready to find the 'essence' of a musical form expressed in a verbal phrase that is only a metaphor must be laid at the door of a 'popular Platonic' aesthetics (to coin a phrase), which tends to fasten on the paraphrases that are set up 'around' a thing, and treat them as the ideas that lie 'behind' the concrete phenomena and manifest themselves through them.

If melancholy is, on the one hand, depicted in the Largo e mesto in extreme modifications—sadness and despair constitute the central contrast in the middle section—and, on the other, transformed from depression (which is the form more familiar to common experience), into the esoteric form of the 'saturnine temperament', a configuration results which is not amenable to a simple 'statement' about the aesthetic meaning of the movement. If we try to extend and refine the verbal definition, sooner or later it becomes unavoidable to place more emphasis on compositional descriptive language and less on aesthetic terminology. If we say, for example, that melancholy takes on a strain of brooding intellectuality in the recapitulation (bar 46), which it lacks in the exposition (bar 3), it implies that an association exists between a complex of technical features (the imitative counterpoint, the use of dissonance and chromaticism) and profundity of thought, which, furthermore, evokes the memory of Bach. The fact that the technical element and its pre-history are grasped by the reflecting mind becomes a condition of the comprehensibility of the expressive character.

The configuration of depressive melancholy and 'saturnine temperament' that underlies the movement would be misunderstood, admittedly, if it was regarded as 'development' from one character to another. It is a matter, rather, of placing different characters, ideas and points of view in relation to one another—as in a drama, unless it is a pièce à thèse—without any one of them being able to claim to be the 'quintessence'.

Although a drama is a goal-directed process, its dialectic remains essentially unresolved. In other words, the structure of a drama is at once and inseparably both teleological and paradoxical: the action presses on towards an end, but leaves behind it the intuition of an undetermined state of ideas, characters, and points of view that reciprocally 'relativize' each other. This undetermined state continues to be realized throughout the dramatic process; and, vice versa, the meaning of the action is not revealed by its ending but by the totality of the stages through which it passes, with all the contradictions that are expressed on the way.

Similarly, the duality of teleology and paradox provides the foundation of the 'dramatic' nature of Beethoven's instrumental works. For that reason it is impossible to take the configuration of characters that are placed in apposition to each other and force it in its entirety into one comprehensive verbal expression (however precisely it may be qualified). Of course it can be useful to explore ways of formulating various degrees of differentiation—as long as we keep in mind that these are only frameworks that we are setting up around the 'content' of the work, and that we must not confuse them with what the work 'says' on its own account. If, in the case of the Largo e mesto, we examine the relationship between elements of 'content' and elements of form from the point of view of the coherence of the work, the middle section appears to be dominated by the element of 'content'—the ramifying of the fundamental mood into contrary expressive characters, linked by their very contrast— but in the final section it seems to be the formal element which is dominant, and governs that of 'content', for here the compositional profundity of thought is the substance of a representation of the 'saturnine temperament'. The decisive factor, however, is not the varying emphasis on one or the other element but the way each continues to affect the other. In isolation, the formal coherence would be as incomplete as the coherence of the content.

3. Aesthetic Logic

The expression 'aesthetic logic' looks self-contradictory, because when Alexander Baumgarten founded the discipline of aesthetics in 1750, his purpose was precisely to provide an alternative to the logic of linking concepts together, by promoting the observations of the senses as a mode of perception that was just as valid. But the impression that an inner imperative association exists to link the aesthetic characters that succeed one another in a sonata-form movement makes it reasonable enough to speak of hidden logic, because the alternative, which is to explain the clearly felt inner relationship of outwardly differing themes by sketching a programme or a narrative, is not very persuasive, although Beethoven's contemporaries quite often had recourse to it.

Christian Gottfried Körner's definition of 'ethos' or 'character' as the quality that ensures the inner coherence of a whole movement produces a terminological quandary, in so far as it is difficult to denominate the nature of individual themes by anything other than the word 'character', too. In the so-called 'character piece', where monothematicism is an essential feature, the character of the piece and the character of the theme coalesce. A sonata-form movement, on the other hand, accommodates a number of thematic characters as a rule—what Hölderlin called the 'variation of tones' (*Wechsel der Töne*)—and to discover the unity of overall character postulated by Körner in the diversity of the themes is often difficult, and sometimes impossible.

A solution suggests itself when we become aware that the notion that thematic characters and their groupings are strictly individual and unrepeatable is something of an exaggeration. While it would be very hard to reduce Beethoven's themes to types—and to do so would in theory overthrow the historical process which led from the varied formulas of the baroque to the individual themes of classicism—at the same time there is no mistaking the fact that the aesthetic substance of the themes consists in the differentiation of characters, of which the number is limited. Therefore to speak of models, which underlie the fashioning and the sequence of the aesthetic characters in Beethoven's sonata movements, is by no means to deny the individuality which constitutes the artistic character of the works.

In the D major Sonata, Op. 10 No. 3, the first subject of the first movement introduces itself with the energy that is regarded, not without justification, as characteristic of the openings of Beethoven's sonatas. The 'transition' (bar 23: it is not actually a transition, because, although it modulates, it presents a counter-theme in B minor) is a cantilena, the second subject (bar 54) has a scherzando character, surprisingly enough, and the closing group (bar 106) adopts a hymnic tone. There can be no question, therefore, of the thematic dualism postulated in sonata-form theory. Each of the four themes contrasts with the other three, and it is not possible to make distinctions between 'essential' and 'incidental'.

At the same time the sequence of aesthetic characters is by no means arbitrary, and it would be an overstatement to speak of a 'sonata quasi una fantasia'. Rather, the grouping of thematic characters—the 'variation of tones'—must have been immediately comprehensible to the eighteenth-century hearers, for the same scheme, 'marcato'–'cantabile'–'scherzando', is the model that underlies the order of the movements within a sonata cycle. (It was from the analogy of thematic character and movement character that Franz Liszt, half a century later, drew the logical consequence of 'double function form': several movements combined in one.)

It is difficult to give the 'variation of tones' an aesthetic foundation without entering the realm of speculation, and contemporaries seem to have evaded the problem, although reflection on aesthetic questions was one of the intellectual passions of the age. Nevertheless, the addition of the minuet to the sonata cycle (initially regarded as an unnecessary disruption in northern Germany) shows that it was felt to be entirely appropriate to supplement the contrast between allegro and adagio movements by a scherzando, in spite of the fact that the original Allegro–Adagio–Allegro scheme is immediately comprehensible and actually resists an interpolation. (It should also be said that in the three-movement cycle the concluding Allegro quite often struck a scherzando note.)

Aesthetic characters are a correlative to formal functions. The cantabile usually acts as a second subject, the scherzando as the concluding group, which tends to be thematically independent. In the D major Sonata, however, the associations between the aesthetic characters and the formal functions have been, as it were, realigned by one phase: it is not a second subject and a concluding group, but a 'transition' and a second subject, that are respectively cantabile and scherzando in character. This does not affect the evident aesthetic rightness that cleaves to the 'variation of tones'. Instead, the formal irregularity has a tonal foundation. The 'transition' begins by presenting its own key, the relative minor, although it goes on to modulate. And the fact that the aesthetic characters which underlie the exposition correspond to changes of key, the configuration of which is scarcely less obvious than the dichotomy of tonic and dominant, makes it possible almost to forget the principle of thematic dualism, although, of course, it represents the norm that is ever active in the background of our awareness of form, and to which the disposition of the D major Sonata represents an exception.

The unorthodoxy of the overall structure, and the 'realignment' of the relationships between aesthetic characters and formal functions, are closely connected with irregularity in the syntactic structure of the themes. The first subject is a period complete in itself, with a repeated consequent clause, but the second subject (bar 54) is open-ended, in so far as the repetition breaks off after five bars. If we accept that the general rule is the opposite, with the first subject presenting the open form of the 'clause', and the second the closed form of the period (because the first is likely to generate motivic development, but the second is not), then it is not unreasonable to seek the explanation for the irregular syntax in the formal irregularity of the fact that the 'transition' is a cantilena. The periodic form of the first subject corresponds to a 'transition', the lyrical character of which gives notice that on this occasion the motivic development that would normally form the continuation of a syntactically open first subject has been abandoned. The evolutionary section is made good to some extent, however, by the fact that the second subject (bar 67) is followed by motivic development. The syntactic structure of a 'clause', although unusual for a second subject, is thus justified. Admittedly, the motive that is developed comes from the first subject, rather than from the second, but an explanation is not hard to find. Firstly, it can be argued that the motivic dependence of the development section on the 'clause' is less important than the abstract syntactic structure as such, without regard to the material (as in late baroque melodic elaboration). Secondly, it is possible to relate the beginning of the second subject to a motive from the first subject, as a variant, in that the up-beat (D–C♯–B–A) can be interpreted as a prolongation of the note a' (Ex. 6.3). Although it appears to have

Ex. 6.3

only a loose association with the notes, the explanation is not complete nonsense, because it brings 'contrasting derivation' to light as the connection between the themes, and that is one of the fundamental principles of thematic dialectic in Beethoven. Additionally, the fact that the second subject is succeeded by a section which elaborates particles from the first subject is arguably confirmation of the inner relationship between the two themes.

Aesthetic characters, formal functions, syntactic structures, and motivic relationships are all thus shown to be parts of a complex network of associations in which we can see the 'inner form' of the movement—to employ a central aesthetic category, which, intangible as it is, has a long tradition. In Beethoven, irregularities are more than mere deviations from the norm, they are starting-points for the construction of a whole that is coherent in itself, and—far from falling short of schematic forms in integrity and inner logic—actually surpasses them.

4. Rhythm and the 'Metrical Foot'

The terms 'affect' and 'character' were used as synonyms in the middle of the eighteenth century, by Mattheson, Marpurg, and

Quantz, although the concept of 'character'—embracing program-matic elements and even tone-painting, as well as the expression of emotions—was really the more comprehensive category.

In setting the two terms up against each other, Christian Gottfried Körner, whose theory of musical aesthetics is the only one that can be regarded as a philosophical counterpart to Viennese classicism, departed from this terminological tradition, which nevertheless persisted alongside his proposals. In his treatise on the repre-sentation of character in music (*Über Charakterdarstellung in der Musik*), published in 1795 in Schiller's periodical *Die Horen*, character is presented as the element which is fixed, enduring, and founded from within, whereas affect is inconstant and motivated by external circumstances. 'We distinguish in that which we call soul something constant and something transitory, the heart (*das Gemüth*) and the emotions of the heart, character—ethos—and a passionate state—pathos. Is it of no importance, which of the two the musician seeks to represent?'[3]

Hard as it may be to make useful distinctions between pathos and ethos in Beethoven's music, it is equally hard to mistake the problem that Körner was addressing. It was posed by Schiller in 1794, in his *Briefe über die ästhetische Erziehung des Menschen*. The affective power of music, working on both the senses and the emotions, evidently stirred Schiller no less violently than it did his contemporaries of the age of *Empfindsamkeit*, and he saw in it a threat to the inner freedom that constitutes the dignity of the human being. Music's power to 'enslave' or 'fetter' (*fesseln*) the listener, in the metaphor beloved of enthusiasts, constituted for Schiller grounds for moral suspicion. Effects that worked directly on the senses and the emotions had to go hand in hand with moral influences, if they were to be aesthetic and not merely pathological. Körner believed that the recognition that pathos in music was counterbalanced by an ethos, the existence of which could be not merely postulated but proved, would allay Schiller's doubts about the aesthetic essence of the effects of music.

In the attempt to define the musical representation of character more precisely, admittedly, Körner entangled himself in a contradiction which deserves mention, in so far as it is not an incidental error on his part, but draws attention to an issue that is inherent in the subject itself.

On the one hand Körner describes ethos as a principle of unity in a diversity of 'passionate states'—that is, he reinforces the antithesis at the centre of his theory with the fundamental aesthetic formula of

---

[3] Repr. in W. Seifert, *Christian Gottfried Körner: ein Musikästhetiker der deutschen Klassik* (Regensburg, 1960), 147.

1. Ludwig van Beethoven (1712–73). Oil-painting by Leopold Radoux (Historisches Museum, Vienna). Beethoven's grandfather served the electoral court in Bonn as a bass singer for forty years, and also as Kapellmeister from 1761 onwards. It was exceptional for a Kapellmeister not to be a composer, and it may have been a talent for administration that earned him the post. The Bonn master-baker Gottfried Fischer, whose memoirs are a reliable source of information about Beethoven's early life, in spite of the late date at which they were written, records: 'Stature of the Hofkapellmeister: a tall, handsome man, long, narrow face, broad forehead, rounded nose, large, round eyes, plump, red cheeks, very serious countenance.'

C. G. NEEFE

2. Christian Gottlob Neefe (1748–98). Engraving by Gottlob August Liebe from a drawing by Johann Georg Rosenberg (photo: Gesellschaft der Musikfreunde, Vienna). Neefe came to Bonn in 1779 as Musikdirektor of the Grossmann theatre troupe, and was the only musician of any standing among those who taught Beethoven in Bonn. It is true that Wegeler wrote in his memoirs that 'Neefe had little influence on the education of our Ludwig; the latter even complained about Neefe's excessively severe criticism of his first essays in composition', but that carries little weight, for Beethoven was liable to claim that none of his teachers had taught him anything. Neefe was both a composer and a writer, and Beethoven had him to thank for introducing him not only to *Das wohltemperierte Klavier* but also to Klopstock's poetry. Above all, however, it was Neefe who instilled in him the aesthetics of the characteristic. In his *Dilettanterien* (1785), Neefe wrote: 'Sulzer, one of our greatest philosophers, and perhaps the greatest aesthetician of our time, complains about halfheartedness in the attempt to imbue instrumental music with greater significance, and it would undoubtedly have become more eloquent long ago, if those efforts had been pursued.'

3. Three Sonatas for Piano, the so-called 'Kurfürst' sonatas; first edition 1783 (photo: Gesellschaft der Musikfreunde, Vienna). The dedication to Elector Maximilian Friedrich, Archbishop of Cologne (in which Beethoven's reference to his age is probably the result of his father's deliberately misleading him), begins: 'Your Most Sublime Grace! Music began to be the foremost of my youthful occupations from my fourth year onwards. From this early acquaintance with the fair Muse, who attuned my soul to pure harmonies, I came to love her and, or so it has often appeared to me, she to love me in return. I have now entered my eleventh year: and since that date my Muse has often whispered to me in hours of dedication "try it, and set down the harmonies of your soul in writing!"' The tendency towards monothematicism exhibitied by these sonatas is significant in so far as it suggests that the principle of 'contrasting derivation' developed from the desire to differentiate what was originally unified, rather than modify material that was originally contrasted.

LUDWIG VAN BEETHOVEN

in seinem 16ten Jahre.

Lith. von Gebr. Becker in Coblenz 1838.

4. Ludwig van Beethoven *c.*1786. Silhouette by Joseph Neesen. Frontispiece to F. G. Wegeler and F. Ries, *Biographische Notizen über Ludwig van Beethoven,* Koblenz 1838 (photo: Bayerische Staatsbibliothek, Munich). Carl Ludwig Junker writes in 1791 of Beethoven's keyboard playing: 'I have heard Vogler, often and for hours at a time, playing the fortepiano (I cannot judge his organ-playing, for I have never heard him on the organ), and I have always admired his exceptional facility, but Beethoven goes beyond facility, he is more eloquent, more pointed, more expressive, in short, more for the heart; that is, he is as good at playing adagio as allegro.' This description tallies with Czerny's view: 'Beethoven's style: the predominant feature is a characteristic and passionate strength, alternating with all the charms of legato lyricism.'

5. Ferdinand Ernst Gabriel, Count von Waldstein (1762–1823). Unsigned oil-painting (Duchcov Museum, Czechoslovakia). Count Waldstein, dedicatee of the Piano Sonata, Op. 53, met Beethoven in Bonn and smoothed his entrée into aristocratic circles in Vienna. The words he wrote in Beethoven's diary on 29 October 1792 are a remarkably prophetic formulation of what writers like J. F. Reichardt and E. T. A. Hoffmann came to call the 'classical triad': 'Dear Beethoven! You are now travelling to Vienna to fulfil the wishes which have so long been denied you. The Genius of Mozart still laments and weeps over the death of her foster-child. She found refuge but no occupation with the inexhaustible Haydn; through him she yet hopes to be united with another. Through incessant industry, may you receive the spirit of Mozart from the hands of Haydn.'

6. Johann Georg Albrechtsberger (1736–1809). Unsigned oil-painting (Gesellschaft der Musikfreunde, Vienna). Albrechtsberger gave Beethoven lessons in counterpoint in 1794–5, while Haydn was away in London. Beethoven was a difficult pupil, to judge by the account of Ferdinand Ries: 'Haydn had expressed the wish that Beethoven would include the words "pupil of Haydn" on the title-pages of his works. Beethoven did not want this, because, he said, although he had received some instruction from Haydn, he had learnt nothing from him . . . Beethoven had also studied couterpoint with Albrechtsberger, and dramatic music with Salieri. I knew them all well: all three thought very highly of Beethoven, but were also on one mind as to his learning. Each of them said that he had always been so stubborn and selfwilled that there were things he had had to learn from harsh experience, after having refused to learn them earlier as the subjects of instruction.'

7. Ignaz Schuppanzigh (1776–1830). Lithograph by Bernhard von Schrötter (photo: Gesellschaft de Musikfreunde, Vienna). Schuppanzigh, a loyal friend of Beethoven through thick and thin, played first violin in the string quartet maintained by Count Rasumowsky from 1808 to 1816. He was evidently the first to perform quartets before the general public, in 1804, and this enterprise had an influence on the Op. 59 quartets of Beethoven, in which, broadly speaking, the composer transformed the genre from music for the private salon to music for the concert-hall. J. F. Reichardt wrote of Schuppanzigh's playing in 1808: 'Herr Schuppanzigh himself has a personal, piquant style, which suits very well the humorous quartets of Haydn, Mozart, and Beethoven; or perhaps it would be truer to say that it has developed out of the whimsical performance appropriate to these masterpieces.'

8. The old Burgtheater on the Michaelerplatz, Vienna. Coloured copperplate by Carl Postl, 1810 (Galerie Liechtenstein). A benefit concert in this theatre on 2 April 1800 was the occasion on which Beethoven broke through to public recognition as a leading composer, to be mentioned in the same breath as Haydn, whereas previously he had enjoyed a somewhat esoteric reputation, confined mainly to aristocratic circles. The programme comprised the First Piano Concerto, Op. 15 (the second in order of composition), the First Symphony, Op. 21, and the Septet, Op. 20, which remained Beethoven's most popular work for many years. The correspondent of the *Allgemeine musikalische Zeitung* wrote: 'In the end Herr Beethoven got his turn in the theatre, and this was probably the most interesting academy for a long time. He played a new concerto of his own composition, which has very many beautiful passages, especially the first two movements. Then they gave a septet by him, which is written with much taste and sentiment. He next improvised in masterly fashion, and finally they performed a symphony of his composition, which contained much in the way of art, novelty and abundant ideas.' Though the terminology is conventional, this review is significant at least inasmuch as Beethoven was by no means always praised in the pages of the *Allgemeine musikalische Zeitung*.

9. Page from the score of the 'Eroica', with the dissonant horn entry four bars before the recapitulation (Gesellschaft der Musikfreunde, Vienna). Fétis thought it necessary to correct the dissonance, and even Ries did not understand it at first: 'At the first rehearsal of this symphony, which was appalling, but where the horn came in correctly, I was standing at Beethoven's side, and in the belief that it was wrong I said: "That damned horn-player, can't he count?—It sounds execrable!" I think I was very close to having my ears boxed. Beethoven did not forgive me for a very long time.'

10. Ludwig van Beethoven. Oil-painting by Joseph Willibrord Mähler (Historisches Museum, Vienna). The first of Mähler's four portraits of Beethoven was painted in 1804–5, and remained in his possession until his death. It depicts him with an allegorical lyre, before a landscape with a Greek temple, and the general impression is idealized; comparison with Horneman's miniature on ivory (1803) shows, however, that a good likeness was not sacrificed.

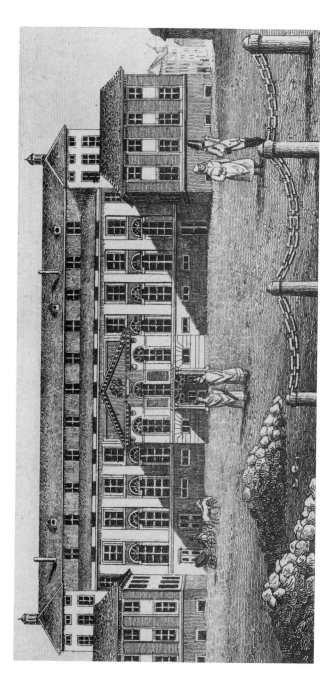

11. The Theater an der Wien. Unsigned and undated steel-engraving (photo: Bayerische Staatsbibliothek, Munich). The Theater an der Wien—where Beethoven was given an apartment in 1803, so that he could work undisturbed on his opera—saw the first performances of the first version of *Fidelio* (1805) and the revision (1806). Sonnleithner's libretto roused the correspondent of the *Zeitung für die elegante Welt* to an outburst of indignation: 'It passes comprehension how the composer could bring himself to give life to this inane and shoddy piece of work by Sonnleithner with his beautiful music. It was for that reason . . . that the effect of the whole could not possibly be such as the composer may well have assured himself that it would be, for the idiocy of the spoken words wholly, or to a very great extent, obliterated the beauty of the sung passages.'

12. Josephine, Countess Deym, née Countess von Brunswick. Unsigned
pencil miniature (Joseph, Count Deym, Vienna). For many decades the
identity of the person to whom Beethoven wrote the letter which he addressed
to the 'immortal beloved', in Teplitz in 1812, was the subject of heated debate
(it is not known if he actually sent the letter or not). It seems now to be
generally accepted that Josephine von Brunswick was the lady.

13. *An die ferne Geliebte.* First edition 1816 (photo: Bayerische Staatsbibliothek, Munich). Fanny Giannatasio, the daughter of the tutor of Beethoven's nephew Carl, wrote in her diary that the composer had spoken to her father of a hopeless love that had possessed him five years previously, and some biographers have seized on this as grounds for linking the song cycle with the letter to the 'immortal beloved'. But the biographical interpretation treads on uncertain ground psychologically, because no one can be sure whether the composition is an expression of emotion, or the outcome of distancing from emotion.

14. Ludwig van Beethoven. Drawing by Johann Peter Theodor Lyser (coll. André Meyer, Paris). Lyser (1803–70), whose drawing was later reproduced lithographically, appears never to have set eyes on Beethoven. The sketch is not a particularly good likeness, and its significance lies in the fact that it represents the 'romantic image of Beethoven': the image of the revolutionary, the genius unconcerned with externals.

Freytag den

K. K. Hoftheater nächst dem Kärnthnerthore.

Große musikalische Akademie

von

Herrn L. van Beethoven,

Ehrenmitglied der königl. Akademie der Künste und Wissenschaften zu Stockholm und Amsterdam, dann Ehrenbürger von Wien.

Die dabey vorkommenden Musikstücke sind die neuesten Werke des Herrn Ludwig van Beethoven.

Erstens. Große Ouverture.
Zweytens. Drey große Hymnen, mit Solo- und Chor-Stimmen.
Drittens. Große Symphonie, mit im Finale eintretenden Solo- und Chor-Stimmen, auf Schillers Lied, an die Freude.

Die Solo-Stimmen werden die Dlles. Sontag und Unger, und die Herren Haizinger und Seipelt vortragen. Herr Schuppanzigh hat die Direction des Orchesters, Herr Kapellmeister Umlauf die Leitung des Ganzen, und der Musik-Verein die Verstärkung des Chors und Orchesters aus Gefälligkeit übernommen.

Herr Ludwig van Beethoven selbst, wird an der Leitung des Ganzen Antheil nehmen.

(Die Eintrittspreise sind wie gewöhnlich.)

Freybillets sind heute ungültig.

Der Anfang ist um 7 Uhr.

15. Programme of the concert in the Kärntnertortheater on 7 May 1824 (Picture archive of the Österreichische Nationalbibliothek, Vienna). The three movements from the *Missa solemnis*—Kyrie, Credo, and Agnus Dei—which, like the Ninth Symphony, were heard in Vienna for the first time, were referred to as 'hymns' because the censor did not permit settings of the mass to be performed as such at concerts. The overture with which the concert began was *Die Weihe des Hause*, written for the opening of the Josephstadt theatre in 1822. With customary malice Joseph Carl Rosenbaum noted in his diary: 'Many boxes empty—no one from the court. For all the large forces, little effect—B's adherents made a noise, the majority remained quiet, many did not stay to the end.'

16. Beethoven's funeral procession. Watercolour by Franz Stöber (Beethoven-Haus, Bonn). Something like 20,000 people accompanied the coffin. The funeral oration written by Franz Grillparzer, which had to be spoken at the entrance to the cemetery, began by pairing Beethoven with Goethe: 'As we stand here at the grave of the departed, we can be said to represent the entire nation, the whole German people, mourning the passing of the one greatly celebrated half of that which remained to us of the vanished glory of our native art, the spiritual efflorescence of our fatherland.'

his time; the fact that familiarity made the formula a commonplace should not be allowed to obscure its original significance:

If music has an abundance of clear signs with which to illustrate a specific state, then it possesses the ability also to represent character. We cannot directly discern what we call character either in the real world or in any work of art whatsoever, but can only deduce it from what is contained in the features of individual states.[4]

Character, as Körner understands or construes it, is not perceptible in tangible musical features of a piece, but must be inferred from the changing affects as the element of unity, operating in the background, as it were, and relating the 'passionate states' to each other. (The means whereby the affects are expressed are established by tradition, and are therefore directly discernible, unlike those of character.)

   The affects that succeed each other in the first movement of the 'Pathétique' Sonata, Op. 13, are unmistakable, and in order to conjure them up before one's eyes, there is no need to yield to the temptation to put them into words: that is, to fall into the 'heresy of paraphrase'. Equally, the overall character indicated by the title of the work really does not need any further comment. Indeed, the titles Beethoven gave to some of his works, or to some movements — 'Sinfonia eroica', 'Pastorale', 'Quartetto serioso', 'La malinconia' — are strangely conventional, suggesting that the aesthetic significance of works without such a title was not deliberately concealed, as Schindler thought, but proved too complex to be expressed in words. It would follow that a clearly perceptible overall character, such as Körner postulated, was an exception rather than the rule.

   On the one hand, therefore, Körner defined character as an inner unity that was not directly presented, but had to be inferred from the configuration of the affects. On the other hand — and this was the cause of the rift that runs through his theory — he attempted to pin down the ethos of a movement in its musical material: that is, to exchange indirect representation (which he initially thought was the only kind possible) for direct representation, or to supplement the former by the latter. 'We notice in the motion of the sound partly differences of duration, partly differences of constitution.' (By 'constitution' [*Beschaffenheit*], Körner means pitch and timbre.) The differences of duration 'are the most important in the representation of character. The regular element in the alternation of lengths of notes — rhythm — indicates the independence of the motion. What we discern in this regularity is constancy in the living being, which asserts its independence in the face of all external changes.'[5] It is not

   [4] 'Über Charakterdarstellung', 155.

   [5] Ibid., 157.

altogether clear which musical phenomenon Körner meant by the
'regular element' (*das Regelmäßige*), which he calls 'rhythm', and
interprets as character. At first it seems that he means the metre that
Hegel in his *Ästhetik*, two decades later, interpreted as the element
that remained identical amid the variations of note-lengths, and
therefore as the analogue of the consciousness of self. But as Körner
goes on, it is revealed that he understands by 'rhythm' not 'empty'
('pure' or 'abstract') metre but 'filled' (or 'rhythmicized') metre:
metre, that is, in the ancient sense of the word. Musical character
expresses itself primarily in the configuration of long and short beats
that predominates in any movement or shorter unit.

Johann Mattheson outlined a theory of musical metres, or 'musical
feet' (*Klangfüße*), in *Der vollkommene Capellmeister* (1739): 'What
the feet signify in poetry is represented by the rhythms in music,
which is why we propose to call them, too, musical feet, because
song goes along on them, so to speak.'[6] Usually, though not
invariably, Mattheson's musical feet begin on down-beats, and he
ascribes specific expressive characters to them: the spondee is
'honourable and serious', the iambus 'moderately merry, not quick
or running', the dactyl suitable 'both for earnest and light-hearted
melodies'.[7] Thus the theory of metre is, as with Körner,
simultaneously a theory of the representation of character, with the
difference that Mattheson, as already mentioned, does not distinguish
between affect and character. By that means he escapes a difficulty
that befell Körner: the fact that while a particular metre like the
iambus or the trochee may dominate a long stretch of a piece of
music, it is quite impossible that it should underlie the entire piece.
The monotony might be characterful indeed, but aesthetically it
would be unbearable.

It is not certain, admittedly, whether Körner, by the words 'the
regular element in the alternation of lengths of notes', meant simple
metre at all, in the sense of a persistent recurrence of one and the same
pattern of short and long beats. Körner's theory perhaps invites the
objection that it misses the point of musical reality and is blindly
borrowed from poetics, but in his defence it can be surmised that,
when he spoke of '*das Regelmäßige in der Abwechslung von
Tonlängen*', he had in mind a difference between concrete durations
of notes and the abstract musical foot that stands behind them, as it
were. In that case, the musical foot would be a structure operating in
the 'background', which can coincide with the rhythmic events in the
'foreground', but does not need to be in agreement with them. A

---

[6] (Hamburg, 1739; fac. repr. Kassel. 1954), 160.
[7] Ibid., 164 ff.

period can be dactylic, without presenting the sequence 'long – short – short' and nothing else.

As an abstract category, 'musical foot' is analogous to the melodic shape which, likewise, is capable of appearing in different concrete forms without the fact that it permits of variation causing it to lose its identity. And it is not an exaggeration to claim that it represents an important, and as yet scarcely acknowledged, means of establishing formal relationship in Beethoven's works.

In the first movement of the Second Symphony, the principal subject (bar 34), the second subject (bar 73), and the final group (bar 114) are related to each other by a common basic rhythmic pattern (♩. ♩|♩♩♩♩). The recurrence of this pattern is unmistakable, as soon as the listener has assimilated the idea of the 'musical foot' as a category of musical hearing (Ex. 6.4). Even an apparently non-

Ex. 6.4

thematic part of the development (bar 198) proves to be thematic, if the musical foot, the basic form of which remains perceptible through changing modifications or concrete relizations, is accepted as a thematic element. (It is appropriate to speak of concrete realizations of an abstract pattern., in so far as the musical foot is not presented in the basic form at the beginning, but already takes a variant or modified form in the first subject.)

The underlying rhythmic structure of the first movement of the 'Pathétique' Sonata can be interpreted either as a complex of two variants of one and the same musical foot, or as two separate but related musical feet: ♪ ♩ ♩ |(♩) and ♪ ♩♩♩ |(♩). The first subject (bar 11) contains both versions side by side, the transition (bar 35) and the second subject (bar 51) confine themselves to the second, crotchet version, and the continuation of the second subject (bar 89) is based on an augmentation of the first variant. (The fact that the lyrical second subject modulates means that it can also be interpreted as a second transition, which gives the tonally closed continuation the function of the 'real' second subject; that is irrelevant in the context of a scrutiny of the rhythmic structure, but has to be mentioned because it causes confusion in the nomenclature of the formal sections; see Ex. 6.5.) It would doubtless be an overstatement if

Ex. 6.5

adherence to a system drove one to claim that one and the same musical foot—in two versions—permeates the entire movement. But in order to confirm the hypothesis that a rhythm that runs throughout the movement is one of the guarantees of its unity, it is enough for a common pattern to be contained in the principal motives of the various formal sections. (The value of rhythm for this purpose can perhaps be set midway between that of 'pure' metre and that of actual note-values.)

After analysis of the 'Pathétique', it is necessary to moderate the objection to Körner's theory on the grounds of contradiction between the definition of character as the element operating in the background to unify changing 'passionate states', and the attempt, in spite of that, to fix character in the musical material. Though it is impossible in theory to ignore the distinction between the aesthetically vague and the materially explicit, at the same time there is no denying the fact that the antithetical possibilities for representing character can coexist in compositional practice. Unity of character in the first movement of the 'Pathétique' can be inferred as the trait common to the various 'passionate states', and, simultaneously, it manifests itself in a recurrent musical foot, by means of which the formal sections are linked together in a musically tangible way.

Unity of character, as postulated by Körner, may not only be based on a recurrent musical foot but also emerge from the dialectic between two differing musical feet. In the first movement of the 'Eroica' Symphony, the rhythm of the first subject, the simplicity of which is in strange and marked contrast to the complexity of the consequences drawn from it, is a trochee. There is some difficulty in identifying a second subject that forms a contrast to the first, because lyricism of any kind is not to be found, and of the two motivic groups in the dominant (B flat major), the first (bar 46), which does not modulate, cannot be interpreted as part of the transition, and the second (bar 83), which is followed by several further sections, cannot be interpreted as a concluding group. We are left with no alternative but to speak of two second subjects of equal standing. There is not the slightest connection in purely intervallic terms between the two, but—and this goes at least some way to explain why there are two of them—they are related by a common musical foot, and one of some substance, moreover: two crotchets form a long up-beat finishing on a crotchet down-beat (Ex. 6.6). (The dotting of the note in the first

Ex. 6.6

second subject is a modification that does not affect the identity or the recognizability of the musical foot.)

If for a moment we employ a terminology of the eighteenth and nineteenth centuries, which arose from the amalgamation of the quantitative metrics of classical poetry and modern metrical rhythmics, we can say that the down-beat trochee of the principal subject is countered by an up-beat trochee in the two second subjects. But the conflict of up-beat and down-beat attributes results in a rhythm which is one of those features of the 'Eroica' which are both characteristic and made prominent by their insistence; in this case it is the syncopated hemiola, the irregularity of which is accentuated by sforzatos (Ex. 6.7). This strutting rhythm is introduced in the

Ex. 6.7

transition, recurs before the concluding group, and reaches a paroxysmal climax in the development.

The syncopated hemiola can be interpreted as a rhythm in which to some extent the up-beat minims of the second subjects and the down-beat minims of the first subject come into conflict. Undeniably, such an interpretation is methodologically risky, because no theory of the developing variation of rhythms exists at present—and the need for one has not even been recognized. But in a description of the formal structure of the exposition, it is scarcely possible to dispense with the hypothesis that the down-beat trochee of the first subject and the up-beat trochee of the two second subjects are blended in the syncopated hemiola, because it enables us to recognize the rhythmic contrast between the first and second subjects as an antithesis that does not merely exist, but actually works itself out. And if the initial premiss of an interpretation contains an element of uncertainty, it will be at least partly justified by the conclusions that it permits us to draw from it.

While Körner looked to character (manifested primarily in rhythm) as the source of unity in the diversity of affects, other aesthetic theorists—those who held to the tradition of the eighteenth century, and could not conceive of instrumental music as an autonomous form, but only as either the representation of a 'content', or an empty, albeit pleasant, noise—sought it in a 'secret programme'. The hermeneutical byways among which Beethoven exegesis strayed from Adolf Bernhard Marx to Arnold Schering become easier to understand if it is recognized that it was the wrong solution to a problem that certainly existed. In Beethoven's works the 'form set in motion by sounding' (*tönend bewegte Form*) always points forward to something beyond the present instant, and in his case, of all composers, it is immediately evident that it is not enough to declare the 'variation of tones' in a sonata exposition a groundless and irrational process, or to seek the unity of the whole solely in the functional coherence of the formal sections, and in the overt or latent motivic relationships of separate themes. Telling a story, whether invented or borrowed from literature, in order to lend the sequence of affects a coherence expressible in words, is, nevertheless, a questionable process that cannot be supported by the musical text. It is more reasonable to seek the solution to the problem in the direction adumbrated in the previous section of this chapter: the succession of expressive characters is based on models like the sequence 'marcato'– 'cantabile'—'scherzando', which, as is shown by the analogy of thematic characters and the character of a movement, acquired a special authority or 'aesthetic logic' in the eighteenth century and beyond.

The theory of 'esoteric programmes' which Arnold Schering pursued to an extreme with inexorable logic is weakened by a second fault, namely that the aesthetic meaning of the interpretation remains uncertain. Schering was convinced that Beethoven used great works of literature as the sources of his inspiration, and to some extent 'followed the text' as he composed (he cited the *Iliad* as the source of the 'Eroica', and Goethe's *Werther* and *Wilhelm Meister* for the C minor Violin Sonata, Op. 30 No. 3, and the F major String Quartet, Op. 59 No. 1, respectively). The interpretation of the interpretation produces a contradiction, however. On the one hand, Schering believes that only knowledge of the 'esoteric programmes' will lead to the removal of 'everything unclear, ambiguous, and confused from these compositions'.[8] In other words, he regards the deciphering of the music as a necessary preliminary to listeners' complete understanding of it, so that they are not left perplexed by formal irregularities which can be explained only by the programme. On the other hand, Schering simultaneously takes the view that the function

[8] *Beethoven und die Dichtung* (Berlin, 1936), 115.

of a programme is fulfilled by the fact of its assuming musical shape, and it can be passed over in silence, its interest being solely analytical, and not aesthetic.[9] The contradiction is blatant but not incomprehensible in its historical context; the interpretation of interpretation has itself become a subject of historical exegesis since Schering's day. In the nineteenth century and in the early part of the twentieth, people could not agree on whether the process and the technicalities of composition were a private matter for the composer, which did not concern the public, or if a work could only be understood thoroughly after its genesis had been reconstructed. It took time for the idea to gain ground that programmes only belong to works as 'aesthetic subjects' if the composer makes them known, and that, vice versa, even programmes that are added later, and are wholly irrelevant to the compositional process, are aesthetically legitimate: in other words, it is not the method of composition that is decisive but the composer's declared aesthetic intention.

5. 'Moral Characters'

It would be very interesting to know Haydn's motives for composing his works, as well as the sentiments and ideas which were in his mind as he composed, and which he strove to express by means of the language of music. In order to know for certain, however, someone would have had to place each of his works in front of him in turn, and the old man found that irksome. But he did say that he had often depicted moral characters in his symphonies.[10]

The biographical memoir of Haydn by Georg August Griesinger[11] is the authority for this quotation of the term 'moral characters'. It looks straightforward enough: one thinks of Molière and La Bruyère, or of the *Moralische Bildnisse* (Moral Portraits) of Christian Fürchtegott Gellert, and it is not hard to imagine a character like 'the miser' or 'the misanthrope' as the subject of a symphonic movement. The depiction of 'moral characters' was admittedly, as the quotation implies, not a general principle for Haydn, but one possibility among others. Moreover, it is not clear how the representation of character related to the expression of emotions, which, according to eighteenth-century beliefs, was the real import of the language of music—as distinct from the language of words, which expressed concepts. Although Griesinger had no pretensions to philosophy, it

[9] Ibid., 51.
[10] A. Schering, 'Bemerkungen zu J. Haydns Programmsinfonien', in his *Vom musikalischen Kunstwerk* (Leipzig, ²1951), 257.
[11] *Biographische Notizen über J. Haydn* (Leipzig, 1810; repr. Vienna, 1954).

cannot be ruled out that he understood by 'character' something similar to Körner's idea of the unity behind a diversity of emotions.

Eighteenth-century musical aesthetics was primarily an aesthetics of opera, and it was by no means a matter of course to turn to unity of character as the possible source of the formal integrity or 'wholeness' that, according to Karl Philipp Moritz, was part of the essence of a work of art. The purpose of the representation of personae in *opera seria* was not directed towards integrated characters, but towards the affects between which the personages are torn. In a case like that of Julius Caesar in Handel's opera, for example, who swings from one extreme 'passionate state' to another in a succession of abruptly altering circumstances, it is impossible to speak of 'character' in the sense of a consistent type. To the idealistic anthropology and aesthetics of the end of the century, the 'lack of character' shown by the heroes of *opera seria*—which did not mean bad character but vacuousness—was deeply suspect. Yet if we keep an open mind we can scarcely deny that the categories that classical anthropology took as its premises, and held up in opposition to baroque psychology—identity of the persona and integrity of character, that is—were based less on empirical facts than on optimistic postulates. The unity and the persistence of ethos was an article of faith around 1800—Körner's treatise *Über Charakterdarstellung* was its testimony in musical aesthetics—but, before long, Heine, Marx, and Nietzsche in turn cast doubt on it, and denounced it as merely the 'mask of character'.

The consistent character who refuses to make concessions to circumstances was represented as rigid and deformed in Molière; it was only with Rousseau that the misanthrope Alceste, who will not subscribe to social coventions, was made a hero. The requirement for consistent, high-principled characters was thus by no means necessarily taken for granted in the anthropologically based poetics of the late eighteenth century.

Furthermore, as soon as we turn from the poetics of spoken drama to the aesthetics of opera, we must take into consideration the fact that there is a peculiar affinity between baroque anthropology, which emphasizes the volatile affect and not the stable character, and the conditions under which music represents character. In brief: for musical reasons, the anthropology of opera has always remained that of the baroque opera. Easy and musically expressive as it is to allow operatic heroes to vacillate between different or contrary affects, it seems correspondingly difficult to milk strongly delineated characters for musical interest for more than the space of an episode. The direct representation of a 'whole' character quickly grows monotonous, and it is scarcely possible, using musical means, to make the indirect representation postulated by Körner—persisting through the variation of 'passionate states'—as clear as the theatre demands. It is not surprising, therefore, that operatic heroes, regardless of the current theory of anthropology, always tend to show 'lack of character'. Weber's Max and Meyerbeer's diabolical Robert are not exceptions, but represent the rule; and to reproach them for 'lack of character' from an idealistic standpoint is beside the point, to the extent that it ignores the musical conditions under which operatic psychology works, and which are stronger than the philosophical principles of any particular era.

Unity of character, which could be overlooked in opera because the unity of the action was the decisive factor, became an acute and urgent problem in the symphony, inasmuch as there was no action to provide an explanation for the different states of emotion. (The practice of inventing a 'secret programme', in order to make the changes of affects comprehensible as a coherent nexus of ideas, was a hermeneutical blind alley, as we have seen.) Körner's attempt to demonstrate that it was possible to represent character in instrumental music—as an alternative to 'telling a story'—therefore fulfilled a need of the time (in addition to its part in answering Schiller's doubts as to how 'inner freedom' could be preserved in the face of the affective power of music to 'fetter' the listener). The aesthetic justification of autonomous instrumental music, as it gained its independence from opera and the aesthetics of opera, converged with a central requirement of classical anthropology.

Admittedly, when Goethe and Kant spoke of 'character' they meant something different from Molière: not a mould bestowed by nature, but a 'self-forming' structure which grew out of the inner freedom of a human being. Kant distinguished between 'empirical' character, founded in nature, and 'intelligible' character, issuing from freedom. If 'empirical' character is subject to a law that it cannot influence, 'intelligible' character proves to be the mould which the human being, according to the *Critique of Pure Reason*, 'creates for himself, inasmuch as he possesses the ability to perfect himself according to the purposes which he has himself adopted'.

It is not certain whether Kant's distinction permits any relevant conclusions to be drawn for musical aesthetics. A character in the older sense, a fixed structure given by nature, can be represented plausibly in music, as countless monothematic 'character pieces' and sonata movements of the eighteenth century demonstrate; that does not mean that these pieces are also underpinned by an intention that does not appear in the finished phenomenon. And the representation of character by a recurring 'musical foot', for which Körner argued, is to some extent a kind of monothematicism at the abstractly rhythmic level. But it must be doubtful whether a 'self-forming' character can be rendered perceptible in music. Although Beethoven adopted the most important idea of classical anthropology, as formulated by Kant, as a conviction that governed his existence, it would be assuming too much to infer an aesthetic maxim from the ethical one. Clear as it is that Beethoven thought of his work as a whole as a contribution to that 'education in humanity' of which Herder spoke, yet it would be futile speculation to interpret the character which, in the formal complexity of sonata form, represents the unity in the diversity of 'passionate states' as being also a 'self-forming' character. Establishing and maintaining a fixed 'ethos' in the face of the vacillations of 'pathos' cannot, it seems, be understood as a process that music depicts, but only as a structure that it has appropriated for aesthetic effects.

7

The 'Underlying Idea'

I carry my ideas around with me for a long time, often a very long time, before I write them down. My memory remains so true the while that I am sure not to forget a theme, even years later, once I have hold of it. I change some things, discard, and try again until I am satisfied with it; then the elaboration begins in my head: expanding, compressing, raising, and deepening; and as I know what I want, the underlying idea never deserts me. It rises, it grows tall, I hear and see the image in my mind in its entire extent, as if cast in a single mould, and all that remains is the task of writing it down, which is accomplished quickly, as and when I find the time, because I sometimes have several things on the go at the same time, but am sure of not confusing any of them with any other.[1]

There is a shadow of doubt about the authenticity of this statement, which Louis Schlösser recorded Beethoven as having made in 1823. For one thing, the assertion that he carried musical ideas in his memory for a long time before writing them down is contrary to his habit of at once noting down in his sketchbooks even rudimentary ideas, the provisional character of which he must have recognized from the first. Secondly, as the 'continuity drafts' show, the 'task of writing it down' quite frequently became bogged down, and, if a difficulty could not be resolved immediately, was broken off for a return to more detailed sketching.

The essential problem presented by the statement does not consist, admittedly, in the difficulty of reconciling it with the evidence of the sketchbooks, but in the complicated relationship of the terms 'theme' ('*Thema*') and 'underlying idea' ('*zugrunde liegende Idee*'). They can scarcely be regarded as synonymous, because we cannot insult Beethoven or Schlösser by putting into the mouth of either the truism that a composer does not forget a musical theme while he is elaborating it. So a distinction must be made between 'theme' (or 'generative idea': '*Gedanke*' [translated as 'idea' in the first sentence of the quotation]) and 'underlying idea'—although, in the continuation of the passage quoted, the word '*Idee*', unqualified, is

[1] F. Kerst, *Die Erinnerungen an Beethoven* (Stuttgart, ²1925), ii, 15.

used as a synonym for '*Thema*' and '*Gedanke*'. 'Theme' obviously means the same thing as H. C. Koch meant by '*Hauptgedanke*' ('principal idea' or 'first subject'), whereas 'underlying idea' refers to an overall conception of a movement that is not yet 'the image in its entire extent'. The difficulty therefore lies in reconstructing a formal conception in such a way that it remains distinct from both the thematic material and the realized form, which constitutes the starting-point for the act of reconstruction.

The distinction between 'theme' and 'underlying idea' recalls some of the articles in Jean-Jacques Rousseau's *Dictionnaire de musique* of 1768. It is an illuminating association, even though, because both Beethoven and Schlösser could have known the dictionary, the possibility that the stylistic idiosyncrasy reveals a debt to Rousseau tells us nothing more conclusive about the quotation's provenance.

Rousseau defines the word 'sujet' at first in such a way as to suggest that he understands by it nothing more than a subject, or theme, in the technical musical sense, and not in the aesthetic sense: a pregnant melodic figure, which is stated at the beginning of a movement as a rule, and to which the remaining elements—variants, 'dissections', antitheses or episodes—relate:

C'est la partie principale du Dessein, l'idée qui sert de fondement à toutes les autres . . . Toutes les autres parties ne demandent que de l'art & du travail; celle-ci seule dépend du génie, & c'est en elle que consiste l'invention.[2]

Rousseau defines the underlying idea of a movement under the headword 'motif', and it is here that he distinguishes it from 'sujet'; a motive is not the same thing as a subject, but, rather, represents a principle that regulates both the nature of the subject and the structure of the form:

Il signifie l'idée primitive & principale sur laquelle le Compositeur détermine son sujet & arrange son dessein. C'est le motif qui, pour ainsi dire, lui met la plume à la main pour jetter sur le papier telle chose & non pas telle autre. Dans ce sens le motif principal doit être toujours présent à l'esprit du Compositeur, & il doit faire en sorte qu'il le soit aussi toujours à l'esprit des Auditeurs.[3]

The 'motive' that should always be present in the composer's mind— like Beethoven's 'underlying idea'—is undoubtedly a formal conception, but it seems also to concern the emotional content expressed in a movement. And in the article 'Dessein', the word 'sujet', too, denominates not so much a specific melodic figure as the inner unity in which the formal characteristics—from melody and

---

[2] *Dictionnaire de musique* (Paris, 1768; repr. Hildesheim, 1969), 455.   [3] Ibid., 302.

harmony to the tonal plan and the aesthetic character—converge. This is a unity which can be based on the subject only if 'subject' is understood to mean not only a melodic 'principal idea' and the compositional working thereof but also and simultaneously an underlying emotion or mood, to which all the structural elements of a movement relate:

Ce n'est pas assez de faire de beaux Chants & une bonne Harmonie; il faut lier tout cela par un sujet principal, auquel se rapportent toutes les parties de l'ouvrage, & par lequel il soit un. Cette unité doit régner dans le Chant, dans le Mouvement, dans le Caractère, dans l'Harmonie, dans la Modulation. Il faut que tout cela se rapporte à une idée commune qui le réunisse.[4]

Rousseau's definitions illustrate a problem that also had an effect on discussion of the concept of the 'poetic idea'—a term Beethoven used, although its importance was exaggerated by Anton Schindler. The problem lies in the difficulty of describing adequately the extent to which the inner unity of a movement is based on the formal concept, on the one hand, and on its expressive content, on the other. It is a commonplace to say that the relationship can be established only in specific cases and not as a matter of principle; however, if the attempt to reconstruct an 'underlying idea', which mediates between the formal and expressive elements of a movement, and—equally— between the thematic working and the finished form, succeeds in the cases of individual works, then it certainly does permit conclusions to be drawn about general categories influencing Beethoven's musical thinking.

We can make an initial, abstractive approach by defining the 'underlying idea' as the manner in which a specific association is made between the development of the thematic material, the design of the tonal groundplan, the disposition of the formal functions, and the succession of the aesthetic characters: a manner of connection which can be traced back to a problem, to which the finished movement is the solution. Analysis achieves its goal if it succeeds in the reconstruction of the question to which the work represents an answer.

The premisses underlying the first movement of the D major Sonata, Op. 10 No. 3, were discussed in the previous chapter, and merely need to be recapitulated. The exposition is in five sections: it consists of the principal subject, a 'transition' (bar 23) which modulates but is a cantilena presenting a contrasting counter-theme, a second subject (bar 54) which strikes a scherzando note, a continuation of the second subject (bar 67) in which motives from the

[4] Ibid., 142.

first subject are elaborated, and a concluding group (bar 106) of a hymnic character and with a melody that was partly prefigured in the continuation of the second subject (bar 87).

The succession of characters—from the energetic attack of the first subject, through the lyricism of the 'transition', and the scherzando quality of the second subject, to the hymnic tone of the conclusion— is the manifestation of an aesthetic logic which is comparable to the sense of rightness—hard to explain but easy to see—that is also illustrated in the arrangement of movements in a sonata cycle.

The first and second subjects are related to one another by contrasting derivation: latently underlying the second subject is the inversion of the first subject's second motive—elaborated in the upper part (bar 54) and unelaborated in the bass (bar 55). The inverted form of the same motive returns in the continuation of the second subject (bar 94), where it is counterpointed by an augmented version of the first subject's opening motive in inversion, so that there is scarcely room for doubt that the motivic association is intentional.

The subdivision of the exposition into five sections, the 'aesthetic logic' in the succession of thematic characters, and the principle of contrasting derivation do not belong to the textbook scheme of sonata form, but they are general premises with a background in tradition; they must therefore be specified when access to the individuality of the work is sought. A characteristic with a lesser degree of abstraction is the phenomenon described earlier as the 'realignment' of the relative positions of the formal functions and the aesthetic characters of the themes. The 'transition' is a cantilena and the second subject a scherzando, whereas in the tradition to which Beethoven referred in the very act of modifying it the second subject was more usually a lyrical section and the concluding group a scherzo. (It could be taken for granted that contemporary listeners would be acquainted with the type of movement by Haydn to which Beethoven's game with tradition relates.)

The first movement of the D major Sonata, as the outline description shows, rests on a configuration of premises which can be defined as the 'underlying idea', if we succeed in comprehending it genetically and tracing it back to a problem which could have been the point at which the conception of the movement started. (It is scarcely necessary to say that the reconstruction is hypothetical.) It would be wrong to suppose that the 'underlying idea' is just one of the elements making up the configuration—the first subject, the motivic association connecting first and second subjects, the aesthetic logic in the succession of themes, or the realignment in the relative positions of formal functions and aesthetic characters. The 'idea' does not consist in a tangible circumstance from which everything else could then be derived, but in a nexus of relations in which the 'foundation circumstances'—the hierarchy of what came first and what came later—are uncertain. It is in no way necessary to conclude that all the premisses and implications which come to light out of the 'given' form, during the reconstruction of the 'form in the process of becoming', were constantly present in the composer's mind while he was writing the piece. From the hermeneutical point of view, however—and independently of psychological considerations—the total configuration of the form-determining elements has to be regarded as the starting-point of the work's conception.

The problem that to some extent 'switched on' the configuration of general premisses in the D major Sonata—that is, set in train the process that led to the realization of the individual form—was a paradox: the ambition, on the one hand, to accomplish a grouping of thematic characters which is as richly contrasted as can be imagined, and, on the other hand, nevertheless, to weave a dense network of motivic relationships which spreads itself over virtually the entire movement. Opposing extremes of divergence and unification were to be compelled to combine, and it is no exaggeration to claim that the exposition of the D major Sonata is a composed-out contradiction. That, and nothing less, is its 'underlying idea'.

Connecting first and second subjects by means of contrasting derivation—that is, mediating the contrast of aesthetic characters by means of motivic logic—is a positively common practice in Beethoven, as Arnold Schmitz demonstrated. But the idea of generating the continuation of the second subject (a passage which lasts for no less than 39 bars) from the elaboration of motives from the first subject—that is, from the insertion of a lengthy piece of development into the exposition—is altogether unusual. And while following the hymnic theme of the concluding group with a lengthy appendix that uses the opening motive of the first subject (bars 114–124) can be explained as a conventional retransition, it receives an additional significance in a context where motivic relationships are being linked in a positively systematic fashion.

The formal idea underlying the movement can be understood as simultaneously a generalizing and a particularizing of the principle of contrasting derivation: individual as it appears to be in the conception of the D major Sonata, it is also unmistakably founded in a method that is typical of Beethoven's compositional thinking. Both the elements of contrasting derivation—antithesis and deduction—are taken to extremes. The grouping of no fewer than four very distinct aesthetic characters goes far beyond what the textbook scheme of thematic dualism recommends, without the question arising of any laxity in the sequence of the musical ideas, as can be the case with some of Mozart's sonata movements. Another departure from the rules is to be found in the extended development of all three motives from the first subject during the exposition: first the opening one, in forward and retrograde motion (bar 67), then the third, extended through three octaves (bar 86), and finally the second, in inversion, counterpointed by an augmentation of the opening motive in inversion (bar 94).

According to Hugo Riemann, the tonalities that confront each other in the exposition of the first movement of the 'Waldstein' Sonata, Op. 53 — the C major of the first subject and the E major of the second — relate directly to each other. In the last phase of evolving his harmonic theory, Riemann experimented with the idea of a system of five tonal functions. The mediant was to be regarded as the equal of the dominant as an alternative to the tonic; and there can be no doubt that the 'Waldstein' directly influenced Riemann in constructing his theory, while behind it lay Moritz Hauptmann's maxim that the major third is also, like the fifth, an 'immediately comprehensible interval'.

In relation to C major, E major emits a radiance that G major would lack: aesthetically, therefore, E major constitutes a correlative to the hymnic tone of the second subject, which presents an extreme contrast to the first subject.

The 'underlying idea' of the movement, however, does not consist in the antithesis of the thematic characters alone, but also in the procedure Beethoven uses in order to mediate between the extremes. The harmonic presentation of the first subject has been the subject of innumerable commentaries; it rests on the foundation of a chromatic progression descending through the interval of a fourth (C–B–Bb – A–Ab–G), which is 'thematic' to at least the same extent as the upper voice is, without necessarily requiring to be described as 'Beethovenian baroque' (Erich Schenk). The harmonic progression is supported by the bass-line, but it is functional nevertheless, and makes sense even without the bass. In the transition the chromatic descent through a fourth in the bass is countered by a chromatic ascent through a fourth in the upper line (F#–G–G#–A–A#–B): the F between the G and the G sharp does not obscure the linear structure of the harmonic progression. But if the bass-line in the first subject is 'thematic', so too is the inversion in the transition. And the common origin of these two contrary-motion progressions is found at the junction of bars 2 and 3, where the descending second in the bass (C–B) encounters the simultaneous rising second in the upper voice

(F♯–G). Thus one of the elements of the opening idea is 'composed out' to produce the contrary motion of the 'thematic' descending and rising fourth-progressions. The goal of the second of these progressions is a chord of B major, which leads, as dominant, to the contrasting tonality, E major. The 'principal ideas which already relate to each other' (and the chromatic progressions must be included in that category) constitute, however, what H. C. Koch called *die Anlage* ('disposition' or 'design'), and Beethoven the 'underlying idea'.

One of the elements making up the notion of the 'underlying idea' is a conception of the association between thematic material and its treatment on the one hand, and form in general on the other. It may seem banal to say that in its fundamental elements the connection is always established from the first. But during the composition of the Finale of the Second Symphony, as Gustav Nottebohm's edition of the sketches demonstrates,[5] it was subjected to alterations and changes of mind which offer information to anyone attempting the reconstruction of the 'underlying idea', precisely because they are experiments with an unusual formal principle.

The 'Kessler' sketchbook, which was a major source for Nottebohm's research, and is now available in a facsimile edition,[6] contains three 'continuity drafts' of the Finale of the D major Symphony. The first two contain the ritornello, the first episode, and the return to the rondo ritornello, in which the principal subject of the eventual version is already established, whereas the second subject is still liable to vary. But only the third draft, comprising the whole movement, has a bearing on the interpretation of the final version. The formal plan is unusual:

A	B	A+	C	A	B	A+	C	Coda
1	24	71	87	105	128	173	191	225

A is the ritornello, B and C a first and a second episode. In the A+ version, the ritornello is reduced to the first part and continues with thematic–motivic working. The coda is unusually long, no less than 63 bars, and, strictly speaking, to call it a coda is a makeshift solution to a terminological quandary.

The formal plan, alternating between a ritornello and two differing and thematically independent episodes, recalls a rondo. The return of the second episode after the fourth ritornello has no parallel, however, in any of the forms of the rondo and sonata-rondo

[5] *Zwei Skizzenbücher von Beethoven aus den Jahren 1801–1803* (Leipzig, ²1924), 13 ff.
[6] L. van Beethoven, *Keßlersches Skizzenbuch*, fac. edn., ed. S. Brandenburg (Munich, 1976) fol. 19ʳ.

classified by Adolf Bernhard Marx. And the formal concept itself is obviously a principle that could well be called a 'double cursus', to borrow a term invented by the medievalists: the whole of a sequence of differing formal sections (A B A+ C) is repeated. It seems, however, that the 'double cursus' did not impress Beethoven as a fully closed form in itself, and the 'coda' provides a counterweight to some extent—so that its length is explained by its function. (Alfred Lorenz might talk of a large-scale *Bar* form, composed of two identical—or nearly identical—*Stollen* and a divergent *Abgesang*.)

The final version of the movement is a sonata-rondo, if a textbook scheme is applied:

A	B	C	A+	Development	A	B	C	A+	Coda
1	26	52	108	120	185	210	236	294	338

The principal subject corresponds to the ritornello of the draft version, the transition to the first episode (B) and the subsidiary subject to the second episode (C). The fact that the transition is thematically independent—Nottebohm called it a 'first subsidiary subject', in spite of the modulation—is a hangover from its origin as a rondo episode. The quotations of the first subject (A+) at the beginning of the development and before the coda are so short that, although the movement is in fact that hybrid, a sonata-rondo, sonata form overshadows rondo form in the general impression it makes.

The coda is a second development section, not merely on the grounds that it quotes the opening motive, but also because the contrapuntal model that underlies large sections of it—complete or restricted to the bass-line—comes from bars 3–6 of the principal subject (Ex. 7.1). But if we think of the development and the coda—

Ex. 7.1

which are very similar in length—as analogous sections, a formal plan comes into view which recalls the 'double cursus' of the third continuity draft, albeit with different dimensions. The entire course of events, from the principal subject, through the thematically independent transition and the subsidiary subject, to the reduced version of the principal subject and the development, recurs in the second part of the movement. Thus one and the same formal idea, that of the 'double cursus', was realized, using the same thematic material, but differently proportioned and following a different formal plan. The draft is primarily a rondo, the final version, on the other hand, primarily a sonata-form movement. The first episode is reinterpreted as a transition, although it is thematically independent, and the coda—a counterweight to the 'double cursus' in the draft version—becomes a second development, rounding off a 'double cursus', in the final version. Thus the 'underlying idea' comprises the thematic material, the sonata-rondo form, and the 'double cursus' principle; however, the functions of the themes, the emphasis on rondo or sonata form, and the proportions of the 'double cursus' were all subjected to profound changes during the process of composition.

8

Form as Idea

1. 'Obbligato Accompaniment' and 'Durchbrochene Arbeit'*

On 15 December 1800 Beethoven wrote to the publisher Franz Anton Hoffmeister, offering him a 'Septett per il violino, viola, violoncello, contra-Bass, clarinett, corn, fagotto . . . tutti obligati'; he added the comment: 'I can't write anything unobbligato, because I came into this world already equipped with an obbligato accompaniment.'[1]

It looks at first glance as if Beethoven meant nothing more than the obvious: no one part can be omitted without destroying the integrity of the piece, and he may have thought it necessary to say it because the Septet, Op. 20, originates in the tradition of the divertimento, but surpasses its limits. But his chosen form of words is eye-catching, even if modified by irony, and makes one wonder if he did not also wish to convey that, even though the work is a septet, every instrument has something independent to express from time to time, almost as in a string quartet. At all events the statement formulates a compositional principle that can be taken for granted in Beethoven as a rule, but was put into words on this occasion because, in the special case of a divertimento, he could not be sure that it would be generally recognized.

The case for accepting the expression 'obbligato accompaniment' as a standard term was argued by Guido Adler in 1911, in his book *Der Stil in der Musik*, because it facilitated the collecting together of the innumerable gradations between polyphonic and homophonic technique characteristic of the Viennese classical style in a single term that was, moreover, historically authentic.

---

* The expression *'durchbrochene Arbeit'* is a metaphor in musicology; it belongs to the vocabulary of a number of crafts such as ceramics and fine metalwork, and refers to decorative pierced work, filigree and the like, all of which have the effect of lightening the texture by literally making holes in it. (Translator's note.)

[1] *Sämtliche Briefe und Aufzeichnungen*, ed. F. Prelinger (Vienna and Leipzig, 1907–9), i, 61.

The other voices are then generally in a subordinate relationship, at the utmost in an intended accessory relationship, to the principal voice, or, in isolated cases, to two, or on very rare occasions to three, principal voices. We are here entirely within the realm of the fundamental stylistic principle of accompagnato, so far as the other voices are concerned. In such an accompagnato, voices put themselves forward, however, with the desire to appear in a more or less concertante role. Sometimes they function as counterpoints, or are content with the external mannerisms of counterpoint, with a complementary manner of rhythmic presentation and style, or descend to the level of harmonic filling. I should like to gather together the entire complex of these almost infinitely variable ways of treating voices under the expression 'obbligato accompaniment'.[2]

Adler distinguishes between principal voices and accompagnato, to which he also assigns, under the expression 'intended accessory relationship' (*intentionierte Beiordnung*), the phenomenon that Arnold Schoenberg called 'secondary voices' (*Nebenstimmen*). As Adler's analysis of fragments from the Andante con moto ma non troppo of the B flat major Quartet, Op. 130, illustrates, the criterion of a principal voice is that it plays a part in the thematic–motivic structure. The thematic and the polyphonic aspects do not match each other quite so perfectly, however, as Adler suggests. That the one voice ranks as the principal voice because it participates in the thematic–motivic working, while another is regarded as merely a secondary voice, in spite of 'functioning as a counterpoint', does not make sense. A figure that is thematic in its structural function may yet emerge aesthetically—in terms of the effect the movement makes—as merely accompanimental.

No less problematic than the distinction of the thematic element from the polyphonic is the attempt to reach agreement on how the concept of 'polyphony' needs to be understood, in order to be usable in analysis. The idea that 'genuine' polyphony, which Adler distinguishes from mere 'functioning as polyphony', implies equality between all the voices is ambiguous, in so far as it can mean either a consistent degree of equality in each superimposed voice, or an approximately equal participation in the melodic or thematic substance. The former is found, even among Bach's fugues, only in exceptional cases like the C sharp minor fugue from Part 1 of *Das wohltemperierte Klavier*; the latter can be called upon even by Beethoven in some of his quartet movements.

The criterion of participation by all the voices in the thematic substance is inadequate, of course, to justify the use of the term

[2] *Der Stil in der Musik* (Leipzig, [2]1929), 267 f.

'polyphony'. At the same time it would be an exaggeration to postulate consistent equality from start to finish, in the sense of equal balance of all the voices in simultaneity. There is no justification for denying the epithet 'polyphonic' to music that consists of functionally differentiated voices with different significances and graduated weights: arias by Bach, for instance, with an expressive and declamatory vocal part, a motivic and figurative instrumental part, a continuo, and a chordal accompaniment.

'Obbligato accompaniment', admittedly, is not really applicable to the configuration of thematic–motivic working and functionally differentiated counterpoint which is characteristic of Beethoven's quartet style, and we are forced to abandon the 'authentic' term although we have nothing to use in its place.

The first movement of the F minor Quartet, Op. 95, begins in unison. The essential element in bar 3 is a complementary rhythm which, independently of the other elements in the fabric of the music, becomes 'thematic' in the development section (bars 66–9). The function of principal voice passes in bars 6–7 from the thematic bass to the melodic upper voice, without it being possible to pinpoint an exact spot where the transfer occurs. In bars 10 and 12, the cello's arpeggio is to some extent an 'amplification' of the first violin's held note; it would not be appropriate to speak of melody and accompaniment, because the melody is formed by the two voices together. In bars 13–17, the opening motive of the principal theme serves as an accompanimental figure, but that does not cause it to cease to be thematic; and at the same time it fulfils the function of mediating the return of the principal theme in bar 18, which would be disruptive in the upper voice without that mediation. In the subsidiary theme (from bar 24), the motive alternating between the lower parts is at first the principal voice and then the secondary one; but the change in function does not necessitate any changes in dynamics. On the other hand it is not perverse to hear the F–Db in the second violin's accompanimental figure in bar 26 as motive, and the viola's Gb–Eb in bar 27 as response, so that it is possible to speak of a lyrical counterpoint, embracing three voices which are graduated in weight.

It is still an exaggeration to speak of 'polyphony', even if the functional differentiation of voices is included among the elements of counterpoint. On the other hand, the term 'obbligato accompaniment' is inadequate to describe a musical texture in which accompanimental figures not infrequently take on motivic significance or hint at a latent lyricism. The mixture of hierarchically ordered counterpoint, thematic–motivic working, and remnants of the 'melody-and-accompaniment' texture (which is 'ennobled' in the quartets, but not dispensed with altogether) evades terminological capture for the time being.

'Obbligato accompaniment' is closely associated, in Adler's description of the Viennese classical style, with *durchbrochene Arbeit*. The latter owes its name, as Riemann wrote in 1913, to 'the kinship with Gothic architecture, for like that it dissolves solid mass into delicate tracery'.[3]

'*Durchbrochene Arbeit*' is defined by both Adler and Riemann as the 'distribution of the principal melodic line between several voices or parts'. But if we consider the most-often cited examples—the second subject of the First Symphony, the principal subject of the Fifth, and the variation theme of the C sharp minor Quartet—the definition is seen to be too narrow, or even misapplied.

In the first place, it is misleading to posit the prior existence of a melody which is subsequently broken down into particles and distributed between the voices or instruments. It would be absurd to have the variation theme of the C sharp minor Quartet played on a single instrument. For while there is no mistaking the continuity presented by the theme, it is equally obvious that the inner unity is not given a priori, but arises out of the motivic dialectics. The particles must be performed by separate voices or instruments, paradoxically, in order for their cohesion to be discernible.

In the second place, the 'dissolution of mass' of which Riemann speaks—and the metaphor is better than the description—is more than the 'distribution of the principal melodic line between several voices or parts'; it consists also, and primarily, in participation in the thematic–motivic substance by all the voices in every register. The fact that the melody can move from the top line to the bass, or to one of the inner parts, means that the vertical 'piercing' or 'perforation' of the divisions between the strata in the music is the corollary of the horizontal 'perforation' of the principal voice.

Separation and connection are thus shown to be two facets of the same process in '*durchbrochene Arbeit*'. The very fact that the motives occur in different voices illustrates the connection between them. The changes of timbre which mark the caesuras draw attention, at the same time, to the complementarity of the segments. And the distribution across different registers signifies both the differentiation and the integration of the musical structure.

In 1860, in *Zukunftsmusik*, Wagner described the first movement of the 'Eroica' as 'a single, perfectly integrated melody':[4] that is, as a

---

[3] *Große Kompositionslehre*, iii (Stuttgart, 1913), 129.
[4] In his *Gesammelte Schriften und Dichtungen*, ed. W. Golther (Berlin, n.d.) vii. 127.

prototype or early example of what he called 'unending melody', one of those elements of music drama inherited from symphonic style. Thus Wagner discerned an uninterrupted continuity among the melodic particles of the various voices, and he saw, in the inner connection that overrides the delineations of motives, caesuras, and changes of register, the element of 'melody' in the essential sense of the word. For Wagner, the essence of a melody worthy of the name was not that it was fully rounded, but that it possessed an openness with the potential to stretch out to infinity. If we accept his generous interpretation, the dialectics of '*durchbrochene Arbeit*' and 'unending melody' can be seen to be characteristic of the entire first movement of the 'Eroica', and not merely of individual themes distributed between various instruments. What Leopold Mozart called '*il filo*' runs through the fabric at every instant.

2. The 'Motives of the Variation'

Variation form was in bad odour around 1800 with those critics who took the artistic character of music seriously, because the technique of elaborating figuration of a greater or lesser degree of virtuosity over a fixed harmonic and metrical framework—which could not be too complicated, or it would cease to be recognizable—encouraged banality. (Not the banality of simplicity, but that of the aesthetic contradiction between substance and pretension, between the simplicity of the harmonic and metrical framework and the grandiose gestures of the ornamentation.) If the set of variations was to be 'ennobled', it was necessary first to enrich the harmonic base, without reducing the ease of comprehension, and then to give the ornamentation a motivic stamp.

The practice of distinguishing between figural and character variations is unsound, because there is no logical dichotomy between the technical term and the aesthetic one. Technically, rather, the opposite of figural variation is the practice of giving the individual sections of a cycle pregnant motivic material. (In a radio talk about his Variations for Orchestra, Op. 31, Arnold Schoenberg spoke of the 'motives of the variation'.) The fact that 'motivic variations', as they might also be called, are character variations at the same time, as a rule—just as the character piece also depends on the elaboration of a single motive—does not alter the need for a terminological distinction.

In the C minor Piano Variations, WoO 80, which appeared in print in 1807, Beethoven solved the problem of enriching the harmonic framework without endangering comprehension, by recourse to the

ostinato variation, with a chromatic descent through a fourth as bass.
(The ostinato is supplemented in the C minor Variations by the
cadence IV–V–I.) While rich harmonies are erected on the ostinato,
they remain effortlessly easy to grasp, because the chromatic descent
through a fourth is a common figure that ensures immediate
comprehension.

The melody is to some extent divided in the upper voices. It is
based on a framework of contrary-motion counterpoint to the
ostinato in the bass. The framework is not an abstract conception
but, in a series of variations, elaborated by motivic working, forms
the only melodic substance derived from the theme (Ex. 8.1). On the

Ex. 8.1

other hand the actual melodic material of the theme, forming the
foreground, so to speak, through which the framework can be
glimpsed, is by no means insignificant. Rather, particles of the theme
can readily become 'motives of the variation'.

Technically, therefore, the C minor Variations are characterized by
the fact that the theme contains no fewer than four constituents
which are all—either in combination or singly—capable of becoming
the material for variations: the chromatic progression in the bass, the
harmonic and metrical scheme, the melodic framework, and the
actual melodic material. And close as the relationship is between
these constituents—together they form the 'theme' of the
variations—it is nevertheless necessary to have a terminological
distinction, for in the individual variations, to express it summarily,
we are faced with a free choice to some extent between the various
attributes of the theme which can be isolated for further examination.

The harmonic scheme is not infinitely variable, but at least in the
third and fifth bars it permits chords to be varied. The supposition
that Beethoven regarded the chords that he substituted as equal in
harmonic function looks plausible when he uses the dominant of the
dominant as substitute for the augmented-sixth chord (bar 5), but
does not seem to be the case with the dominant-seventh chord and its
substitute, the Neapolitan sixth (bar 3).

As a rule, the abstract melodic framework provides the melodic
substance of the variations, and it is to some extent made concrete by
the fact that it advances out of the background into the foreground,
and is not just contained in the melody but actually constitutes the

melody itself. Nevertheless, as has already been noted, the motivic material of the theme acquires a significance independent of the melodic framework. In Variation V, bar 7 of the theme—which can be read as the inversion of the opening motive—is reinterpreted as a 'sighing' figure, and forms the 'motive of the variation', and the highest notes in each bar correspond to the melodic framework of the theme. The motive underlying Variation XVIII is the demisemiquaver figure from the theme, spread out over two octaves. And in Variation XVII the three-note motive of bars 1–2 (C–Eb–D) and bars 3–4 (E–G–F) is continually elaborated in dense imitations.

The contrary motion between the ostinato and the melodic framework can be replaced by parallel motion, in which the bass-line may be adapted to match the upper voice (Variation XII) or, vice versa, the upper voice to the bass (Variation III). And in Variation XXV the motivic material of the upper voice develops out of the idea that it simultaneously contains both the melodic framework and a parallel to the bass ostinato.

If the chromaticism in the C minor Variations is thematic as a whole, an extreme of chromaticism is achieved when Beethoven equips each of the individual notes of the chromatic progression of the upper voice in turn with lower appoggiaturas (Variation IX, bars 3–5; Ex. 8.2). As the analysis shows, the fact that the variation cycle

Ex. 8.2

is based on a fourfold frame, rather than on a single one, does not by any means amount to 'overdetermination' leading to restriction of the potential for motivic development. On the contrary, Beethoven retains the freedom to choose between the ostinato, the harmonic scheme, the melodic framework, and the actual melody as the primary basis for any one variation. None of the constituents is continually present, because sufficient reference to the theme—and 'theme' is the essential factor in all four premisses—is ensured if a choice from among the thematic features is recognizable as the substance of a variation.

The fact that all the constituents of the theme can be altered or suppressed without endangering the thematic connection ensures that phrases able to function as the motive of a variation can be coined in almost unlimited quantity and variability, without the necessity of referring back to an established harmonic or melodic scheme. The essential idea of the C minor Variations—an idea that can truly be called dialectical—consists therefore in accumulating the attributes, and thus acquiring the possibility of choosing between them—obtaining, that is, a freedom of movement to formulate motives of

particular variations that is unthinkable when a single framework
provides the backbone of a cycle.

3. A forgotten formal idea[5]

Beethoven's C major Piano Sonata, Op. 2 No. 3, has rarely been the
subject of analysis (unlike Op. 2 No. 1, cited as the classic example
in almost every theory of sonata form). Op. 2 No. 3 is felt to
exemplify the virtuoso, extrovert sonata, whereas the more esoteric
type circles around problems of 'musical logic'. Yet the recapitulation
of the first subject in the first movement raises questions that are not
satisfactorily answered by the simple explanation, accepted by every
formal theorist, that any changes when a theme returns are to be
understood as the consequences of its 'history' during the
development section.

The first eight bars of the theme are almost identical in the
exposition and in the recapitulation. The continuations (bars 9–20
and 147–54) are significantly different, however, and the difference
cannot be ascribed to any change in the modulation. (Bars 21–6 and
155–60 correspond literally, without transposition.)

The provenance of the elements in bars 147–54 is not hard to
determine: the bass at first (in bars 147–8, transposed in bars 149–50)
takes up the upper voice from bars 145–6. The upper-voice
counterpoint to that (bars 147–8 and 149–50) comes from bar 20 of
the exposition: a diastematic element and a rhythmic element from
this source—the chromaticism of the lower voice and the syncopation
of the upper—may be said to be combined in bar 147 in a single line.
The upper voice of bars 147–8 (and 149–50) is then transferred to the
bass (bars 151–2, and fragmented in bars 153–4). The counterpoint to
that (upper voice in bars 151–4) consists of a chain of leaps of a sixth;
the interval as such comes from bar 148, which is still close enough in
time for the association to be perceived, while the outline pitch-
progression that generates the sixths makes up a chromatic tetrachord
(D–C♯–C–B–B♭–A), corresponding to the outline progression of the
second subject from the exposition. Furthermore, the upward chain
of sixths recalls the downward sequence in the 'display episode' of the
second subject-group in the exposition (bars 69–71).

Innocently 'empirical' as this analysis may appear, it entails a
number of premises that are anything but self-evident. In the first
place, the statement that the chromaticism of one voice and the

[5] This section was first published, with the title 'Eine wenig beachtete Formidee', in
*Analysen: Beiträge zu einer Problemgeschichte des Komponierens. Festschrift für Hans Heinrich
Eggebrecht zum 65. Geburtstag*, ed. W. Breig, R. Brinkmann, and E. Budde (Stuttgart, 1984),
248–56. This shortened version is reprinted with the kind permission of Franz Steiner Verlag,
Wiesbaden and Stuttgart.

syncopation of the other voice in bar 20 are 'combined' in bar 147
contradicts the normal concept of motivic development, which
implies the dismemberment of an original diastematic-rhythmic unit
into its constituents but not the contrary process: the generation of a
secondary unit out of originally separate elements. In the second
place, the 'skeletal' structural function of the chromatic fourth-
progression appears to serve as justification for an excessively vague
association between a lyrical second subject and an, if anything,
martial continuation of the first subject. And thirdly, the hypothesis
that separate constituents of the exposition are grouped together and
made to mediate each other in the recapitulation, without the process
having been prepared by events in the development, is hard to
reconcile with the concept of 'development form' that all the theorists
of form propound as something to be taken for granted in Beethoven.
It would require a measure of force to make the connection that has
been described here—in so far as it exists at all—conform to the
concept of 'developing variation' (Arnold Schoenberg), or
'contrasting derivation' (Arnold Schmitz), or the unfolding of a
'motivic cell' (Rudolf Réti), or to think of it as a station in a 'history
of a theme' stretching from the exposition, through the development,
to the recapitulation (August Halm).

The case is, rather, that heterogeneous and separately expounded
motives and constituents are referred to one another and mediated by
one another in retrospect, and the substance of the mediation—the
thing that goes beyond mere combinatory art—consists in the
chromaticism: the feature common to the motive derived from bar 20
and the outline progression that originated in bars 27–32.

The substratum—the chromaticism—is admittedly less decisive
than the formal idea that underlies the described procedure—that is,
the idea of linking originally heterogeneous elements and allowing
them to interpenetrate at a secondary stage; the chosen stage is not
the development but the recapitulation, and the development is not
used to justify what is done.

The motivic process described above, which turns the
recapitulation of the first subject in Op. 2 No. 3 into a formal-
theoretical brain-teaser, makes little or no difference to the basic
premiss of Beethoven's musical thought, namely that form—in so far
as it is 'spirit', in Eduard Hanslick's phrase—should appear as a
'consequence' and a goal-directed (teleological) process. But it
appears to necessitate a reduction in the scope of the concept of
'process', which is associated with 'musical logic', a category filled
ever fuller over the years by theorists from Johann Nicolaus Forkel to
Arnold Schoenberg and Boris Asafyev. The retrospective, second-
stage combination and mediation of motives and constituents of a

theme can scarcely be interpreted as a process—regardless of how
narrow or wide a conception of the term we may have—because the
term entails or suggests the idea of an original substance which
continues to maintain its identity as the 'subject' of the course of
action, the underlying factor in all the changes and modifications that
ensue. But an original substance, from which 'consequences develop'
(as constituents of musical form), is precisely what does not exist in
the case of the passages under examination in Op. 2 No. 3. And after
it has been demonstrated, by means of a second, supplementary
analysis of a sonata-form movement, that the principle in question is
one that is wholly characteristic of Beethoven (alongside his thinking
on origination and development), I shall conclude with the attempt to
illustrate and make plausible the interpretational model that underlies
the analyses, by recourse to the distinction made in historiographical
theory between the history of processes and the history of events.

Beethoven's G major Piano Sonata, Op. 14 No. 2, has been the
object of numerous interpretations, which have, admittedly, focused
less on the work than on Beethoven's comment, referring to the 'two
principles' underlying the first movement. (Transmitted by Anton
Schindler, the comment was long regarded as the authentic
expression of a formal idea of Beethoven's, although it has now fallen
prey to critical doubt.) On the other hand, the fact that the
movement contains a structural problem, the solution of which is
more difficult than the decoding of the celebrated comment, has
remained largely ignored, the more so because it concerns a section in
the sonata form—the concluding group of the first movement—
which rarely attracts the attention of the analyst in other works
besides this one.

The first seven bars of the concluding group (bars 47–53) contain
five motives (a^1 b^1 b^2 c a^2), stated at first in the upper voice and then
in the lower. The third of these, with a different opening note, is a
sequential version of the second; and the fifth, even though it
overlaps with the fourth, is recognizable as a recurrence of the first
(Ex. 8.3). The procedure Beethoven used in constructing this group

Ex. 8.3

recalls Op. 2 No. 3: deriving motives from separate constituents of
the exposition, combining them in unexpected ways, and using them

to mediate each other. And the attempt to work out an analysis which aspires to more than the recording of 'data'—which, strictly speaking, do not even attain to the status of 'musical facts' without a hermeneutical system of references—comes up against the same problem as in the case of Op. 2 No. 3 (the earlier work by three years): the problem of justifying the interpretational model which must be adopted if the associations which the analyst thinks he perceives are to be recognized as a segment of 'musical reality'.

Description in itself, as with Op. 2 No. 3, is not difficult. The chromaticism of motive *a* originates in the bass-line of bars 40–43, played only an instant earlier (F♯–G–G♯–A). On the other hand the rhythmic figure, the three-quaver anacrusis, is the outcome of a longer 'prehistory', reaching back to the beginning of the movement. The sonata starts with a motive that hovers between a three-semiquaver and a five-semiquaver anacrusis, because of the discrepancy between the placement of the barline and the entry of the harmony (Ex. 8.4). In bar 5 the 'proper' metre—with a three-

Ex. 8.4

semiquaver anacrusis—is expressed unambiguously. In bar 9, however, the five-semiquaver anacrusis—augmented to five quavers—is taken up again and, thanks to note-repetition, functions as an independent rhythmic motive. (Bar 11 shows that the augmentation is intended, for there the diminution of the repeated-note figure to a five-semiquaver anacrusis restores the original rhythmic value, which establishes the alleged connection retrospectively to some extent.)

The other possible interpretation of bar 1 is not abandoned, however. It is clearly enough manifested in a number of three-quaver anacruses (bars 25, 29, and 40), again appearing as rhythmic motives rendered independent by note-repetition. And the three-quaver anacrusis is the element that mediates between the various motives in the concluding group of the exposition; exactly like the chromaticism in the recapitulation of the first subject in Op. 2 No. 3, it acts as the 'common denominator' of the heterogeneous constituents: the substratum in the process of assimilating elements of disparate origins.

Motive *b* of the concluding group originates in the continuation of the second subject (bars 33–4), but is repositioned by one quaver in the bar, so that the chance of recognizing it is reduced but not eliminated. Finally, motive *c* can be understood as an augmentation of notes 3–6 in bar 1: that is, as a segment of the principal idea. (The characteristic, distinctive sequence of intervals and the identity of the pitches mean that the connection is in no way 'abstract' in any negative sense, in spite of the intervening distance.)

Admittedly, as with the analysis of Op. 2 No. 3, the mere act of pointing to the notes does not oblige anyone else to accept the motivic connections described here as 'musical facts'. And once more the difficulty is not in the discovery of relationships—which some analysts seem to think is an end in itself—but in making reasoned distinctions between 'real' and 'fictive' derivations.

In the first instance the analysis is merely a hypothesis. The simplest reason for accepting it is the number of analogous cases. It is not just one element that is extracted from an earlier context, but three, which are then made to relate to each other unexpectedly in the concluding group, and it is done by subjecting all three to the process of rhythmic alteration: motive *a* by diminution, *b* by repositioning within the bar, and *c* by augmentation. And the outcome of the modifications is a rhythmic assimilation: the three-quaver anacrusis, whose 'prehistory' has been narrated, proves to be an integrating feature, a common trait which unites the constitutents of the concluding group, in spite of their heterogeneous origins.

The technique of integrating independent and separate elements of an exposition at a later stage—and not in the development but in the concluding group—is, however, the expression of a way of musical thought whose basic pattern—as in Op. 2 No. 3—is not to be found in the concept of 'development form' all too often attributed to Beethoven.

The idea that musical form is a process is so firmly established in the theory of music, and in musical perception (which is influenced by the theory), that it calls for a certain effort to recognize that it is not a matter of an 'evident' state of things—that is, one that demonstrates what it is by reference only to itself—but of the interpretation of a state of things, and an interpretation, moreover, that cannot be accepted as a matter of course. Undoubtedly music— as an event in time, or one in which time is implicit—proceeds, but not everything that 'proceeds' (or 'goes forwards') is a 'process'.

The concept of 'process' is associated in the theory of music with the 'organic' model, one of the characteristic models of nineteenth-century ways of thinking. The principle is that, from an original, given substance—a theme, a 'motivic cell', a '*Grundgestalt*'—there 'grows' a form, which 'develops' over a period of time; the 'growth' is determined by what Aristotle called 'entelechy': potential that sets its realization as its goal. Thus—tacitly, but all the more effectively and compellingly for the musical consciousness and its forms of reaction—'process' implies on the one hand the idea of a 'source subject', which generates the musical development, and on the other hand that of a 'goal-directed lawfulness', which underlies the course the development takes (we could also speak of 'lawfulness without laws', to borrow a Kantian paradox).

The attempt to make a different interpretational model comprehensible and plausible is intended to supplement, not replace, the conventional one. What is questioned is not the dominance of development form in Beethoven—even in the sonata movements that have been cited, and notably in their developments—but merely the exclusive application of the model adopted by Adolf Bernhard Marx from Goethe's morphology.

Undoubtedly, the description of the alternative model turns out to be metaphorical, but that is inevitable. (It is unnecessary to seek justification in the argument that the descriptive terms of today are the metaphors of yesterday, and that today's metaphors are the descriptive terms of tomorrow.) Linguistic orientation towards the form of observation that is called 'history of events' in historiography does not by any means imply that the analyst believes he is reconstructing the language in which Beethoven thought 'about' music, but only that he is feeling his way towards a mode of expression which might be appropriate to Beethoven's thinking 'in' music, and reveal more than it distorts. (That a descriptive language cannot avoid distortion when it attempts revelation is a dilemma no analyst can escape, unless he takes refuge in Hans Keller's 'wordless analysis'.)

In the theory of historiography, 'history of events' differs from 'history of processes' in two things in particular. Firstly, it starts out from a number of relatively mutually independent subjects; secondly, it regards a historical event not as the result of a goal-directed development, but as the outcome of an action in which agents and forces work with and against each other—without, as a rule, any of the actors foreseeing that outcome.

The claim that it is both possible and worthwhile to apply the above to musical contexts—the assumption, that is, of an analogy which, of course, must not be 'forced' any more than other interpretational models of musical formal theory—means, therefore, that we are not obliged to interpret a musical movement as a

'development', when we want to demonstrate that it 'goes forward' as
an integrated and coherent entity. It is also possible to understand the
inner connection by looking back from the end: a position where the
motives and elements that have gone before conjoin to some extent in
a musical configuration which represents an 'event', inasmuch as the
light it sheds backwards enables earlier events to be seen as
constituents of a 'history'.

9

The 'New Path'

There are few aesthetic commonplaces that nobody will dispute, but they must surely include the maxim that musical form is not so much architectural as linear. The statement needs qualification, however, if it is to serve the purposes of analysis or historical commentary. This chapter will investigate the proposition that, in works written in and after 1802, Beethoven expressed the processual character of form in a way that justified his speaking of a 'new path' or a 'wholly new style'; but the thesis remains vague and impalpable for as long as the ideas that commingle in the concept of 'musical process' are not examined.

The fact that music extends in time justifies the postulate that musical form must be perceived as linear, but it is not a sufficient reason for speaking of music as emphatically processual. The temporal quality of music is an unchanging fact, but the divergent consequences that have been drawn from that fundamental datum are far more important. The components of a musical continuum emerge one after another, but that does not prevent a listener from perceiving them alongside one another. The principle of correspondence—the combining of phrases, clauses, and periods by allowing concordant and antithetical elements to interlock in such a way that the impression is created of complements and correspondences—favours the transformation of a temporal phenomenon into a quasi-spatial one, indeed it encourages it. On the other hand, it is only possible to speak meaningfully of a process, as opposed to a mere course of events, when the temporal quality of the music—the succession of things one after another—does not constitute a resistance against which the form must assert itself but, quite the reverse, composes the substance of the form, so that the components appear to proceed from one another, and a 'logical', rather than an architectural, principle predominates.

Musical 'logic', on which the processual character of individual works is founded, can be defined, broadly, as thematic-motivic working in relation to a harmonic-tonal development. In other words, the process represented by a 'logical' form is the epitome of the consequences drawn from a thematic substance, acting in reciprocity with a harmonic course which is the vehicle for the thematic elaboration—the generation of variants.

According to Martin Wehnert,[1] a 'theme' is to be understood as a Gestalt to which reference is made (*Bezugsgestalt*; the equivalent term in English usage is 'source-shape'). Metaphorically speaking, therefore, a theme is not solely an idea from which consequences issue but also the text underlying a commentary which constantly returns to the starting-point. The movement described by a commentary is circular, rather than linear. Thus a rounded, clearly delineated theme, the prerequisite on the one hand of a musical form as process, proves on the other hand to be a hindrance when a goal-directed course is intended, rather than elaboration or prolongation. And one way of describing the compositional problem that Beethoven was trying to solve around 1802—in combination with other problems—is as the difficulty of designing musical forms that create an impression of processuality in an emphatic sense by being simultaneously thematic and non-thematic: thematic to the extent that a thematic substance is the prerequisite of a formal process; non-thematic in so far as the composer avoids setting down a fixed, pregnantly delineated formulation at the beginning of the work to provide the 'text' for a commentary. In brief, the 'thematic material' is no longer a 'theme'.

If we define musical form as process, therefore, we can distinguish three elements: firstly, the banal observation that forms extending in time are linear forms; secondly, the circumstance, arising from the historical context, that the processes as which the forms of eighteenth- and nineteenth-century instrumental music were established were 'thematic processes'; finally, the specific fact that in some of Beethoven's works, dating from after 1802, processuality created by the use of 'non-thematic' thematic material appears particularly pronounced.

Carl Czerny relates that 'around the year 1803' Beethoven said to Wenzel Krumpholz: 'I am not very satisfied with what I've written to date. From today I intend to enter upon a new path.' The implication is that he had already decided the direction of the new path. Czerny comments: 'Shortly after this event his three sonatas, Op. 29, appeared, in which we can discern the partial fulfilment of his resolve.'[2] The sonatas in question—Op. 31, not 29—were composed 1801–2 and printed in 1803 (so that it is likely that Beethoven made the remark to Krumpholz in 1802, rather than 1803).

[1] 'Thema und Motiv', in *Die Musik in Geschichte und Gegenwart*, xiii (1966), col. 282.
[2] *Erinnerungen aus meinem Leben*, ed. W. Kolneder (Strasburg, 1968), 43.

There is some debate as to what Beethoven meant by the 'new path'. Ludwig Misch defined the 'new' that was achieved around 1802, at the beginning of the 'middle period', in terms of musical form: he related the remark made to Krumpholz to the 'structural idea' of the first movement of the D minor Sonata, Op. 31 No. 2.[3] Philip Downs, on the other hand, put an ethical, rather than a formal, interpretation on the 'new path'. He included the 'Eroica', Op. 55, in his discussion (undoubtedly rightly, for much of it was composed in 1803), linked the concept of the 'new path' with the admissions of the approximately contemporary Heiligenstadt Testament (dated 6 and 10 October 1802), and emphasized that Krumpholz, as depicted by Czerny, was an intelligent enthusiast, not a musical expert, so that an exoteric, ethical significance is more plausible than an esoteric, formal one.[4]

In interpreting the human ethos of the 'Eroica' as the essential element in the 'new path', however, Downs overlooks that Czerny cites Op. 31, not Op. 55, as the documentary statement of the 'new': that is, a work not intended for a mass audience. Secondly, Krumpholz played the violin in the Hoftheater, so he was not an amateur who would not have understood a 'structural idea'. Finally, Downs's reading looks even less likely when the 'new path' is compared to the 'really wholly new style', to which Beethoven referred in connection with the variation cycles, Opp. 34 and 35.

In October 1802, at approximately the same period, therefore, as when he may have confided in Krumpholz, Beethoven wrote to Breitkopf & Härtel:

I have made two sets of variations, one of which can be reckoned as eight variations, the other thirty. Both of them are worked out in a really wholly new style . . . As a rule I only hear it from others when I have new ideas, and never know it myself. But this time it is I who must assure them that the style in both works is entirely new, and it's mine.[5]

There can be no doubt that the 'really wholly new style' is meant in a formal, not an ethical, sense here. A style (*Manier*)—a way of writing or a compositional technique—is the means of realizing a formal idea. (It is significant that Beethoven felt he needed to draw attention to the presence of his innovation in two cycles of variations; the low standing of the genre at that time meant that nobody would have expected to find anything essentially new in them.)

---

[3] L. Misch, 'Das "Problem" der d-moll Sonate von Beethoven', in his *Beethoven-Studien* (Berlin, 1950), 55.

[4] P. Downs, 'Beethoven's "New Way" and the Eroica', in *The Creative World of Beethoven*, ed. P. H. Lang (New York, 1971), 83 ff.

[5] *Sämtliche Briefe und Aufzeichnungen*, ed. F. Prelinger (Vienna and Leipzig, 1907–9), iv, 6.

Whether, as I would claim, the 'new style' and the 'new path' can be equated, or at least closely related to each other, is admittedly not something that can be decided by theoretical criteria, but only by means of analysis of some of the works: the Piano Sonata, Op. 31 No. 2, the Variations, Op. 35, and the 'Eroica' Symphony, Op. 55. The first movement of Op. 59 No. 3, composed between 1804 and 1806, will also be included, so that the string quartet is not left out of consideration; the purpose of the exercise is to reveal a formal idea that transcends differences between genres. If it can be shown that, underlying the symphony, the string quartet, the sonata, and the variation cycle, there is one formal idea that, on the one hand, is common to all these works, regardless of the differences between the genres, and, on the other hand, is a means whereby they, as witnesses to a new stylistic phase, are distinguished from earlier works, then it is surely reasonable to suppose that there is an analogy between the 'new path' that was entered upon in Op. 31, according to Czerny, and the 'really wholly new style' of Op. 35, and to interpret the 'new path' as a matter of compositional technique and form, just as we do the 'new style'—for which no other interpretation is possible.

The first movement of the D minor Sonata, Op. 31 No. 2—an analytical challenge—has been written about so much that yet another discussion is wellnigh inexcusable. In this context, however, it fulfils a function in respect of other works in a way that no other piece would. The difficulties that arise when the movement is referred to the schema of sonata form are positively labyrinthine, yet at the same time it would not be appropriate to set sonata form aside and describe the movement as possessing simply a form *sui generis*. Its paradoxical relationship to the traditional model is actually part of the formal idea of the work. What is specific is realized in a fragmented relationship to what is general, and it is the latter that determines the expectations of the listener—the 'implied listener'—that Beethoven had in mind.

The argument as to whether the 'real' first subject is stated at the opening of the movement—the arpeggiated triad in the 'largo' and the 'bald' scalar motion in the 'allegro'—or in bars 21 ff. is a waste of time; it requires a decision when the whole point is that decision is impossible, and ambiguity should be understood as an aesthetic quality. The opening contains the thematic material of the movement in a rudimentary form. The second subject is there as well as the first, yet the passage is not a subject itself, in either a syntactic or a 'gestural' sense. The 'largo' motive contains a 'protoform' of the first subject, which appears more clearly shaped in bars 21 ff.; the 'allegro' motive contains a 'protoform' of the second subject, which is presented in bars 42 ff. The 'gesture' made by the opening, however, is like that of an introduction.

Yet it would be equally unsound to regard bars 21 ff. as the 'real' first subject. For one thing, it is an evolutionary episode, in terms of both the syntax and the harmonic-tonal scheme: a modulating transition with thematic-motivic working; and for another, the passage does not return in the recapitulation. On the other hand, the close connection between the evolutionary episode and the development is characteristic: at first, for ten bars, the development takes the form of a transposition of the evolutionary episode; then it presents an analogous construction; as early as the nineteenth bar of the 'allegro' it reaches the tonic, and does not leave it again, thus using the same motivic material as the evolutionary episode to carry out the contrary modulation.

Nearly all the formal sections occupy a twilight world, in which it is difficult or impossible to make unequivocal pronouncements about their functions. Is the opening of the movement a theme or an introduction? Do bars 21 ff., despite their modulation into the dominant, present an exposition of the first subject in a melodically rounded, but syntactically open, shape? If a commentator decides that the modulating passage beginning in bar 21 is a first subject, is he obliged to conclude that the beginning of the development is simultaneously a recapitulation of the first subject, substituting for the recapitulation that fails to arrive later? As a conclusion, that may sound absurd. But if a modulating evolutionary episode can be called the exposition of the first subject, then a modulating development, which is a mirror image of the evolutionary episode, can equally well be regarded as a substitute for the recapitulation of the first subject.

Beethoven does not expect his implied listener to resolve the paradoxes, but to recognize them as the formal idea of the movement. Anyone who feels confused by the sonata should not try to impose on it an unambiguous solution, which would be incorrect by virtue of being imposed; rather, the ambiguity should be perceived as an artistic factor—an attribute of the thing itself, not a failure of analysis. The very contradictions of the form constitute its artistic character.

The beginning of the movement is not yet a subject, the evolutionary episode is one no longer. Nowhere, in fact, is there a 'real' statement of the first subject. But because Beethoven avoids 'presenting' the themes, and goes straight from a protoform to developmental elaboration, the form *is* process. Nowhere is the thematic material 'given', in the sense of a text on which a development section comments; rather, it is involved in developmental process from first to last—either as anticipation of thematic working to come, or as consequence of thematic working already past. It exists exclusively in transformations, in which it is a function, a dependent variable of the linear formal course; it has no existence as a substantive structure, or a source-shape to which the thematic-motivic working refers back. The motion described by this movement is exclusively goal-directed, not circular.

The innovation in the D minor Sonata, to which Beethoven's remark to Krumpholz obviously referred, is the radical processual character of the musical form, the technical correlative of which is the abrogation of the traditional concept of theme. What underlies the movement is less a 'theme' than a 'thematic configuration', a grouping of elements—the arpeggiated triad and the 'bald' scalar motion—which are in effect 'pre-thematic' at the opening, and already 'post-thematic' in bars 21 ff. and 42 ff.: consequences, not premisses.

A formal idea similar to that realized in the D minor Sonata by dint of profound changes to sonata form is, however, characteristic of the 'Eroica' Variations, Op. 35, within the circumstances of a different genre. The variations of the work are not based on a single, 'closed' theme, a clearly outlined melodic-harmonic source-shape, but on a configuration of components which are categorically independent of one another: a bass theme, a melodic theme, and a harmonic-metric framework or 'skeleton'.

The 'really wholly new style' that Beethoven demonstrates in Op. 35 emerges as the outcome of a process of sifting and reinterpreting traditions. The independence of the bass theme derives from the model of ostinato variations, the self-sufficiency of the harmonic-metric framework from variations on the outline, and the elaboration of the melodic theme from figural variations. It is not the origin, however, but the unusual function of the elements that determines their meaning.

Beethoven calls the exposition of the bass theme as such—without the melodic theme—'Introduzione col Basso del Tema'; he emphasizes its introductory and preparatory character, not its expository role. In sections *a due*, *a tre*, and *a quattro*—with the number of voices progressively increasing, that is—the bass theme is supplemented by changing counterpoints; however, while these contrapuntal changes recall the tradition of ostinato variations, they diverge from it in so far as their formal meaning is not contained in themselves; it lies in the preparation of the melodic theme, the—as it were triumphal—entry of which is their goal. Contrariwise, the exposition of the melodic theme is less a presentation and a statement than an outcome and a consequence or culmination of a development: the *a due* section foreshadows the melodic shape of bars 1–8 and 13–16 of the melodic theme, the *a quattro* section the demisemiquaver motion of bars 9–12.

A constantly changing selection of components taken or wrested from the thematic configuration is subjected to further working or quotation within the individual variations. In Variation II, bars 1–4 are underlain by nothing but the harmonic-metric framework, but in bars 6–8 the upper notes of the right-hand figuration combine to form a quotation from the bass theme—a reminiscence in an unexpected region. In Variation III, the harmonic-metric framework is not only the foundation of the variation technique but also its subject: bar 5 of the harmonic skeleton is missing from the variation, bar 6 takes its place as fifth bar, and bar 7, by augmentation, is expanded to form both sixth and seventh bars. Thus Beethoven takes his harmonic-metric framework to pieces: the harmonic framework, without forfeiting its identity, is repositioned in relation to the metric. It would scarcely be exaggerating to call the variation cycle *in toto* an analytical process: a breaking-down of the thematic complex (bass, melody, and skeleton) into partial structures, and partial structures into elements.

There is a particularly drastic example of the analytical character of the variation technique in Variation VI, in the first section of which the melodic theme is used untransposed (that is, in E flat major) and almost unchanged (in bar 7 the note E♭ is altered to E♮) to act as the upper voice in a harmonic progression that begins in C minor and modulates to F minor, and is thus alienated in harmonic-tonal terms. (The same principle underlies the coda of Variation XV.) If we are not afraid of terminological anachronism, we can say that in Variation VI Beethoven exchanges the complex categories—such as 'rhythm' and 'melody'—of classic–romantic musical thinking for parameters like 'duration', and 'pitch' (in the sense of intervallic material independent of harmonic identity); for the implied listener is undoubtedly intended to be as conscious of the intervallic structure of the melodic theme as of the harmonic-tonal alienation. (In Variation X bars 9–12 reproduce the original rhythm of the bass theme without creating the slightest suggestion of a diastematic association:)

The replacement of the traditional theme by a thematic configuration and the breaking-down of the partial structures into their individual elements are signs of a musical thinking that is directed towards radical processuality of form. The thematic substance is analysed, not elaborated. It does not provide a text on which the variations comment (in circular motion); rather, it forms a complex of attributes from which an ever changing selection of components are wrested to play their part in a formal process that, so to speak, devours the thematic substance.

Although it might be thought that there can be no direct comparison of a sonata movement with a variation cycle, the analogies that spring into view during the interpretation of Op. 31 No. 2 and Op. 35 justify relating the 'new path' of the D minor Sonata closely to the 'really wholly new style' of the 'Eroica' Variations. In both works the openings are simultaneously thematic and provisional: introduction and exposition commingle. Both works are underlain by a thematic configuration instead of by a theme in the traditional sense. (True, Beethoven called the melodic theme of the 'Eroica' Variations a 'theme', but it does not serve as the channel for development to the extent that is expected of a variation theme.) The concept of the 'thematic configuration' makes it possible to relate the monothematicism of the variation cycle (which can be broken down into its elements) to the bithematicism of the sonata movement (which is contained in the movement's opening); that is, the forms are rendered commensurable in terms that override the differences between the genres. The unusual thematic structure, however, is the correlative of the processual character of the form.

The outstanding characteristic of the first movement of the 'Eroica' Symphony has always been felt to be that the musical form is a process in the emphatic sense, an urgent, unstoppable forward motion. Beethoven's Third Symphony represents a 'qualitative leap' beside the two earlier ones, and his contemporaries were already well aware that with it he had entered upon a 'new path'. While the inherent proximity to Op. 31 No. 2 and Op. 35 in certain decisive traits is, therefore, unmistakable, the thematic structure of the 'Eroica' nevertheless requires discussion if the kinship between the formal idea of the symphony and the principle realized in the sonata and the variation cycle is to be made clear.

To say that bars 3–6 present the principal theme is an oversimplification that ought not to be permitted even in a concert programme note. (Saying that it is not so much a theme as a motto is evasive and, far from resolving the quandary, merely states it.) There is no answer to the question as to where the principal theme is stated. Bars 3–6, presenting a motive of pastoral character, are 'not yet' the exposition, and bars 15–22, in which the principal motive returns, sequentially repeated on the second and fourth degrees, are 'no longer' the exposition: the motivic material has already been developed instead of being stated as a theme in the syntactic form of a period. Beethoven goes directly from the 'protoform' to the 'derivation', in a way not significantly different from how he does it in Op. 31 No. 2, without the theme having been 'really' expounded at all.

Bars 3–6, briefly, constitute neither a 'theme' in substance, nor an 'exposition' in function. What underlies the movement is not a theme but, in Beethoven's 'new style', a thematic configuration. In the symphony it consists of the contrast between the arpeggiated triad of the principal motive and the chromatic progression through a second, into which the principal motive is unexpectedly diverted in bars 6–7; the contrast is thus as elemental and as abrupt as the antithesis between triad and scalar motion in Op. 31 No. 2.

The chromatic element appears in divers forms, as a rising or falling succession of semitones, and with various functions. In bars 6–7, as a descending succession of semitones starting from the fundamental of the principal motive, its role is to undermine the tonality, thus demonstrating the provisional character of the opening, and putting its expositional character in doubt (Ex. 9.1). Later, in bars 15–20 (Ex. 9.2) and bars 37–42 (Ex. 9.3), as a succession of semitones starting

Ex. 9.1

Ex. 9.2

Ex. 9.3

from the tonic or the fifth of the principal motive, it leads to sequential elaboration of the principal motive. (In relation to the rather static character of the pastoral motive, it represents the 'developmental element', the propulsive, dynamic component in the thematic configuration.) It is as an augmentation of the semitone sequence—the 'developmental element'—that the shift of the principal motive, from C minor via C sharp minor to D minor, should be understood (Ex. 9.4). The chromaticism, which is a melodic continuation of the principal motive in the exposition, determines the scale-degrees of its harmonic progress in the development.

On the other hand, the chromatic element is not confined to the thematic working of the principal subject group, but simultaneously provides the latent framework (F–E–E♭–D) of the first subsidiary

Ex. 9.4

subject (bars 46 ff.) and the substance of the second (bars 83 ff.). The thematic configuration permeates the entire texture. The principal motive is thus not 'thematic' in itself but in its dialectical relationship to the chromatic 'developmental element'. And the subject of the 'developing variation' is not only the Gestalt of the motives but also their relationship to one another. The chromatic progression through a second may ascend or descend, it sets off from the fundamental or the fifth of the principal motive, and forms either the melodic continuation of the principal motive or a groundplan of the harmony.

The thematic configuration of the first movement of the 'Eroica' is not 'given' anywhere, in the sense of a text set out for commentary; instead, it is entirely absorbed into the process for which it provides the substance. Even the apparently innocuous statement that the principal theme reaches its ultimate shape in the coda is open to question, in so far as it implies that that is not only the last Gestalt but also the 'real' or 'definitive' one. The triumphal expansion, in repetitions which appear to find it impossible to end, is specifically finale-like: the principal motive has reached an end that represents a culmination. But what is decisive is that even the last station of the formal process is a station like all the others, and that the theme never appears in a 'real' or 'definitive' Gestalt, either at the beginning or at the end; instead, it constitutes throughout, at every moment, a function—a dependent variable factor—of the formal process.

The C major Quartet, Op. 59 No. 3, has been described by Ludwig Finscher as a reflection, from a composer's point of view, of the social position of the string quartet in the years following 1800.[6] On the one hand, the genre was gradually moving out of the private

---

[6] 'Beethovens Streichquartett opus 59,3', in *Zur musikalischen Analyse*, ed. G. Schumacher (Darmstadt, 1974), 122 ff.

into the public domain, and on entering the concert-hall it showed a tendency to emulate the symphony or the *quatuor brillant*: that is, to strike a symphonic or concertante attitude. On the other hand, it would have been wrong to sacrifice the genre's aesthetic aspirations, the stylistic heights it had reached in Haydn and Mozart. And it was the antithesis between the attraction of the exoteric and the esoteric ambition that proved productive in the case of Beethoven's Op. 59 No. 3, where it is presented dialectically. The quartet makes use of symphonic or concertante means as a way of presenting itself to the general public, but at the same time it incorporates those same means in a skilled artistic construction that only connoisseurs can appreciate. The exoteric acts as the vehicle for the esoteric, without its own effectiveness being diminished.

The attributes that characterize the 'new path' in other works—the provisional opening to the movement, the radically processual character of the musical form, the dissolution of the traditional concept of form, and the functional ambiguity of the formal sections—are also found in the first movement of Op. 59 No. 3, though they are modified here by the special nature of the genre. The 'really entirely new style' that Beethoven developed around 1802 extends to the string quartet as well.

The slow introduction, built on the framework of a descending chromatic progression in the bass, is tonally ambiguous, and motivically it is virtually shapeless, apart from a three-note figure marked with a trill. But the tonality is still vague at the beginning of the 'allegro vivace' (bars 30 ff.), and the listener begins to wonder whether it is the exposition of the first subject or a second introduction, especially as the melodic gesture is rhapsodically concertante.

On the one hand, bars 30 ff. are tonally unstable and syntactically irregular: an antecedent clause, five (1 + 4) bars in length and not capable of reduction to a more orthodox four bars, is transposed up by one degree to D minor, the subdominant of the relative minor, instead of being supplemented by the addition of a corresponding consequent clause to form a closed period. On the other hand, the motivic substance of bars 30 ff. is what the development feeds on, and what the later sections of the exposition already continuously refer back to (bars 57, 65–75, 91). Thus, if 'theme' is defined as a Gestalt to which reference is made, bars 30 ff. represent a point of reference for other things, but do not attain to the character of a Gestalt; they are thematic and pre-thematic at the same time.

The effect achieved by bars 43 ff. is equally ambivalent. The fundamental tonality is clearly stated, if not too clearly; but the motivic material is meaningless in two senses: the melody is banal and the form is inconsequential. Although this is the first clearly delineated thematic shape of the exposition, it can scarcely be described as a theme, in the sense of a 'subject' for 'working out'. And the quasi-orchestral expansiveness of bars 43 ff., too, argues against, rather than for, interpretation as a first subject. Firstly, the textural and dynamic contrast between bars 30 ff. and bars 43 ff. acts like a chamber-music equivalent of the symphonic contrast of concertino and tutti, and suggests to the listener who is a connoisseur of Haydn's symphonies that the opening of the 'allegro vivace' should be taken as a theme, for in Haydn it is the concertino, not the tutti, that has thematic function. And secondly, the melodic banality may make listeners who are mindful of the aesthetic ambitions of the genre look back and recognize the differentiated content of bars 30 ff. as the thematic substance (in spite of the lack of tonal and syntactic stability), and, if they do so, the development will confirm the recognition. (The melodic banality is justified by the formal function of bars 43 ff.—the function, that is, of providing the counterweight to bars 30 ff.; hence it must not be judged as an aesthetic quality in isolation but only in its context.)

The thematic concept is, so to speak, split in Op. 59 No. 3, just as it is in Op. 31 No. 2. Bars 30 ff. expound thematic 'substance', but thematic 'Gestalt' is not achieved until bars 43 ff. Bars 30 ff., as a rudimentary protoform, do 'not yet' really present a theme; bars 43 ff., as a noisy tutti following a melodically differentiated concertino, do so 'no longer'. The former is too provisional, the latter too devoid of content, to count as the theme in the full sense of the word.

These very qualities of the provisional and the banal are, however, closely bound up with the exoteric aspect that Finscher interpreted in terms of social history: the turn towards a general public. The rhapsodically concertante gesture of bars 30 ff., which is even more pronounced in the recapitulation, is exoteric, as is the symphonic expansiveness of bars 43 ff. The configuration formed by the relationship between the two elements is, however, wholly esoteric: the characteristics of the 'new path' or the 'new style'—the dissolution of the traditional concept of form by the division of the 'source-shape' into its parts of 'point of reference' and 'Gestalt character', and the ambiguity of the formal sections—are elements of skilled artistry understood only by initiates.

The 'new style', the fundamental elements of which can be illustrated by examples in Opp. 31 No. 2, 35, 55, and 59 No. 3, is thus revealed as a general concept transcending the frontiers between genres, without it becoming necessary for the analyst to make his descriptive categories so abstract as to be void. On the contrary, concepts like 'thematic configuration' and 'formal ambiguity' are sufficiently concrete to be used as the means of defining a stage in the history of composition: 'after 1802'.

At the same time, the 'new style' came into existence under the drastically disparate conditions of the individual genres in a multitude of differing forms: generic distinctions were still crucially important in the early nineteenth century. Or to express it in converse terms: the 'new style' presented a means of solving totally different problems that altered from one genre to the next, and were the outcome of the individual histories of each genre.

The orchestral apparatus becomes a creative medium in the 'Eroica' Symphony. Far from being a mere vehicle for presenting thematic substance in an effective manner, the orchestra in this work is actually the driving force that turns unpromising material into a structure deserving the epithet 'symphonic'. The manifestation of the orchestral factor, the specifically symphonic trait, is the correlative in the 'Eroica' of the meagreness of the thematic substance. Beethoven—taking the 'new path'—does not expound a theme, but sets off from a protoform that is not yet a theme, eschews a true exposition, and comes to a development that it is too late to call a theme; this move takes on a specific significance in the symphonic genre: the processual character of musical form at which the 'new style' aims is realized in the process of deploying the orchestra. That the principal motive is heard at the start on the cellos alone, then alternates between woodwind and strings (bars 15 ff.), before it finally extends to the whole orchestra (bars 37 ff.), ought not to be interpreted solely as movement towards a climax achieved through instrumentation, for it is a matter of the orchestra's presenting itself in the course of a formal progress, the structure of which is partly a function of an orchestral apparatus itself. The apparatus is, however, the expression and the vehicle of the Beethovenian symphony's aspiration to address an audience that represents humanity, in both the intensive and the extensive senses of the word: the humanity in each individual and humankind at large. The formal character of the 'new style' is simultaneously aesthetic in the 'Eroica', and the aesthetic character is simultaneously social. (That is not to support Philip Downs's argument, however, that the concept of the 'new path' was primarily ethical, rather than a compositional and formal matter.)

If the symphony displays the heroic aspect of the turn towards a mass public, the genre of the piano variation unveils its pathetic side.

The variation cycle was an inferior form around 1800, and it is no accident that the two works of which Beethoven boasted that they were composed in a 'really wholly new style' were of that genre. The composer who wanted to say something original and serious in a genre at the bottom end of the musical market had to spell out his intention, because nobody would have been expecting it. The 'new style' is thus deployed in piano variations as a way of ennobling a genre that had come down in the world. The technique of brilliant elaboration was replaced in Op. 35 by that of thematic working: the separation of the theme into a bass theme, a melodic theme, and a harmonic-metrical framework enabled Beethoven to pick out a different group of components from the thematic configuration for use in separate variations, instead of being tied to a single formula. In Variation II, for example, a new version of the harmonic framework grows from a quotation out of the bass theme, disguised in upper-voice figuration. But the thematic working is the technical stamp of a high stylistic level, represented by the piano sonata, and barred to the piano variation. By restructuring a successional form as a developmental form, Beethoven made an aesthetic claim on behalf of variation form which should be understood as opposition to a commercially rooted debasement.

The 'new style', which had an exoteric trait in the symphony, and, contrariwise, an esoteric trait in the piano variations, became involved in the string quartet—in Op. 59 No. 3—in problems inseparable from the nature of the genre, which arose from the attempt to mediate between an esoteric tradition—that of an art form intended for a private circle of connoisseurs—and a new function: that of music to be played at public concerts. The difficulty was compounded by the fact that the mediation was not effected by compromise, but by a dialectics in which the means signalling the turn towards a larger public were simultaneously subjected to a structural idea possessing a sophistication that went beyond even the traditional degree of differentiation.

Paradox and ambiguity, alienation and irony are categories that contradict the ideas we commonly form about musical classicism; surely their origins lie in a mannerist theory of art, which it appears questionable to apply to works of Beethoven's 'middle period'. But it would be wholly wrong to accuse this interpretation of the 'new path' or 'new style' of claiming priority over the fundamental recognition that classical form is based on equality and a reciprocal relationship between differentiation and integration, or to leap to the conclusion that the purpose of the description is to rehabilitate the exhausted commonplace that Beethoven smashed musical form. Forms that rest on paradox and ambiguity, like the first movement of Op. 31 No. 2, certainly do not need to be 'free', or even 'fragmented': not infrequently they present themselves with a wholeness that feels classical.

It is as if the aesthetic or musical theorists who believe it is their duty to defend Beethoven against the foolish charge of having smashed musical forms often get caught in the same metaphorical trap that confuses their opponents: the idea that a musical form is a kind of shell or casing inside which one must either accommodate oneself, or which one must smash. If we are to discuss formal problems in the case of Beethoven, however, we must acknowledge that the image of the shell is misconceived.

Traditional formal schemata were like a 'subject' for composition to Beethoven: they were neither adopted not rejected, but were used as material which changed its function according to the context in which it found itself. Elements of a slow introduction, included in the thematic configuration of a sonata movement, change their purpose, without the memory of their original function being extinguished. On the contrary: if listeners who are familiar with the tradition first interpret the 'largo' bars in Op. 31 No. 2 as an introduction, and only later recognize them as a component of the thematic configuration, then that is concordant with Beethoven's formal idea that the 'largo' bars are thematic, certainly, but in a provisional formulation. Introduction and exposition permeate one another. The ambiguity requires the listener 'implied' by Beethoven to possess both an awareness of tradition and the ability to see beyond the customary.

We would therefore mistake the significance of traditional schemata if we regarded them exclusively as the vehicle of heuristics. Rather, as elements in the tradition of the various genres, the models are absolutely essential (without our being obliged for that reason to adopt a categorical 'essentialism' in musical formal analysis). The fact that Beethoven distanced himself from them—that he, so to speak, 'composed out' the historical movement away from them, and treated it like a rough draft for his own modelling of forms—in no way means that the traditional models lost all substance. On the contrary, the use of formal principles like paradox and ambiguity will be void and ineffectual, unless the traditions that play a part in the artistic strategy of a work are still alive for the listener.

IO

Fidelio

1. Idyll and Utopia[1]

According to classical and romantic aesthetic theory, an essential qualification of those works that belong to the 'imaginary museum' of the great art that transcends history is that they should be unrepeatably individual. Hence, if the tradition of its genre is so deeply ingrained in a work that the work can be explained in terms of that tradition, then it is commonly regarded—at least in recent musical history—as a sign of inferior rank. Works that outlive their time, and claim a place in the repertory, are expected to be *sui generis*.

But a genre can be regarded as more than a formal law to which the individual work is subject; it can also be 'material' used by a composer in the realization of an idea he has conceived for a specific work. (The particular use can consist in modification; or it can happen, as in the case of the opera *Così fan tutte*, that a work 'reflects' its genre, rather than 'belonging to' it.) In the case of Beethoven's *Fidelio*, it can be shown that one of the important factors determinining the special character of the opera is an idiosyncratic mixture of genres. (Even though at first sight the mixture appears aesthetically questionable, it had already become something very like a new tradition.)

Historians have settled that *Fidelio* is representative of the 'rescue opera', the French model of which, as manifested in works by Luigi Cherubini, undoubtedly had an influence on Beethoven. But the rescue opera, in which the spirit of the French Revolution assumed musico-dramatic shape, is a paradoxical genre in that, on the one hand, it reflects the pressing reality of the historical moment to a degree that is unusual in opera, while, on the other hand, the motive of an amazing rescue, defying the laws of probability, is reminiscent of the 'marvellous'. The 'marvellous' constitutes one of the fundamental concepts of aesthetic theories of opera precisely because

[1] This section was first published, with the title 'Idylle und Utopie', in *Neue Zeitschrift für Musik*, 1985, fasc. 11, 4–8.

it renders the criteria of everyday reality irrelevant to sung drama, for it provides justification for improbabilities 'out of the spirit of music'. The trumpet-call in *Fidelio* that announces the arrival of the Minister, and hence the rescue, provoked Bertolt Brecht to parody, with the arrival of 'the monarch's mounted messenger' to save MacHeath from the gallows in *Die Dreigroschenoper*; but unlike Brecht, who despised the whole genre, Ernst Bloch took opera seriously as a historico-philosophical phenomenon, and regarded the trumpet-call as one of the most compelling examples of 'Utopian pre-semblance'—the aesthetic anticipation of social hope.[2]

We encounter further paradox when we attempt to define the sense in which *Fidelio* is a political opera. If we take the text of the libretto literally, and in isolation from the music—which is aesthetically impermissible—then the revenge Pizarro wreaks on Florestan is a purely private affair: Florestan is the only person whose name does not appear on the list of prisoners. But the trite conclusion that the guilt or innocence of the other prisoners is therefore an open question is refuted by the music of the prisoners' chorus and the finale of the second act: there is no escaping the feeling that injustice has been done to people who express themselves in such music. But if all the prisoners are victims of injustice—and the music does not allow any possible alternative—then, behind Pizarro, who uses his position for mere personal revenge, there loom the dark, shadowy outlines of an unjust state, where political opponents are thrown into gaol *en masse*. And then the Minister, who is the representative of that state, turns out—in accordance with the function of the 'marvellous' in operatic aesthetics—to be a fairy-tale figure who fulfils all the hopes invoked in the opera, contrary to any kind of probability. The music performs a dual function: because its language is incomparably more powerful than that of the text, it enables the private quarrel to open out into an affair of state, by which alone *Fidelio* is made a truly political opera; at the same time, it removes the political drama from the sphere of reality into that of the 'marvellous', which is opera's native soil.

But if the weight of the political element—up to the unlooked-for rescue—is oppressive, the note of insouciant comedy struck by some of the vocal numbers is even more disconcerting, for a twentieth-century audience, at least. The presence of the duet for Marzelline and Jaquino (No. 1) and Rocco's aria (No. 4) in the same opera as Leonore's 'Abscheulicher, wo eilst du hin?' and Florestan's 'Gott! welch Dunkel hier!' strikes us as a clash of styles, and the attempt to encompass that clash in an integrated production style makes the problem worse. Rather than gloss over the discrepancy, we should

[2] *Das Prinzip Hoffnung* (Frankfurt am Main, 1959), 1295–7.

try to understand it in terms of its historical context, but it remains incomprehensible without reference to the dramatic theory of the Enlightenment and its psychological and socio-historical motives.

According to the eighteenth-century conceptions with which Beethoven grew up, the action involving Jaquino, Marzelline, Leonore, and Rocco is a *comédie larmoyante*, while the drama played out between Leonore, Florestan, Pizarro and Rocco is a *tragédie bourgeoise* (in which a 'happy ending' is perfectly possible). Far from being regarded as radically different, both types were included in the category of *genres intermédiaires*, and commended by dramatic theorists of the Enlightenment like Denis Diderot and Louis-Sebastien Mercier as the only genres suited to the spirit of the age.[3] *Comédie larmoyante*, or 'sentimental comedy', differs from the comedy of Molière in seeking to touch the hearts and sympathies of the audience, instead of raising laughter over errors and vices. 'Bourgeois tragedy', or 'domestic tragedy', differs from traditional tragedy by its location in a middle-class milieu, rather than among royalty or aristocrats. Thus, for all their superficial difference, from the point of view of social psychology the two types of drama represent the same thing. Instead of being cast as Pantalone, a figure of fun for others—whether the nobility or the common herd—the bourgeois *père de famille* becomes in the hands of Diderot an object for understanding and sympathy; and, at the same time, the middle classes stake a claim to a tragic destiny, which, until the middle of the eighteenth century, had been regarded as the aesthetically and socially sanctioned privilege of kings and great lords.

Gotthold Ephraim Lessing placed a strictly symmetrical construction on the *genres intermédiaires*, as complementary manifestations of the same tendency.

There [in the *comédie larmoyante*] it was thought that the world had laughed in comedy and hissed tasteless vice off the stage for long enough; the idea was formed of at last allowing the world to weep for once, instead, and take noble pleasure in quiet virtues. Here [in the *tragédie bourgeoise*] it was felt unreasonable that only rulers and persons of high rank should awaken our terror and pity.[4]

Twentieth-century commentators on 'bourgeois tragedy' have interpreted its shift of emphasis from the ruling to the middle class as political or ideological in inspiration, but for Lessing it was a matter

---

[3] P. Szondi, *Die Theorie des bürgerlichen Trauerspiels im achtzehnten Jahrhundert* (Frankfurt am Main, 1973), 181.
[4] *Abhandlungen von dem weinerlichen oder rührenden Lustspiele* (1754), quoted Szondi, *Die Theorie*, 152.

of aesthetic effectiveness, bearing on drama's purpose to touch the audience and arouse its sympathy.

The names of princes and heroes can give a play pomp and majesty; but they add nothing to its power to move us. It is only natural that the misfortune of those whose circumstances are closest to our own will penetrate furthest into our souls; and if we feel compassion for kings, we feel it for them, too, as men and not as kings.[5]

The traditions of eighteenth-century drama provide a historical background which makes it easier to understand some of the differences between the three versions of *Fidelio* than when the attempt is made to explain them exclusively in terms of aesthetic impressions *per se*. The duet for Leonore and Marzelline (No. 10 in the first version, No. 9 in the second) was cut in 1814, and it can be argued that Beethoven and Friedrich Treitschke wanted to avoid the risk of allowing a banal dramatic formula—Jaquino loves Marzelline, who loves Leonore, who loves Florestan—to be all too obvious. But if, instead of accepting that the reason for the cut was solely a desire to retouch the dramaturgical surface, we go back to the fundamentals of classical dramatic structure—to 'action' and 'dramatic dialectics'— then at first sight there appears to be no reason for it at all. The duet sets out the 'dramatic dialectics' that Leonore is compelled to deceive and confuse Marzelline in respect of the very emotion that provides the impulse for all her own actions; that 'dramatic dialectics', however, is the primary force driving the 'action', which consists of the steps taken by Leonore to rescue her husband.

But the classicist premiss does not fully serve the work, and, to the extent that it does not, the cutting of the duet is revealed as dramaturgically justified, without it being necessary to imagine Beethoven and Treitschke consciously taking an eighteenth-century line on dramatic theory. The central structural category of the *genres intermédiaires* was neither 'action', nor 'dramatic dialectics', but the 'tableau'; and the aesthetic legitimation of the tableau was its ability to touch the audience's hearts. 'Over and over again in Diderot's bourgeois dramas, time seems to stand still; moved, with tears in their eyes, the characters contemplate one another and themselves, and permit themselves to be contemplated by those around them, who include the members of the audience.'[6] It would be hard to formulate a more accurate description of the function and character of the quartet in *Fidelio* (No. 3, 'Mir ist so wunderbar'). It would not be an overstatement to claim that certain essential features of the

---

[5] *Hamburgische Dramaturgie* (1767–9), no. 14.
[6] Szondi, *Die Theorie*, 116.

tableau achieve the aesthetic reality proper to them only in opera: the suspension of time, which is fundamental to the *pezzo concertato*, and a general emotionalism permitting even insoluble conflicts of feeling, such as the confusion in Marzelline's heart, to be veiled by tears. (Apart from a brief allusion to it by Rocco, Marzelline's misfortune—a catastrophe for sentiment—is not referred to in the finale of the second act, amid the general jubilation in which she, too, joins. The tableau, in which she takes the place allotted to her, is aesthetically more important than the—at least temporary— embarrassment her tragi-comic destiny ought to cause.)

The aesthetic theory of the eighteenth century focused primarily on effects, rather than on the issue of the work as structure, and the essential premisses of that theory are still valid for *Fidelio*. Judged strictly as a stage action, Sonnleithner's libretto is a disgraceful piece of botching. The only way to obtain a fairer view of it is to interpret the dramaturgy as the result of a psychological calculation, and the basis, in turn, for its being possible to set the text to music at all. There is nothing in the concatenation of events to justify Florestan's stature as a principal character; he has to be one, because the dramaturgy is wedded to the range of different voice types, but his role in the action is nothing more than to be the passive, suffering object of the confrontations between Leonore, Pizarro, and Rocco. However, when the dramatic scheme is one in which the most characteristic scene is the tableau, and when the purpose of the tableau is to move the audience to tears, then Florestan's prominence is justified.

The tableau (it was hardly by accident that the 'tableau vivant' became a popular party-game in the early nineteenth century) is every bit as much the musical freezing and prolonging of a moment as the exit aria in a Metastasian *opera seria* of the eighteenth century. An account of musical history based on the premiss that, in the course of developments leading from the eighteenth to the nineteenth century, the stasis of a series of musically depicted affects, following one after another, was gradually replaced or alleviated by the dynamic force of a dramatic action that spread out of the recitatives and invaded the arias and ensembles as well, is distorted and one-sided, in that the element of contemplation, resisting the trend towards such dramatization, was constantly being revived in the tableau. The effort to transform opera into a type of drama where the substance consists in an action that presses forward to an end, kept in motion by a tragic or comic dialectics, appears to have been circumscribed by something inherent in the very nature of music. The vehement busyness that, in the early nineteenth century, took possession even of some 'numbers'

in musically closed forms had a counterpart in the evolution of the
pezzo concertato, in Beethoven as much as in his musical antipodes,
Rossini.

The conditions under which the audience in the theatre may be not
just fleetingly touched but moved to tears were outlined by Lessing
in a letter to Friedrich Nicolai, in terms that are equally applicable to
opera:

To be touched is when I have no clear thoughts of either the perfections or
the misfortune of the object of my feelings, but only an obscure conception
of both; thus the sight of any beggar, for example, touches me. He stirs me
to tears, however, only if he makes me better acquainted with his good
qualities and with his misfortunes, both at the same time, which is the true
art of arousing tears. For if he acquaints me first with his good qualities and
later with his misfortunes, or vice versa, then he indeed touches me more
strongly, but not so much as to elicit tears.[7]

The passage sheds much light on the art of libretto writing, as it was
understood in the tradition of the *genres intermédiaires*. Clumsy as
Sonnleithner was in the construction of a coherent dramatic action
and the dialectics to motivate it, there can be no mistaking his
endeavour to fulfil Lessing's psychological-cum-dramaturgical
postulate in the dialogue preceding the trio (No. 5, Marzelline–
Leonore–Rocco: 'Gut, Söhnchen, gut'), in which we learn of the
wretched fate that has befallen Florestan, and also of the noble mind
of the man who 'dared to speak the truth boldly'. We should not
allow the faded, old-fashioned language of the dialogue to hide from
us the fact that even a minor servant of the Tenth Muse was
consciously practising the technique, described by Lessing, of
intertwining emotional motives so as to arouse tears of compassion
that are simultaneously tears of admiration. In a dramaturgy that was
primarily a matter of psychology, the sensibility in *comédie
larmoyante* and the pathos in *tragédie bourgeoise* ultimately had a
common goal, which was why the two genres could be combined
without causing a stylistic clash: that goal was an emotion in which
pity was mixed with sympathy and even admiration.

The dramaturgical difference between *comédie larmoyante* and
tragédie bourgeoise corresponds broadly to the social-cum-
psychological distinction between the bourgeois Rocco, who adapts
himself to the prevailing circumstances, although painfully aware of
their corruption, and the *citoyen* Florestan, who 'dares to speak the
truth boldly', and suffers the consequences that such boldness

---

[7] Letter dated 29 November 1756, quoted Szondi, *Die Theorie*, 161.

attracts under an unjust regime. But if we want to understand this historically, nothing could be more inappropriate or wrong than to oversimplify the social-cum-psychological distinction, and apply modern ideological critical criteria in accusing the bourgeois—who takes refuge in an idyll when catastrophe looms overhead—of indirect, passive inhumanity. Beethoven and his librettist were far from ridiculing Rocco's praise of money as the means of ensuring domestic happiness (No. 4), or denouncing the principle that professional duties must be carried out even in the service of blatant injustice, as long as the limit of personal wrongdoing is not overstepped (No. 8), as a perverted ethos converted into inhumanity by abstract acceptance. Rocco has nothing to be ashamed of as he takes a place in the second finale that is his by right, not only as the principal bass, but also as a character in society.

The inner agreement of the *genres intermédiaires* gets over the (perhaps only apparent) clash of styles in *Fidelio*, but it is only possible truly to understand the interlocking of *comédie larmoyante* and *tragédie bourgeoise*, if we recognize that the idyll in which Rocco, Marzelline and Jaquino try to shelter, and the Utopia for which Florestan and Leonore are fighting, are, in the last instance, two aspects of the same thing. The opera's subtitle in the first and second versions, 'die eheliche Liebe' (married love), seems quaintly old-fashioned now, but it ought to be taken more seriously than it usually is. The praise of *amour conjugal* in the French original by Jean Nicolas Bouilly, on which Sonnleithner based his libretto, made such an impression on contemporaries that one enthusiastic lady made up her mind on the spot to marry Bouilly; and 'married love' is the essence both of the political Utopia glorified in the final tableau of *Fidelio*, and of the idyll in which Marzelline will surely find the domestic happiness she seeks, even though her first dream has been so rudely destroyed. The bourgeois drama, in Lessing's *Emilia Galotti* as in Schiller's *Kabale und Liebe*, was always torn between the impulse to rebel against social hierarchies and the longing for a seclusion in which they could be ignored. And just as the urge to rebel was provoked by disruption of a family's (actual or desired) happiness, so, too, the rebellion was ultimately directed towards the restoration of that happiness. Private happiness, as a refuge, was the antithesis to bourgeois political activism and its barricade-building, but at the same time—as the epitome of the dream of humanity fulfilled—was also the true goal of politics. And we will not fully understand the inner unity that binds together and reconciles the dramaturgical genres and their social-cum-psychological implications, unless we recognize that the idyll was not so banal and meaningless by the standards of the early nineteenth century as it seems today, and the Utopia was not so exclusively political.

2. Musical Symbolism and Motives of Reminiscence

A music historian's eagerness to discover or construct 'prehistories' quite often leads to phenomena being forced into an unnatural relationship, while the questions to which they provided an answer in their original historical context are not even asked.

In view of the fact that the use of motives of reminiscence had been richly developed in the French revolutionary opera which was Beethoven's model, it makes perfectly good sense to look for recurring musical symbols in *Fidelio*. But to 'stylize' Beethoven as a precursor of Wagner is to distort the nature of the issues that underlie the motivic technique of the opera.

The chromatic progression through a third or a fourth, which had been an established, commonplace figure, expressing death, sorrow, and lamentation, in countless works since the Baroque, was interpreted by Ernst Bücken,[8] and even more emphatically by Erich Schenk,[9] as the essence of a 'leitmotivic' technique by means of which Beethoven had anticipated, or at least foreshadowed, Wagner's procedure. But the premiss that the primary goal that Beethoven pursued with his motivic technique was the establishment of associations across the boundaries of separate sections of his work is not really as self-evident as it obviously appeared to Bücken and Schenk. Rather, if we want to build an adequate reconstruction of the issues involved in the use of motives of reminiscence and leitmotivs, we need to recognize that motivic associations across large stretches of a work, and the formal integration of motives within individual closed-form numbers, are, to a very great extent, mutually exclusive. In Wagnerian music drama, the leitmotiv became the essential form-building element at the moment when Wagner abandoned the 'number'. The example of *Der fliegende Holländer*, and, above all, Erik's account of his dream, could be used to demonstrate that the motives of reminiscence—which are not leitmotivs at this stage—are mere interpolations, irrelevant to the formal structure of the individual numbers, to an extent that is in direct ratio to their success in establishing more far-reaching associations.

The question we need to ask, therefore, unless we insist on forcing

[8] *Der heroische Stil in der Oper* (Leipzig, 1924).
[9] 'Über Tonsymbole in Beethovens "Fidelio"', in *Beethoven-Studien*, ed. E. Schenk (Vienna, 1970), 223-52.

upon Beethoven problems he never set himself, is this: did he use recurrent musical symbols primarily in the context of individual numbers, or in that of the whole work?

Integration within a number was fraught with problems, in so far as the chromatic figure that Schenk took as his example is not a clearly delineated, concrete motive, but an abstract structure; rhythm, direction (up or down), and length can all vary, and its metaphorical significance is no better defined, for all its localization within what Kurt Huber called a 'sphere'.[10]

At any given moment the figure's significance is concrete and specific, because of its relation to the text and the dramatic situation. But its outlines grow hazy in the overall context, and it is obvious that a figure equally adept at expressing the domestic misery lack of money can cause ('traurig schleppt sich fort das Leben', p. 65 of the score in the old *Gesamtausgabe*), Pizarro's death threat (pp. 206–7) and Florestan's suffering (p. 171), is not up to the role of the motive of reminiscence which creates, from within, a network of motivic–symbolic relationships across the expanse of an entire opera.

It would of course be over-hasty to deny each and every association that consists of abstract (rhythmically varied) chromaticism, on the grounds that it cannot be strictly proved, unlike those that take the form of the recurrence of rhythmically identical motivic shapes. Whether or not different, rhythmically and motivically concrete realizations of the chromatic figure may properly be related to one another, inside or outside the limits of a number, depends in no small measure on the formal functions of the motives: a substantial association (in the sense of a motivic one, with contingent symbolic significance) and a formal association are two aspects of the same thing.

In the introduction to Florestan's aria, the sighing figures Db–C and F–E (bars 11–12) are products of the tetrachord F–E–Eb–Db–C (bars 1–8) and also of the comparably chromatic counterpoint (bars 6–10: Gb–F and F–E); this constitutes a recognizable association, in spite of the drastic difference in the rhythmic patterns. Once the listener has become conscious of the semitonal structures—regardless of rhythm—as motivic material, and not just intervallic phenomena, he encounters them everywhere; even the positively baroque chromatic figure painted by the word 'Leiden' (suffering) at the end of the recitative proves to be integrated into the form (rather than sticking out from its context as an expressive element).

In the quartet, No. 14, which constitutes the peripeteia of the drama, the chromatic motives are independent of each other from the

[10] *Musikästhetik* (Ettal, 1954), 192–7.

point of view of both form and content, and appear to be nothing but momentary musical symbols, bearing only on the immediate text. Pizarro's vengeful outburst is underlain by a chordal progression of interlocking seconds, which are based upon chromatic third-progressions: G–G#–A–Bb and Bb–B–C–C# (pp. 206–7; Ex. 10.1). A

Ex. 10.1

little later, a chromatic progression rising through a fourth expresses Leonore's resolution in the face of death (p. 209; Ex. 10.2). And

Ex. 10.2

durch · boh · ren mußt du   erst die · se   Brust

Pizarro's threat, once again, involves a chromatic outline sequentially repeated (p. 216; Ex. 10.3). There does not appear to be any

Ex. 10.3

ge-teilt hast du mit ihm das Le-ben, so tei · · · le nun, ____ so tei · le   nun den Tod mit   ihm, den Tod mit ihm.

connection between the three passages, yet the fact that they are all products of the principal orchestral idea, which, as the expression of Pizarro's determination to carry out his fell deed, constitutes the formal substructure of the quartet up to the trumpet-call, justifies the argument that the chromaticism—as an abstract structure realized in various concrete motivic forms—is a kind of second subject or counter-theme. (The conferring of thematic—or 'sub-thematic'— significance on abstract elements is one of the characteristics of the 'new path' on which Beethoven entered in 1802–3.)

At the beginning of the trio, No. 5, the chromaticism is one element in an elaborately differentiated motivic structure (Ex. 10.4).

Ex. 10.4

Gut, Söhn-chen, gut

The principal motive ('Gut, Söhnchen, gut') is complemented by a chromatic progression through a third, and a diatonic progression through a fourth. The subsidiary motives are in quavers at first, and then (with the chromatic third-progression inverted) in minims, sounding simultaneously in contrary motion (bars 8–9; Ex. 10.5).

Ex. 10.5

das   Herz wird   hart

Later, the chromaticism of the subsidiary motive is transferred to the principal motive (bars 29–32; Ex. 10.6). Prepared formally by the

Ex. 10.6

augmentation (bars 8–9), dramatically the transfer means that the courage Leonore asks for includes the strength to bear the anguish of compassion. The symbolism of bars 29–32 (where the motives are blended) is identical with that of bars 8–9 (where they are simultaneous).

The chromatic motives are formally integrated again in the dialogue between Leonore and Rocco which makes up the middle section of the Finale, No. 10; at the same time, however, a motivic reference is made to something beyond the context of this number. The chromatic third-progression is associated both with Florestan's suffering and with the threat of death hanging over him (pp. 142–4; Ex. 10.7). The connection between the rising vocal phrase and the

Ex. 10.7a

stets   we · ni · ger zu   es · · sen   gab.

sfp   *sfp*   *sfp*   *sfp*

Ex. 10.7b

Nein,   gu·ter Jun-ge,   zittre nicht,   zum   Mor-den,   zum   Mor · den dirigt sich   Roc·co nicht

sfp   *sfp*   *sfp*   *sfp*

descending bass progression is unmistakable, because of their proximity and the dramatic association. But the fact that the text

('Zum Morden dingt sich Rocco nicht') contains an obvious allusion back to the duet for Rocco and Pizarro, No. 8 (p. 108; Ex. 10.8),

Ex. 10.8

suggests a connection between the chromaticism in No. 8 and No. 10. The analogy in the dramatic content—Rocco's refusal to commit murder, and the later reference to that—and the motivic similarity (which admittedly only becomes apparent because of the dramatic analogy) are presented with uncommon clarity.

Rocco's exclamation 'Der Gouverneur!' in the trio, No. 5, is a special case. The pause on the fermata makes it clear that a thought has suddenly struck Rocco, and the musical formulation stands out accordingly from the formal context (p. 77; Ex. 10.9). The

Ex. 10.9

chromaticism is conspicuous here, and unless we interpret it as a simple expression of the fear that Pizarro inspires—the motivic combination depicting Pizarro symbolizes both his authority and terror—then the supposition that Rocco's sudden thought may be a premonition of Pizarro's murderous intention, though hypothetical, is not far-fetched. Rocco anticipates what he learns only later (in No. 10), and he uses it then to implement a plan (that Leonore shall join him in the work he has to do in the deepest dungeon), which he puts into words in No. 5 ('Der Gouverneur soll heut' erlauben, daß du mit mir die Arbeit teilst'). Regardless, at all events, of whether we interpret the chromaticism simply as an element in a personal symbol relating to Pizarro, or add to that Rocco's premonition of Pizarro's plan to murder Florestan, the fact remains that the motive has an association outside the limits of this number, and at the same time—I am tempted to say, for that very reason—it stands out from its context inside the number.

As a rule, Beethoven tends to create formal integration within the individual, closed-form numbers. The chromatic figure in the trio, No. 13, which appears in a number of different rhythmic variants, is open to interpretation as the substance of a motivic association, in spite of the differentiation within the limits of the number. But its expressive character—pity—does not permit it to be linked to the chromaticism in numbers in which it illustrates the threat of murder. The reference back from No. 10 to No. 8 and the anticipation of No. 8 in No. 5 are exceptions (the feature is isolated in No. 5, while it is formally integrated within No. 10).

Thus the antithetical nature of significances in separate numbers is the corollary of the concentration on associations within numbers. And the fact that formal relationships exist within a single number— between analogous formal elements, or between elements and their products—is in turn the condition which makes it at all possible to interpret different, rhythmically and motivically concrete realizations of the abstract chromatic structure as versions of one and the same substance—using the word in the sense both of motivic matter, and of dramatic significance.

Church Music and the Religion of Art

꒳꒷

We have no means of knowing whether Beethoven ever read E. T. A. Hoffmann's essay 'Alte und neue Kirchenmusik' (Church music old and new), but, to judge by the respect he expressed towards Hoffmann in a letter dated 23 March 1820,[1] it is not at all unlikely (he did read the *Allgemeine musikalische Zeitung*, in which it was published in 1814). At all events, we arrive at a better understanding of the *Missa solemnis*, if we suppose that Beethoven's attitude towards the issues of church music was similar to Hoffmann's—unconsciously, in his musical decision-making, if not consciously, in his theoretical reflections. Recourse to Hoffmann's essay can be justified in terms of the history of ideas, by the conclusions to which it leads in discussion of the *Missa solemnis*.

On the one hand, Hoffmann—like Beethoven—felt that the tradition of Palestrina was the only 'true' style for church music, yet did not believe that it could be revived: 'It must be a sheer impossibility that a composer today could write like Palestrina or Leo, or even like later masters such as Handel. That time, above all when Christianity still shone in its full glory, seems to have vanished for ever from the earth, and with it has gone the sacred dedication of artists.'[2] On the other hand, in his essay on Beethoven's Fifth Symphony (1810), he interpreted absolute, instrumental music in the sublime style as what Nietzsche was later to call an '*opus metaphysicum*', and in that respect he differed from Beethoven's understanding of himself. But after ascribing a metaphysical substance to sublime instrumental music, it is hardly surprising that the writer integrates the style of instrumental music into that of liturgical music:

One thing is certain, that when music rises up in the composer of today it will scarcely do so other than in the adornment furnished by the rich

[1] *Sämtliche Briefe und Aufzeichnungen*, ed. F. Prelinger (Vienna and Leipzig, 1907–9), ii, 305.
[2] E. T. A. Hoffmann, 'Alte und neue Kirchenmusik', in his *Schriften zur Musik*, ed. F. Schnapp (Munich, 1963), 229.

abundance we now enjoy. The splendour of the manifold instruments, some of which make such a glorious sound in the lofty vault, shines forth everywhere; and why should we close our eyes to the fact that it is the ever-moving World Spirit itself that has cast this splendour into the mysterious art of the latest age, as it labours on towards inner spirituality?[3]

In spite of the marked exterior differences in the styles of the 'true' church music of earlier centuries and modern instrumental music, there must be a hidden inner affinity which makes a union between them appear possible and meaningful.

Music that by its nature is an '*opus metaphysicum*', or may be interpreted as such, does not merely adorn the liturgy, when it serves as church music, but is itself a part of worship, 'quite apart from the fact that music meant for worship is meaningless without worship— for this music is itself worship, and therefore a missa in the concert hall, a sermon in the theatre . . .'.[4] And, in terms of Schleiermacher's thesis that the basis of religion is emotional experience, Hoffmann's interpretation is not unorthodox theologically.

Hoffmann steers very close to the awkward question as to why, if a kind of music is 'religion'—or a path to it—by its nature, it still needs a liturgy to serve, in order to become 'sacred music'. But he evades it, and this weakens the line of his argument. On the one hand he states—several times—that the music is 'itself worship' (so that, as Mendelssohn felt when Bach's *St Matthew Passion* was rediscovered, the concert hall can be said to have become a church). On the other hand he contrives to suggest that, for the very reason that it is itself worship, the music needs the *forms* of worship, and that it is only in the church, not the concert hall, that it can find the purpose that makes it 'religious'.

The problems Hoffmann saw—or at least sensed, and shied away from—are twofold: the difficulty of mediating between old church music and modern instrumental music, and the inner contradictions of a music which places itself at the service of liturgy, as '*opus metaphysicum*', but is 'itself worship', so that it turns the concert hall into a church. They seem to have been Beethoven's problems, too. The *Missa solemnis* was intended for the enthronement of Archduke Rudolph as Archbishop of Olmütz (Olomouc). However, when he failed to finish it in time for that, Beethoven had no objection to letting Prince Galitzin have it for a concert in St Petersburg, or to performing three of the movements himself—the Kyrie, Credo, and Agnus Dei—in a concert given in the Kärntnertortheater, together with the Ninth Symphony.

[3] Hoffmann, *Schriften*, 232.
[4] Ibid., 234.

Liszt, at a later date, in the Gran Mass, was to mediate between the styles of old church music and modern instrumental music by transferring techniques and structures from the symphony to the mass, but Beethoven did it by discovering a leaven of modernity in the archaism that was his guarantee of churchliness, and thereby the music passed the test of the aesthetic maxim that music must be new to be authentic.

Modernity on the further side of symphonic style is the sign of inner affinity to Beethoven's late style. There is scarcely a trace of thematic-motivic working or developing variation anywhere in the work, so that the problem of establishing formal connections between separate sections was intensified in a way that made it necessary to find unusual solutions that went beyond the techniques of the 'middle period'.

It is not enough to speak of a deliberately archaic motet style, adopted by Beethoven in order to conform to generic norms that he took more seriously than most of his contemporaries. The fact that motives or melodic components that have an unmistakable musical symbolism ('in unum Deum', 'omnipotentem', 'descendit') pass imitatively through the voices, or are expanded sequentially, is undoubtedly an acknowledgement of *stile antico* and the traditions of the genre. But the mere stringing-together of motivically unconnected sections, as in the sixteenth century, when the continuity of the text sanctioned it, was scarcely possible in the 'age of thematic processes' without the loss of formal coherence, to which no one was more sensitive than Beethoven. Even non-thematic forms were affected to some extent by the habits of thought instilled by thematic process. To dispense with long-term associations, linking sections of the work from within, was unthinkable. At the same time the demands of the text and musical symbolism required the motivic material to change constantly; consequently, the connectedness was not generated in the motivic material itself, or on its outer surface, but at a semi-latent, submotivic level. And it is this resort to submotivicism that is the basis of the specific modernity which makes the *Missa solemnis* a late work in the emphatic sense of that term.

The almost complete absence of thematic–motivic working or developing variation does not mean, therefore, that the sections of the mass are simply aligned side by side like so many musical pictures, linked solely by the text.

The structural idea of allowing the word 'Credo'—and with it the musical 'Credo' motive—to recur before 'in unum Dominum' (bar 37) and 'in spiritum sanctum' (bar 268) is a unifying technique derived from the Austrian tradition of the 'Credo' mass. (The view that, by the insistence of the constant repetition, Beethoven was attempting to stifle his own religious doubts, cannot be proved or disproved, although the investing of a convention with subjective significance cannot be categorically ruled out.) And over and above the 'Credo' motive, the first two sections of the movement (bars 1–123) are connected by the analogous, symbolic repetitions of notes at 'in unum Deum' and 'in unum Dominum'.

The fact that a generic tradition or a symbolic intention provides a reason for motivic recurrence does not rule out the alternative, formal interpretation—that it is a measure to prevent the motet style from disintegrating into small sections—but is its corollary. The 'Credo' motive is not a theme, however, leading to a development, but a motto, repeated but not elaborated. The other motives, too, in so far as their principal characteristic is their symbolic significance, are scarcely well-suited to thematic–motivic working in isolation from the text. (The separation of the final bars of the 'consubstantialem' fugato theme for sequential treatment in bars 82–6 is less a sonata technique than a fugal one.)

Although they remain semi-latent, the submotivic relationships are of fundamental importance, because they establish formal musical coherence, even without reference to the antithesis between the symphonic style that is in abeyance in the *Missa solemnis*, and the motet style that Beethoven adopted, without fully trusting it to support the burden he wanted it to bear.

Bars 1–2, preceding the first statement of the 'Credo' motive, appear to do no more than establish the tonality, like the opening chords of the 'Eroica', while the 'Credo' motive itself—veering between B flat major and F major—presents it less positively. The opening reappears in bars 14–15, however, in the modified form of a three-note figure (G–F–D), which recurs in bar 24, and can be shown to constitute the substance of a long-term association: the downwards-hurtling three-note motive G–F–D on 'descendit' (bars 114–17) is contracted, when it recurs in the orchestra (bars 120–3), in such a way that not only does the outline of the opening of the movement appear, but also the original version of the word 'descendit' (bars 98–9) is recalled (E♭–D♭–B♭).

Another feature that can be interpreted as a submotivic structure is the means whereby the words 'Patrem omnipotentem' (bars 17–19) are related to 'omnia facta sunt' (bars 83–6), with the motion from G to A♭ at the earlier juncture providing the model for the G–C/A♭–D♭ sequence at the later. If we further note that the arpeggiated triad at

'Deum de Deo' (bars 61–70) recurs as an instrumental figure at 'Qui propter nos homines' (bars 90–111), it is scarcely an exaggeration to speak of a dense network of submotivic associations.

The structure based on submotivic associations differs from symphonic form in that it is not 'dynamic'. Although the sections are linked, they do not proceed out of one another, but line up next to one another, like sections in motet style. The word 'process' cannot be used, because a formal process exists when consequences are drawn from thematic–motivic 'data'. The musical figure which creates a connection between bars 1–2, 14–15, 24, 98–9, and 120–1 is not a 'datum' that is developed, and the musical association that links these bars cannot be understood in terms of a 'consequence'. A group of notes, apparently serving only an introductory function (bars 1–2), acquires motivic or submotivic significance (bars 14–15 and bar 24); a chance to refer back to the three-note figure (bars 98–9) is at first sacrificed for the sake of vivid symbolism on the word 'descendit', but the reference is brought in eventually, emerging out of a variant on the 'descendit' motive: a variant which enables the end of the movement to recall its opening—no question, the sheer number of the references that pass to and fro between the elements like threads in a fabric creates associations, and weaves coherence, but it is not a formal process. For one thing, it is a matter of common intervallic material presented in various rhythmic forms, and not of fixed rhythmic patterns and varying intervallic material, as in Beethoven's thematic–motivic processes. For another, the temporal structure is not goal-directed, not 'teleological'. Beethoven does not proceed from data that give rise to consequences, but uses a technique of referring back in order to reveal only in retrospect the formal significance of the things that are recalled.

In the 'Et incarnatus' Beethoven appears to have assimilated the conventional association of the liturgical and the archaic, the origins of which lie in the stylistic division into *'prima'* and *'seconda prattica'*; this would correspond to the resolution he made at the beginning of his work on the *Missa solemnis*: to go through 'all the monks' church chorales' with regard to 'perfect prosody', 'in order to write true church music'.[5]

It must be admitted that the Dorian melody of the 'Et incarnatus'—an example of 'style quotation' which, nevertheless, does not come from the chorale repertory—is an ambivalent construction. The context in which it is found is at least as important as the inherent historical implications, and the initial effect of the

[5] A. Schmitz, *Das romantische Beethovenbild* (Berlin and Bonn, 1927), 96.

context is unsettling. The 'fluttering' flute solo, interpreted by Ignaz von Seyfried in 1828 as the representation of the dove of the Holy Spirit[6] — by no means an absurd comparison, is not 'old style': an example, as it might be, of baroque hypotyposis. Rather, it evinces a metrical freedom, or the appearance thereof, that, if anything, looks forward to the motive of the Wood Bird in Wagner's *Siegfried*, or the 'Scène au champs' in Berlioz's *Symphonie fantastique*.

In the context of the Credo, the Dorian mode is one of the many departures from the norms of classical style which positively pile up in the 'Et incarnatus' and the 'Crucifixus'. Some of these features point backwards, historically speaking, some forwards. In other words, the church mode is not the 'old style' that Hoffmann was convinced could never be restored, but a 'conscious negation' of major/minor tonality.

Attempts to reinstate the church modes in the nineteenth century usually laboured under the disadvantage that it proved impossible to hold on to their original significance, however faithful the imitation or copy. Even with so well-informed and sympathetic an apologist as Carl von Winterfeld,[7] terms like 'Dorian sixth' and 'Lydian fourth' betray that he instinctively thought of degrees that diverged from the major or minor scales as 'characteristic' components of the church modes — whereas to a musician of the sixteenth century, the seventh or the fourth was as essential a feature of the Dorian mode as the sixth. In the nineteenth century, the Dorian was involuntarily perceived as a picturesque alternative to the minor, and, for that reason, was a leaven of modernity, in accordance with the aesthetic maxim that the evolution of music consists in the overthrowing of conventions. Beethoven shared his contemporaries' way of hearing things, and to some extent he also 'composed it out'.

The cadence in bar 131 is not a Dorian clausula but an imperfect cadence, V–VI in F major. It is obvious that for Beethoven the characteristic harmonic feature of the motive 'ex Maria virgine' — which can be regarded as a combination of 'Et incarnatus est' and 'de spiritu sancto' — was the chord-progression from G major to F major, which sounded particularly 'modal' to nineteenth-century ears because it transgressed the rule that the subdominant should precede the dominant, not follow it. The sixth was highlighted as the most conspicuous element of the Dorian mode by Beethoven's placing it, as the third of G major, in an awkward relationship to F major,

    [6] W. Kirkendale, 'Beethovens Missa solemnis und die rhetorische Tradition', in *Beethoven-Symposion Wien 1970*, ed. E. Schenk (Vienna, 1970), 133.
    [7] *Johannes Gabrieli und sein Zeitalter* (Berlin, 1834; repr. Hildesheim, 1965), i. 73–108.

judged by the tonal norms. The perception of the sixth as the 'characteristic' degree of the Dorian mode—quite alien to sixteenth-century thought—is thus underlined by tonal means.

As stated above, the divergences from the norms of classical style positively pile up. The intricate syncopation in the flute solo (bars 134–44) undermines the metre; the choral recitation (bars 141–2) shows a similar ametrical propensity; and in the 'Et resurrexit' (bars 188–93) the metre becomes irrelevant. The 'rhythmic prose' of this last, illustrating the adoption of a stylistic element of vocal polyphony, is basically more surprising than the resort to church modes, for the tradition of the latter had been kept alive in treatises on counterpoint. Rhythmic periodicity persists more stubbornly in musical instincts than tonality does, and therefore can only be overruled by drastic measures. (In view of the fact that it coincides with the use of 'modal harmony', there cannot be any real doubt that the 'rhythmic prose' is a deliberate example of 'style quotation'.)

The 'rhythmic prose' is associated not only with 'modal harmony'—a feature of 'old style'—but also with other forms of metric disruption, that is, with an element of modernity. Spread out across three bars (bars 143–5) and different parts, the presentation of the chord of D major at the start of the 'Et homo factus est' is equally effective in undermining or disrupting the metre, although in this case, it is done by completely different means. In addition, the 'Et homo factus est'—the 'andante' after the 'adagio'—begins with a phrase that is unmistakably a consequent, a concluding formula: the formal position and the syntactic character are mutually contradictory. The opening of the 'andante' thus takes on the quality of an outcome, and this can be interpreted as an expression of the meaning of the text, the representation of something resulting from something that preceded it: the unconventional syntax has a semantic significance.

The superimposed rhythms in the 'Crucifixus' form an extremely complicated pattern, which distinguishes the orchestral parts from the rhythmic regularity of the vocal parts. Contrariwise, the modified repetition of the orchestral music from bars 167–72 in bars 173–78 is disguised by the fact that the vocal motives are repositioned metrically: instead of reaching from the third beat of a bar to the second of the next, they run from the second of one bar to the first of the next.

The juxtaposition of the archaic and the modern seems to be quite unmediated; yet it can be shown to be mediated if we accept the hypothesis that, while Beethoven regarded the old modes—and the 'rhythmic prose', too, no doubt—as a guarantee of 'true church music', he thought of the archaic as a leaven of modernity, a 'conscious negation' of the norms of classical style. But if the old is 'subsumed', preserved, and simultaneously changed, in the new, it gives an aesthetically and technically tangible meaning to E. T. A. Hoffmann's historico-philosophical speculation that the 'spirit' of old church music could persist, transformed, in the new.

12

'Subthematicism'[1]

The question of Beethoven's late style has driven some writers to take
refuge in the safe but stale controversy as to whether the composer
was 'classical' or 'romantic'; but where the literature has faced up to
the issues surrounding an oeuvre that towers up disconcertingly out
of the period of restoration following the fall of Napoleon, emphasis
has always been placed on the contradictions with which the works
are fissured. Moritz Bauer[2] discovered in the late string quartets and
piano sonatas a 'metaphysical trait', informing all the music, and a
propensity for abstraction, revealed in the recourse to canonic and
fugal techniques, but also a 'striving for vocal expression', manifested
as much in instrumental recitative as in the tendency to give a lyrical,
songlike character to the first subject in a sonata movement, as well
as to the second. The dialectics, which even the most soberly
empirical historians of music feel obliged to discuss, can be pursued
down into minute details of the musical texture: a texture in which an
improvisatory impulse encounters an accumulation of strettos,
diminutions and augmentations, or abrupt outbursts of extreme
expressivity stand in a paradoxical relationship to the procedure,
observed by T. W. Adorno, whereby conventions are 'left
untouched', instead of being 'permeated and overpowered by
subjectivity'.[3]

But while Beethoven's late style has always been acknowledged to
be a disquieting phenomenon, seeming to detach itself from its
context in musical history, and provoking—for that reason—
biographical and, in the fullness of time, psychoanalytical
interpretations, on the other hand it is clear that the 'transition to the
late period' has never been recognized as a stylistic phase in its own
aesthetic right. The word 'transition' is in fact wholly inadequate to
denominate a development that is distinct from the periods of the

---

[1] This chapter was first published in a slightly different form, with the title 'Cantabile und
thematischer Prozeß: der Übergang zum Spätwerk in Beethovens Klaviersonaten', *Archiv für
Musikwissenschaft*, 37 (1980), 81–98.

[2] 'Formprobleme des späten Beethovens', *Zeitschrift für Musikwissenschaft*, 9 (1926–7), 341.

[3] 'Spätstil Beethovens', in his *Moments musicaux* (Frankfurt am Main, 1964), 13.

middle, 'heroic' style, and of the late, 'esoteric' style alike; but, admittedly, its independent existence and significance only come to light when we focus the argument on historical and compositional issues, instead of yielding to the siren song of the biographical method.

The conventional view that Beethoven's oeuvre falls into three periods has fallen into disrepute, but has by no means been expunged from the general consciousness; indeed, Beethoven's own reference to the 'new path' on which he entered in 1802–3, and the profound caesura that can be sensed in the years around 1816, go some way to justify it, in spite of everything. But when the attempt is made to elicit the governing principles of the late oeuvre from the works themselves—and not from the external conditions and circumstances of their composition—this convenient scheme proves to be an obstacle, because it disguises, or at least obscures, the individual nature and the historical significance of the works between Op. 74 and Op. 97. This group of works was, to a certain extent, Beethoven's 'last word' when Schubert began to compose; in other words, it represented the current state of musical thought to which an ambitious young composer—one who wanted to orient himself by the great music of the immediate present—had to relate. In the 'Harp' Quartet, Op. 74, the 'Archduke' Trio, Op. 97, and the two piano sonatas, Opp. 78 and 90, Beethoven struck a 'new note' which, by virtue of the fact that Schubert took it up, became the 'romantic note', although that still does not mean that Beethoven can be classified as a 'romantic'. This has gone almost entirely unremarked by biographers who have clung to the familiar three-period scheme, and treated Op. 78 as a 'minor work' by comparison with the 'Appassionata'; but composers like Schubert and, later, Mendelssohn, recognized it as something that had relevance for them: a distinct stylistic phase which served to clear yet another new path, rather than—like the middle period before Opp. 74 and 78—acting as a conclusion and a finish, and allowing scarcely any sequel. Beethoven, so to speak, relaxed the strict consequential logic of thematic-motivic working, in order to make room for a lyrical emphasis which permeated whole movements, instead of being limited to their second subjects. This was contrary to the spirit of sonata form that August Halm discovered in the works of the middle period. The lyricism that is confined to an enclave in the classical sonata became the predominant structural principle, causing a crisis for the idea of thematic process; but if we approach the history of composition as a history of issues, we will find it possible to interpret the late works as the resolution of that crisis.

The history of instrumental music is to no small degree a history of thematicism and the functions it fulfils: the compositional substance, that is, which gives a movement its formal integration from inside itself; for, unlike vocal music, the source of integration cannot lie outside, in a text. The concept of 'theme', however, the central category of the specifically instrumental style that developed during the seventeenth and eighteenth centuries, enters a curious twilight zone in some works of Beethoven's last years. In the first movements of both the B flat major Quartet, Op. 130, and the A minor Quartet, Op. 132, the first subject (if we can still call it that) consists of the configuration of two ideas, one adagio and one allegro; and the adagio component, despite its historical origins in the slow introduction, is by now integrated in the thematic material, in which it balances the allegro component. But in the A minor Quartet, beyond the obvious contrast of adagio and allegro—from which a rhapsodic effect emanates—a four-note group (G♯–A–F–E) asserts itself latently as the true fundamental idea of the movement, the element which unites all its parts. It presents itself directly— 'thematically'—at the beginning of the 'adagio', and while it remains half hidden in the 'allegro' it unobtrusively—'subthematically'— permeates the motivic fabric. Admittedly, it does not become clear that the influence of the four-note group stretches across the whole movement until, instead of settling for the first 'concrete' formulation, we define the fundamental idea as an 'abstract' configuration of two (rising or falling) semitone steps with a variable interval between them. The more comprehensive formulation may seem vague and intangible, but it encompasses an element of musical reality, and it leads to recognition of the fact that the fundamental idea of the A minor Quartet is not confined to the one work, but returns in modified versions in other late quartets: in the C sharp minor Quartet, Op. 131, the B flat major Quartet, Op. 130, and the *Große Fuge*, Op. 133.

The fact that the fundamental idea of the A minor Quartet retreats into latency in the 'allegro' can be seen as a sign of a profound change in the concept of 'theme', which is closely connected with the propensity for abstraction that has always been observed in Beethoven's late style. The actual formal process—the guarantee of coherence and continuity in instrumental music—withdraws, so to speak, from the surface of the music (which seems to be riven with contrasts like the one between adagio and allegro), into its interior: into a 'subthematic' realm in which threads are tied criss-cross at random, instead of the musical logic manifesting itself as the commanding, goal-directed course of events—as in the works of the middle period. The teleology of the form is no longer turned ostentatiously outwards, with the emphatic gesture of the 'heroic style'.

The 'subthematic' can on the one hand be understood as a special form of the 'thematic'—to the extent that we understand by a 'theme' the substance or subject of the 'dissertation' as which instrumental music presents itself in the great tradition of Haydn and Beethoven; but it differs from 'thematic', in the colloquial sense of the word, by reason of attributes which we can describe (as I already have) by words like 'abstract' and 'latent', and the metaphor of form as a network. To say that a musical idea and the process to which it gives rise remain 'abstract' means that individual, isolated musical elements, detached from the rest, trigger the composer's thinking. The fundamental idea of the A minor Quartet is strictly speaking less a 'theme' or a 'motive'—that is, a 'concrete' melodic-rhythmic construct, generated from an assembly of intervals, a configuration of durations, and an ordered system of accents—and more an intervallic structure, independent of rhythm and metre and with variable durations and accents, which permeates the music and links its parts together from within. Even the expression 'intervallic structure', colourless as it may seem, is still not abstract enough for the phenomenon under consideration: the fact that not even a specific series of intervals that could be identified by the letters of the alphabet by which notes are known, but only a formula as nebulous as 'the configuration of two rising or falling semitone steps with a variable interval between them' serves as the substratum of the 'subthematic'—the stratum into which thematicism's function of establishing musical coherence has to some extent withdrawn.

The latency of the 'subthematic' element is the aesthetic aspect of the phenomenon of which the technical manifestation is the abstract nature of the associations and connections: as the substance underlying the network of relationships grows less distinct, so it retreats from direct perceptibility into the shadows of the 'darkly felt'—as they said in the eighteenth century. But although the network of relations that gives Beethoven's works in the late style their 'deep structure' evades simple, unreflecting perception, it by no means signifies that the network or the structure itself is a figment of the imagination, as the detractors of musical analysis would like to think. The latent structure is unquestionably an element of the musical reality, although verification, if it is possible at all, can only be indirect. The purpose is not served by conscious and detailed perception of the alleged associations, of the kind that almost invariably requires study of the score. The decisive criterion on which alone analysis of the 'deep structure' can be based is the sheer impossibility of explaining the compelling impression of formal integrity that emanates from a piece like the first movement of the A minor Quartet, in spite of the rhapsodic laceration of the surface, unless it is assumed that there is a network of latent relationships. It is an aesthetic criterion, and needs no empirical justification in the psychology of perception in order to be valid and sufficient in an argument conducted on musico-historical lines.

If, therefore, the latency of musical 'deep structures' is in no way an index of a lack of aesthetic existence, on the other hand one of the fundamental paradoxes of the late style is the fact that the abstract nature of the 'subthematicism' is the corollary of a tendency to which it would appear at first sight to stand in exclusive and direct opposition: a tendency for thematic lyricism to permeate allegro movements. In other words, the emergence of lyricism from its enclave in the second subject, to invade the first, and the withdrawal of formal process into the 'subthematic' inner realm of the music, there to continue to exercise its cohesive function, prove to be complementary. The configuration of lyricism and 'subthematicism' encompasses the problems that clamoured for a solution in the period of 'transition'—in the group of works between Op. 74 and Op. 97; and the solution is among the governing principles sustaining the late works.

A rapid survey of the tempos underlying the opening movements of Beethoven's piano sonatas is enough to show that the works of the transitional and late periods differ markedly from those of the middle period (in the narrower sense imposed by hiving off the 'transition') by a tendency to be slower and more songlike. (This rule is broken, however, by certain central works, such as Opp. 81a, 106, and 111.) On the one hand, in sonatas marking Beethoven's 'new path' from Op. 31 onwards, the predominant tempos are typically 'allegro vivace' (Op. 31 No. 1), 'allegro' (Op. 31 Nos. 2 and 3), 'allegro con brio' (Op. 53), and 'allegro assai' (Op. 57); on the other hand, in the later works, we find tempos and characters like 'allegro ma non troppo' (Op. 78), 'with vivacity and with pronounced feeling and expressiveness' (Op. 90), 'rather lively and with the warmest feeling' (Op. 101), 'vivace ma non troppo' (Op. 109), and 'moderato cantabile molto espressivo' (Op. 110).

The F sharp major Sonata, Op. 78 (1809), begins with four bars marked 'adagio cantabile', which break off abruptly, but the lyrical quality seems to carry on into the 'allegro ma non troppo'. The unresolved seventh (b') in bar 6 is carried over the last crotchet (g♯') to form a four-note group with bar 7 (b'–a♯'–d♯''–c♯''); the intervallic substance of this group comes from bar 4, the last of the 'adagio cantabile' bars. Of more importance, admittedly, for the inner coherence of the movement—for the underlying, 'subthematic' weave—is the four-note group that follows immediately afterwards, in bar 8 (f♯''–e♯''–d♯''–c♯''): the outline of this fourth-progression is as evident in the transition (bars 18–19: g♯'–f♯'–e♯'–d♯') as it is in the second-subject group (bars 28–9: a♯'–g♯'–f♯'–e♯'). The fact that it is overlain contrapuntally by a rising tetrachord in the transition, and hidden—as a higher-level fourth-progression (a Schenkerian *Quartzug*)—in 'prolongations' in the second subject, does not mean that the analysis is straying into the musically unreal; rather, it is characteristic of the propensity for abstraction which is the corollary of the lyricism in Op. 78, a paradigmatic work of the 'transitional phase'. The relationship between this lyricism and the goal-directed process of thematic working is precarious: the tetrachord is a 'motive' to start with, but later, in the second subject, it is a mere 'structure', not emerging from latency, yet retaining its function of ensuring inner coherence.

The significance of the 'subthematicism', as the technical counterweight to the lyricism of the theme, reveals itself most plainly in the development, which Schubert would undoubtedly have built up from digressive modulations of the cantilena, but which offered scarcely anything for Beethoven's teleological formal thinking to work on. After two attempts, rapidly abandoned, at minor-mode variations on the theme (bars 39–40 and 43–4), the central section of the development involves a process of paring-down, in which the dotted rhythm of the theme's opening is the only feature of the principle idea left. Contrariwise, the source of the diastematic structure (bars 47–50: e♯–f♯–f♯–g♯, and the sequential repeat d♯–e–e–f♯) is not the lyrical antecedent phrase of the theme but its unremarkable consequent, and the continuation or appendix of the consequent (bars 9–10, and bars 13 and 15: a♯'–b'–b'–c♯''). It is, admittedly, precisely because the connection of the consequent to the antecedent is weak (bar 12 represents an inversion of bar 8) that the expectation is aroused that further consequences will be drawn from the consequent later: indirect logic, that is, compensates for the lack of direct connectedness.

Thus, after a few bars of manifest motivic working, in the development the thematic process retreats into the 'subthematic' realm, where it adopts the structure of a network in which the connecting threads cross at random. And there is no mistaking the connection between the suspension of the 'processual' (in the narrower sense of the word—the urgent, dynamic quality

characteristic of the works of the middle period) and the lyrical
nature of the theme, which is the kind of musical idea that might be
infinitely expanded in the manner of Schubert, but scarcely lends
itself to Beethovenian striving for a goal and a result.

The connection that has been described here, between bars 9–10 on
the one hand, and bars 13 and 15, and 47–50 on the other, is
undoubtedly 'abstract', for neither the metre nor the harmony remains
unaffected: an up-beat version is replaced by a down-beat one,
and the melodic scale degrees of the exposition (T^3–D^7–D^7–T^5)
are exchanged for others in the development (D^5–T^3–T^3–D^7).
Nevertheless, if the purpose of analysis is to enable music to be
experienced as a satisfactorily coherent whole, it is necessary to insist
on the idea of the aesthetic reality and effectiveness of
'subthematicism', because otherwise a work in which Beethoven's
formal conception marks a second 'new path', after the
'Appassionata', is abandoned to the popular belief that it is a
rhapsodic piece of minor importance.

Arnold Schmitz identified the principle of 'contrasting derivation'
as one of the pillars of Beethoven's formal thinking: manifest or latent
motivic relationships are employed to connect themes that threaten to
diverge, so that the dialectics that keeps the formal process going has
a foundation in an inner unity that rests on the 'deep structure' of the
movement. Admittedly, as soon as we attempt to deduce the meaning
of the principle from its historical premisses, we discover that it is by
no means certain whether the contrast or the derivation is the primary
element—that is, if we must start from a 'dualistic' or a
'monothematic' conception of sonata form. The principle sustains
two interpretations: as a means of preventing contrast from
disintegrating into a welter of unrelated parts, by mediating between
them, and as an attempt to justify the dialectics of sonata form in the
face of an aesthetics that, in the interests of unity of affect or
character, took monothematicism as the norm.

In the E flat major Sonata, Op. 81a, for example, the principal
motive (G–F–E♭) underlies not only the introductory 'adagio' (bars
1–2), but also the first and second subjects of the 'allegro' (bars 18–
19, and 50–52), and the result is an inner integrity which can be
understood as the musical consequence of the unity of affect or
character postulated in eighteenth-century aesthetic theory. The fact
that this fundamental musical idea is stated so clearly, and employed
programmatically, up to a point (enough for it to be 'heard' to
express the word 'Lebewohl'), is admittedly, in the overall
conception of the movement, nothing but one extreme of the
manifold spectrum of forms the idea assumes, at the further end of

which the motive wellnigh evanesces. There is a bold reharmonization in the 'adagio' (bars 7–8), and the third-progression G–F–Eb is expanded to form the fifth-progression Ab–G–F–Eb–D in the 'allegro' (bars 17–19), which conceals the origin of the motive; both these are means of steering the motive towards latency, without robbing it of either its technical role or its aesthetic effect.

Thus in Op. 81a the element of contrast, which forms part of the dialectics of sonata form in terms of the principle of 'contrasting derivation', does not lie in the themes themselves. These are presented, rather, as variant versions of a single fundamental musical idea, in the spirit of the monothematic tradition which in Beethoven goes right back to the first of the 'Kurfürst' sonatas (in E flat major). It is only if we include in the analysis a 'subthematic' structure, accompanying the themes like a shadow, that the contrast comes to light. In the process whereby the musical form is generated as coherent discourse, the thematic third motion itself is scarcely more important than the 'subthematic' element that takes the shape of the chromatic fourth motion, the 'lamento' bass. The configuration of the diatonic third motion and the chromatic fourth motion (in other words, manifest 'thematic' working and latent 'subthematic' working) is the form that Op. 81a gives to the relationship between lyricism and abstraction. This is the relationship that we have already observed in Op. 78, where it takes a different form but has an analogous significance; it is characteristic of the 'transitional period' between Op. 74 and Op. 97, and it represents a formal problem, the need to solve which is one of the premisses of the evolution of Beethoven's late style.

The chromatic fourth-progression is first stated in the 'adagio' (bars 2–3) as a counterpoint to the continuation of the 'Lebewohl' motive, and then provides a counterpoint to the first subject of the 'allegro' (bars 17–19). But it is, above all, in the transition, which is laid out like a development, and in the development proper, that the fourth-progression shows itself to be an active element in the formal process, and not merely a contrasting or complementary feature: the thematicism and the subthematicism are mediated with one another. In the transition the fundamental idea moves from the major (G–F–Eb) into the minor (bass-line of bars 35–6: Gb–F–Eb), and is then compressed into a sequence of semitones (bars 37–8: Gb–F–E); in the development the modulation is underlain by a chordal progression which should be understood solely as the 'composing out' of a chromatic third-progression, and not in any harmonically functional sense (bars 77–90: Db–C/C–Cb/Cb–Bb). As a result it is clear, even more than clear, that although the chromaticism is never a theme, in the sense of appearing in a thematic Gestalt, nevertheless, as a 'subthematic' structure, it has as great an influence on the formal process as the themes that can be seen from outside to sustain the musical development.

It is not hard to demonstrate that the dialectics of thematicism and subthematicism is inseparable from the relationship of lyricism and abstraction in Op. 81a, as it is in Op. 78. The 'Lebewohl' motive, the movement's motto, is distinctly 'singable', both in its melodic gesture and on account of the way we involuntarily 'hear' it reproduce the word 'Lebewohl' (only an absolute-music purist would deny that this is part of the aesthetic substance). And in spite of the tendency to half-conceal the fundamental idea, this singableness spreads from the 'adagio' into the 'allegro', if a sympathetic interpreter, who understands music as audible coherence, takes pains to bring out the motivic relationship between the sections, and, thus, the lyrical quality of the related motives.

On the other hand, Op. 81a differs from Op. 78 in that the lyricism does not represent the least obstacle to the dominant principle of the middle period, whereby the themes are subjected to insistent thematic-motivic working in the development and in the coda. Op. 81a is backward-looking in this respect: a 'thematic dissertation'. It looks as if the brevity of the fundamental idea enabled it to be integrated wholly into the musical process, while at the same time the memory of its lyrical quality was preserved in the imaginary text ('Lebewohl') that it 'sings'.

Chromaticism again serves as the 'abstract' counterweight to the lyricism—'abstract', in that rhythm, metre, and harmonic identity turn out to be independent of the intervallic structure, and can be varied or replaced. The chromaticism intervenes in the evolution of the main musical idea, in a constantly changing relationship to it—as a counterpoint to the continuation of the theme (bar 3) and to the theme itself (bar 17), as a generator of melodic coloration and transformation (bar 37), or as the background for modulating motion underpinning thematic development (bar 77). It can be said without exaggeration that very nearly every station in the life-story of the lyrical theme is marked by a change in the function of the chromaticism, which accompanies the theme as a 'subthematic' structure. (There is an unmistakable analogy to the first movement of the 'Eroica', but the formal conception of 'Les Adieux' differs from that of the symphony in the lyrical element, which is characteristic of the works of the 'transitional period'.)

The heading in German above the first movement of the A major Sonata, Op. 101, *Etwas lebhaft und mit der innigsten Empfindung* ('rather lively and with the warmest feeling'), is like a translation from the Italian, undertaken with a view to restoring the description of character that the Italian terminology originally conveyed, but which had gradually been worn down to a mere indication of tempo. Even without the heading there would, admittedly, be no argument about the lyricism of the melody (the word 'theme' is scarcely adequate). The cantilena extends in an unbroken continuum to bar 25, flowing on over the interrupted cadence in bar 16, which would scarcely be a 'point of rest' even as a regular cadence, like a Wagnerian 'endless melody'. If the title 'sonata' is taken literally as a formal prescription, then those twenty-five bars should be subdivided into a first-subject group, a transition, and a second-subject group, but few listeners are likely to be aware of that unless they have previously been rash enough to undertake the wellnigh insolubly difficult task of a formal analysis of the movement. The consequent clause of the 'first subject' (bar 5) is inseparably melded together with the 'transition', which modulates to the dominant; and the 'second subject' (bar 17), as already mentioned, is a component of a cantilena which does not permit any sense of a new beginning to arise. Only the closing group (bar 25) stands out with any degree of independence from what has gone before it.

But if it may be said that the concept of 'theme' is subsumed in that of 'melody' in Op. 101—as if the 'allegretto ma non troppo' (the Italian version of the heading) was not the first, but the second, slow, movement of a sonata—the aesthetic and technical counterweight to the lyricism, the 'subthematicism', acquires a function or a significance which goes even further than that which it has in the 'transitional' works Op. 78 and Op. 81a, precisely because the lyricism of the main voice puts the processual character of the sonata form at risk. The 'subthematic structure'—concealed in subordinate voices, and 'abstract' in that the rhythm and the harmonic identities can be varied and exchanged for others—consists in Op. 101, as in Op. 81a (and Op. 90), of a chromatic progression, through a third in this case. It first appears in bar 1 as a counterpoint in the inner voices, being thus half-latent, even if in a formally expository position. In bars 9–10—and similarly, if less conspicuously, in bar 14—it serves to mediate the transition to the dominant, having changed direction from descending to rising. And in the 'second subject' (bar 17), as a regular progression in dotted crotchets, in relation to a quaver figure, it even forms the true substance of the musical idea. (The second-subject role of bar 17 is confirmed in bar 88, in the coda, where insistent quotations give the melodic idea a weight that makes it imperative to think of it as a theme.)

But while the 'subthematicism' in Op. 101 thus serves to link together the 'themes' or melodic components of the cantilena, its central function is to reconcile the contradiction between the lyricism and the principle of sonata development. The separation of bars 1–2, and later of bar 2 alone, from the melodic context, and the sequential and transformational working of the motives (bars 35–48) are, of course, perfectly 'normal', even paradigmatic, developmental processes: examples of paring-down and liquidation. But the motives are lyrical and contemplative, and they lack the dynamism which made thematic–motivic working seem an urgent, goal-directed activity in Beethoven's middle period—with the reconstruction of the theme as the telos and end-result. It is only thanks to the influence of the 'subthematicism' that the development gets moving at all in Op. 101, instead of 'tarrying' as a 'fair' (if not necessarily Faustian) moment: the chromatic third-progression—vastly augmented, but still perceivable—secretly directs the course of the modulation (bars 35–45: E–E♯–F♯–G). (There is a correlation between the step E–E♯ and the rewriting of the melodic motive c♯'–b–g♯ as a chord: a permutation of dimensions which positively anticipates the New Music of the twentieth century; the progression from F sharp minor to the dominant seventh chord on A would scarcely be plausible without the semitone step F♯–G, which has its foundation in the 'subthematic structure'.)

The elaboration of the descending-second motive from bar 2 does not lead directly to the recapitulation, the first bar of which consists of rising seconds, but only through the mediation of 'subthematicism'. The fact that the change of direction in bars 48–9 coincides with a re-entry of the chromatic third-progression in the bass, far from a meaningless accident, proves to be one move in a far-reaching compositional calculation. In bars 53–4 the rising semitone of the 'first subject' is extended sequentially to form a chromatic third-progression (G♯–A–A♯–B); in bars 55–6 the first subject appears in the minor—that is, with quasi-chromatic shading; and in bar 58, at the start of the recapitulation, the descending chromatic third-progression in turn provides a counterpoint to the rising diatonic seconds of the theme. Thus the components of the opening of the movement are present 'abstractly' in bars 48–9: 'simply' as rising and falling semitones (with a rhythm, and a harmonic identity, that are different from those in the 'first subject'); they are then mediated with one another and, as it were, superimposed in bars 53–4, finally regaining their original form and function in bar 58, as a rising diatonic melody with a descending chromatic counterpoint. In a movement where lyricism rules out goal-directed development with the return of the first subject as the end-result, it is the dialectics of thematicism and subthematicism alone that makes it possible to introduce the recapitulation convincingly at all. (It sometimes happens in Schubert that the recapitulation is merely 'placed' at the end, but that is out of the question in Beethoven. In his way of formal thinking, lyricism could not be simply allowed to go its own sweet way: its paradoxical relationship to thematic process was interpreted as a challenge that had to be met.)

If the continuity of the cantilena half-conceals the ground-plan of sonata form in Op. 101, in Op. 109, contrariwise, it is the extreme contrasts of tempo and character breaking up the musical surface that make it hard to discern that the movement is an example of the form at all. Eight bars of 'vivace ma non troppo', which last scarcely long enough for more than a fleeting impression of a theme to emerge, are followed by seven bars of 'adagio espressivo'; discovering the outline of a sonata exposition in the apparently rhapsodic succession is all the more difficult because the syntactic structures of both the first and the second subjects are irregular. The 'vivace' really comprises nine bars, the last of which overlaps the first of the 'adagio' by what H. C. Koch would have called *Takterstickung* (the elision of bars); these nine subdivide as 2 + 2 + 2 + 3, in which the third phrase is not the start of a consequent but a variation of the second, transposed by a fifth, so that the modulation to the dominant occurs in the theme itself. In the 'adagio'—the second subject—the fourth bar of the antecedent is identical with the first of the consequent (bar 12: it is only possible to speak of 'antecedent' and 'consequent' at all because of the analogy between bars 9 and 12, and bars 11 and 14).

The qualifying of the word 'vivace' by 'ma non troppo' is almost redundant, because the Lombardic rhythm forming a kind of underlying pattern prevents excessive speed in any case. But out of the dotted rhythm (notated with descending stems), which predominates in all the 'vivace' sections, Beethoven produces a motive in regular crotchets (notated with ascending stems), put together from rising thirds and falling fifths. The motive (G♯–B–E–G♯–C♯–E–F♯–G♯) makes a lyrical effect in so far as the contrast with the Lombardic rhythm gives it the character of a sustained melody. (The concept of lyricism, or 'cantabile', in the eighteenth and early nineteenth centuries, and especially in the type of movement known as a 'singing allegro', included the idea of melody contrasting with simultaneous quicker figures, as well as melody composed of sustained notes.)

While the motive of thirds and fifths forms the melody of the 'vivace' sections, and a melody with a lyrical flavour at that, it does not mean that the thematicism in Op. 109 is exhausted in the motive of the top line. In the bass there is a stepwise progression, not unlike a passacaglia, spanning the octave from e' to e, which is no less important than the melody, and the Lombardic rhythm that elaborates it. (Bar 51 in the recapitulation shows that the B in the bass of bar 3 is a substitute for F♯.) It would be an overstatement to claim that the bass progression is the 'real' theme of the movement, but it indicates the direction that an analysis needs to take, if we wish to discover the outlines of a processual form that is governed by the idea of thematic-motivic logic, behind the apparently rhapsodic surface of the movement.

In the development—or the middle section that takes the place of a development—the stepwise progression, divided into tetrachords, emerges in the upper voice, and moving now in the opposite direction—that is, rising instead of descending (bars 18–21, and 26–36). The association should not be dismissed as mere coincidence, even though it looks nebulous at first sight, given the abstract, general character of stepwise progressions in regular crotchets. For one thing, in the coda, which acts as a kind of second development, the descending (bars 66–9) and rising (bars 70–7) progressions confront each other directly, so that the coda acquires a function in the thematic process as the consequence and result of exposition and development. Secondly, the association with the stepwise progression in the bass offers the only chance of enabling the development, in so far as it is one, to be comprehensible as such. The lyrical thirds-and-fifths motive does not emerge in a recognizable form anywhere in the development, except in two bars at the beginning (bars 16–17). The analyst is therefore left with no other choice but to speak of either a non-thematic fantasy on the Lombardic rhythm, or a thematic dissertation on the stepwise progression in the bass.

There are those who suspect that there is an element of system for system's sake in analytical methods regulated according to the idea that music is the coherent organization of pitches. Such a sceptic, faced with the first movement of Op. 109, might yet doubt whether the octave progression in the bass really represents the 'true' theme, and whether it is a theme at all. But in the second movement of the sonata, a Prestissimo, it is quite obvious that the musical structure was conceived from the bass upwards. The top line, a motivic medley of arpeggiated chords and suspensions, rises above a descending octave progression (lightly decorated by non-harmonic notes), which for weight and emphasis is the equal of any baroque passacaglia bass (bars 1–8). And in the development, which only briefly alludes to the

motive from the top line (bars 66–7), the bass progression—which, so
to speak, lifts itself up from the foundations of the music to its
surface—forms the entire substance of a 'thematic dissertation',
compounded of a dense contrapuntal mixture of imitations, strettos,
and inversions (bars 66–104). It would be absurd, therefore, to deny
that the bass is thematic. And the Prestissimo sheds light back on to
the first movement's 'vivace' sections, if we accept the hypothesis that
the thematic-motivic linking of the movements of a cycle is one of the
determining characteristics of Beethoven's late style, so that a
circumstance that is only indefinite in the first movement, to begin
with, becomes more plausible there, too, when it is displayed
unmistakably in the second.

The lyricism which shapes, or at least colours, the thematic
material in some works of the transitional and late style, thus placing
it in a precarious position *vis-à-vis* the formal process, is even more
evident in the penultimate piano sonata, Op. 110. Its prominence in
this work makes its earlier manifestations appear in retrospect to be
stations along an evolutionary path, in the course of which a problem
receives a progressively more distinct, clearer-cut profile. In Op. 110
Beethoven seems to find the direction 'moderato cantabile'
insufficiently eloquent on its own, and first qualifies it by a 'molto
espressivo', then—desperately concerned lest the sonata should
appear simplistic, if it is not presented properly—adds 'con
amabilità'.

If, therefore, on the one hand, the lyricism is accentuated and
exposed to such an extent that the concept of the 'theme' is partly
subsumed in that of 'melody', on the other hand, the first-subject
group of the exposition, bars 1–12, is abruptly split in bar 4 by a
caesura and a fermata, with the result that an essential characteristic
of lyricism—the continuity of the melodic line—comes under threat.
And the rift in the fabric clearly serves the restitution of the 'thematic'
character: because of the very fact of the split between bars 1–4 and
5–12, the combination of the melody from the first group and the
accompaniment from the second, which occurs in the development
(bar 40), has the effect of a reconciliation, a harmonization such as is
possible only when there has been rupture. The fact that a musical
idea can contain a dialectical barb, instead of presenting a smooth
onward   flow   to   which   listeners   can   abandon   themselves
unreflectingly, is one of the traits which decisively distinguish a
theme from a melody—or, to express it hyperbolically, musical
drama from musical lyricism.

It is not that there is any lack of associations and links between bars
1–4 on the one hand, and bars 5–12 on the other. Bar 10 is a repeat

of bar 3 (the metric-syntactic difference, namely that bar 3 is functionally a 'third' bar and bar 10 a 'second', qualifies their identity, but does not negate it); the harmony and bass progression (A♭–B♭–D♭–C) are analogous in bars 1–3 and 5–8; and the rhythmic pattern of the start (♩. ♫♫ |♩ ♩), slightly changed, also underlies the continuation. It might even be claimed—though not without an element of strain—that bars 5–8 are as much the consequent of bars 1–4 as they are the antecedent of bars 9–12, and thus, by a change of syntactic function, serve to hold the two divergent segments of the first-subject group together. (This meets the requirement underlying the perception of a period: that the two half-clauses should relate to one another by means of common material while the cadential harmony is reversed—I–V in the antecedent, V–I in the consequent.) It hardly matters, however, what syntactic category we apply: the connection between bars 1–4 and 5–12 is scarcely deniable, as such. It is nebulous at first, but not non-existent. And the acknowledge-ment of its existence allows far-reaching consequences to come into view, through which alone it is possible to see that the Moderato cantabile an apparently rhapsodic movement, threatening to disinte-grate into emphatically lyrical elements on the one hand, and mere figuration on the other—does in fact manifest the musical logic that is one of the aesthetic and technical norms of the sonata genre.

The connections are, admittedly, abstract: the beginning of the transition (bars 12–15) rests on the same harmonic foundation (A flat major: $I-V^4_3-I^6-V^7$) at the beginning of the movement (bars 1–4); the harmonic repetition in bars 1–2, 5–6, and 12–13 acts as the counterpart to a continuous rhythmic intensification (the beat is divided first into quavers, then semiquavers, and finally demisemiquavers). In view of their abstract nature (and the harmonic framework is too banal to register), these associations may seem at first to be of only incidental interest, exercising little influence on the impression the listener has of the form, and insufficient, at all events, to justify the concept of 'thematic-motivic process'. But it is precisely as an abstract and 'subthematic' course of events that they complement the lyrical cast of the musical ideas—exactly as in other sonatas of the transitional and late period. In movements where the predominance of lyricism prevents, or at least inhibits, processual, goal-directed discourse, it is the network of 'submotivic' relationships that justifies the sonata's pretensions to be an example of musical logic, and not a rhapsodic fantasy.

That the harmonic agreement of the first-subject group with the transition is not a trivial coincidence is revealed in the recapitulation (bars 56–9), where the theme from the start of the movement and the demisemiquaver figuration of the elaboration are superimposed, so that they are heard simultaneously. The perspective gained in the recapitulation is aesthetically decisive, for it is essentially in retrospect that musical form falls into shape. The exposition, too, looks different from this vantage point: things that appeared at first to be juxtaposed without relation, and joined together only by frail 'subthematic' threads, turn out unexpectedly to be complementary: first-subject group and transition may be said to be two sides of the same thing. The construction of abstract associations—the recourse to categories with a high degree of generality, such as 'harmonic foundation', or 'underlying rhythmic pattern'—is not, as it seemed, a quirk of analysts in love with system for system's sake, but stands revealed in the recapitulation as an essential element of Beethoven's formal thinking: an element which proceeds from the fact that the composer can use abstractions exactly as he does themes and motives.

When a thematic—or 'subthematic'—connection reaches across from one movement to another, as in Op. 109, that is one of the traits of a musical logic that is less a goal-directed process than a network, the strands of which can radiate in all directions. Associations that take this form are, however, as already mentioned, the corollary of a lyricism that beckons us to linger in contemplation, and eschews the drama of determining the present from the vantage point of the future.

In Op. 110, the connection of two separate movements of the cycle—the Moderato cantabile and the closing fugue—is less explicit than in Op. 109, but one senses it nevertheless, and it makes its aesthetic effect. The intervallic outline of the fugal subject, or of its start (Ab–Db–Bb–Eb), is prefigured in the first subject of the first movement, although the absence of the first note (C) in the Finale may be said to render the connection latent. (It is also possible, but not unavoidable, to discern the continuation of the fugal subject in bars 1–4 of the Moderato cantabile.)

The material association of the first movement and the concluding fugue is closely related to a functional one, which is manifested as the inner connection between two realizations of the principle of recapitulation. At the end (bar 185), after the fugue proper, the fugal subject has assumed the shape of a triumphant 'cantabile', and—by contrast with the first subject of the first movement—this lyricism is 'achieved', the product of a development, not simply 'given'. And the antithesis of the smoothly flowing melody and the animated countersubject, which characterizes the cantabile in the Finale as a 'singing allegro', involuntarily brings to mind bars 56-9 of the first movement: the startling moment in the recapitulation when the first subject and the demisemiquaver figuration from the transition are presented simultaneously. The counter-subject to the 'cantabile' of the fugue's closing section is also thematic, however. For the clear separation of two fourths (C–F–Eb–Ab), which derives from the subject, and has been diminished by stages in the concluding section of the fugue proper (appearing in dotted crotchets in bar 137, in quavers in bar 152, and in semiquavers in bar 168), is finally reduced to an inconspicuousness which signifies a retreat of the thematic into the 'subthematic'. But the common origin from which both the 'cantabile' and its 'subthematic' counterpoint grew was the fugal subject itself, which has contained from the first a vague reminiscence of the first subject of the Moderato cantabile; in its final version, which calls to mind the recapitulation of the first movement, that theme embraces not the fugue alone but the complete cycle, so that at the end the cycle sheds the deceptive appearance of rhapsodic succession, and proves to be fully integrated and densely worked.

13

⚞❧

Late Works

❧⚟

1. What is a Late Work?

The concept of composers' 'late works', derived essentially from the oeuvres of Bach, Beethoven, and Liszt, forms a category that we will only understand if we try to get to the bottom of the configuration of archaizing and modern elements that have gone into it.

'Late works' do not belong, in terms of either cultural or musical history, to the eras in which chronology has placed them, yet they do not find spiritual homes in other eras. Bach's *Kunst der Fuge* and *Musikalisches Opfer* seem just as awkward and out of place in the age of *Empfindsamkeit* as Beethoven's late string quartets in the Romantic era or Liszt's late piano works in the 'neo-Romantic'.

The correlative of the chronological 'homelessness' of late works is an anticipatory modernity. Yet they do not establish a direct tradition, of which they could be said to be the earliest examples, and hence they are not progressive in the usual sense of the word. The influence of Beethoven on Mendelssohn's early string quartets, Opp. 12 and 13, is an exception to the usual course of history, which leaves a gap between the time when these works were written and the era that assimilated them. And the form their influence takes is not so much that they lay a foundation for later work, as that they are validated by later developments which they have done little or nothing directly to generate. Their after-history is discontinuous.

The sense of 'timelessness' that emanates from late works is profoundly different from that attributed to 'classic' works. When its aesthetic validity matures in the later existence which is its true life, the classic work seems to be detached from the age in which it was written, and the historical conditions in which it came into being fall away from it. It is characteristic of a late work, on the other hand, that already, while it is still new, it is inwardly alien to the age to which it outwardly belongs. It is not in its aesthetic survival alone, but even in its historical origins, too, that a gulf separates it from the age that gives it a date.

The outcome, however, of the paradox that the 'timelessness' of a late work is already manifest in its historical genesis, and not first—like a classic work—in its aesthetic maturity, is a strange and elusive relationship to past and future alike. The 'archaizing' element—that is not the right word, but there is no better alternative—does not mean that the past is 'summoned up' by means of contrapuntal techniques or church modes, but that it is still 'present' in a particular sense. The distinction between past, present, and future fades and becomes unimportant. Nothing would be more mistaken than to extract what is archaizing in Beethoven's late quartets—the 'Lydian mode'—and what is modern—the abstract nature of the four-note figure that roams through them, like a harbinger of the twentieth century—and set them up in mutual opposition. Rather, the aesthetic 'present' proves independent of the chronological distinctions between 'past' and 'future'. The modernity of a late work is not a matter of the 'introduction' of something that is yet to come: with Bach, Beethoven, and Liszt alike, it was not discovered in them until the future it anticipated had long become the present.

The dialectical antithesis of subject and object appears to be resolved in a classic work, but in a late work it is a vigorous source of dichotomies. The fact that some commentators on Beethoven speak of extreme subjectivity, and others of a retraction in objectivity, is not a chance difference of opinion but the sign of an ambivalence inherent in the facts of the matter. In a certain sense we could speak of the dialectics being in suspension: the subjective element is no longer 'subsumed' in the objective, and the objective element, vice versa, is no longer 'justified' by the subjective—it is no longer the case that either is 'transformed' into the other, but, rather, that they directly confront each other.

The fugal exposition in the first movement of the C sharp minor Quartet, Op. 131, borders on the mechanical, technically speaking, as subject and answer alternate at regular four-bar intervals (although there is an irregularity, in that the answer appears in the subdominant, so that subject and answer can be said to have exchanged roles). But the fugue is directed to be played 'molto espressivo', and its schematic and objective facet is countered by an affective and subjective one: the counterpoints of the exposition are not independent voices, each with its own identity, but patchworks of motives that serve no other purpose than to accentuate the expressive quality of the chromatic theme. The decisive factor is the transient effect of the chromaticism (vn. 1, bars 6–7; vn. 2, bars 10–11), not the continuity of the voice-leading. Thus fugal mechanism and motivic expressivity are not sublimated in a '*style d'une teneur*', but left to confront each other as discrete attributes.

2. 'Con Alcune Licenze'

The final movement of the 'Hammerklavier' Sonata, Op. 106, is on the one hand, as the composer said, a fugue 'con alcune licenze', and, on the other, a 'ricercare' deploying all the devices of contrapuntal technique: inversion and retrograde, augmentation and stretto. Interpretation of the fugue can begin with the attempt to grasp the relationship between free and strict counterpoint as an expression of the historical situation of fugue in the 'age of the sonata'.

The strangest manipulation to which Beethoven subjects the theme—over and above the traditional 'arts'—consists in conspicuous repositioning of accents within the bar (inconspicuous shifts are also found in Bach, where they do not so much undermine the metre as serve to indicate weak articulation thereof). In the second development (counting the exposition as the first), the originally down-beat-accented theme enters on the third of the three beats in the bar as subject (bar 52), and on the second as answer (bar 65). There is a certain wilfulness in this change of accent, but it serves a formal function in a context wider than that of the fugue alone, by drawing attention to the relationship between the fugal theme and the first subject of the first movement, which was previously hidden by the metrical difference between them (Ex. 13.1). Although the

Ex. 13.1

connection is restricted to three notes, the emotionally charged and dramatic leap makes it aesthetically real. And the fourfold appearance, in different keys, of the three-note head-motive on its own (bars 48–51), before the subject enters in its entirety in the second development, emphasizes both the metrical realignment, and the isolation and highlighting of the notes common to the fugal theme and the first subject of the first movement.

While the second development, therefore, is characterized by metrical variations, which reveal wider associations, the third (bar 94) is underlain by an augmentation of the theme which, like the shifts of accent, is not merely a demonstration of contrapuntal skills, but belongs in the context of motivic relationships. A fragment of the countersubject is already related to a motive in the theme as early as the exposition (bars 31-2; Ex. 13.2). And it is certainly no accident

Ex. 13.2

that, at the end of the second exposition (bars 71–9), it is precisely the suggestion of augmentation that is expanded sequentially: the 'segment' in the second development anticipates the third. Furthermore, the connection is underlined by the prominence of parallel sixths in both sections.

Motivic relationships constructed from an abstract element like parallel sixths in stepwise motion are a technique of sonata form, rather than of fugue. The boundary between sonata and fugue is seen to be especially fluid in the fourth development, which is based on the theme in retrograde (B minor bars 153–8, and D major bars 162–7). The use of the head-motive (the last three notes in the retrograde version) as a counterpoint (bars 154 and 163) might be interpreted as a fugal technique, but the direction 'cantabile', turning the original character of the head-motive into its direct opposite, causes the inversion to become an embodiment of the principle of 'contrasting derivation', which emanates from the 'spirit of the sonata'. Using repeated statements of the head-motive to confront its own retrograde version (bars 159–161) is another dramatic, sonata-form-like procedure.

In addition to the *rapprochement* of sonata form and fugue, another feature characteristic of Beethoven's late works is the affinity of both principles—and they are indeed principles, not merely forms—to the cycle of variations.

Without straying into byways of wilful speculation, we can compare the divers forms the theme characteristically adopts in individual fugal developments with what Schoenberg called the 'motives of the variation'. In the 'Diabelli' Variations, Op. 120, quite small segments are detached from the theme, and made the 'motive' of individual variations, while rhythm is the distinctive feature as a rule: the whole course of Variation 28, for example, is governed by the semitone figure from the two-quaver up-beat to bar 1 and bar 5 of the theme.

If, in the fugue of Op. 106, the internal structure of the theme has a dramatic plasticity that Bachian purists regard as unfugal, on the other hand it is sometimes almost impossible, because of the dominance of the sequential structure, to pinpoint the exact moment at which thematic development turns into motivic transformation. The distinction is secondary in so far as the difference between thematic development and 'episode' is less decisive than the fact of common motivic material, comparable to the motive of a particular variation. When the theme is developed in augmentation, the stepwise parallel sixths are the most prominent feature, overriding the boundary between theme and 'segment', which tends to be random. Thus it is augmentation of the theme—a principle from contrapuntal tradition—which, in the consequences Beethoven draws from it, leads away from fugal style, and makes possible the transition to variation form.

The primacy of rhythm is characteristic of the motives of particular variations, and from that vantage point it becomes possible to regard the interpolated 'non-thematic' sections (bars 85–93 and 130–52), which it would be arbitrary to bracket together with the 'segments' under the heading of 'episode', as formally integrated: like the second development, they are based on the contrast of quaver and semiquaver movement.

3. Abstraction

There is agreement in the popular and the scholarly literatures on music that late works—Beethoven's quite as much as Bach's or Liszt's—show a tendency towards the abstract. It would appear that the meaning of the word 'abstract' is self-evident in a musical context, as it is never discussed; yet if an attempt is made to define it, it proves curiously diffuse and intangible. In common usage, the authority on unclear terminology, it means little more than a tendency towards strict counterpoint, combined with renunciation of rich sonorities. (The concept of counterpoint is accompanied by a vaguely mathematical association, which persists all the more stubbornly in the mind, the less it is justified.)

At first examination, the meaning that 'abstraction' has in logic is of very little use to musical analysis. We understand by an abstract element something quite specific, which can be thought of in isolation, but never exists in reality without being attached to something concrete. Thus a harmonic function that is not realized in a specific chord is abstract, or—as in dodecaphonic music—a configuration of tonal attributes that is not localized in particular pitches, but only in pitch-classes, is abstract. But contemplation of the terms of musical theory from a logical standpoint appears to be just a pastime, unlikely to have any useful outcome. No immediate enlightenment on the nature of musical structures is to be gained from recognition of the fact that intervallic succession divorced from rhythm is as abstract as rhythm divorced from intervallic succession. Yet there is a way of escape from the dilemma that the commonly adopted concept is vague, while application of the philosophical concept is fruitless. Study of the 'Diabelli' Variations, Op. 120, reveals that there are phenomena which positively force the analyst to adopt the philosophical concept, with the result that the truism that Beethoven's late works tend towards the abstract is substantiated in a way different from the customary one.

The following is concerned with nothing more than bars 9–12 of the theme. If we do not shrink from a certain pedantry, these few bars can be broken down to produce a number of features, some of which are concrete and some abstract (Ex. 13.3). The motive E–F–A

Ex. 13.3

remains a concrete figure, even if it is taken from its context, whereas the sequence as such, if separated from the melodic shapes and chords in which it is realized, is an abstract structure which is nevertheless, in Variations 21 and 17, a musical reality conveying the association between the theme and the variation.

Admittedly, a concept of abstraction that is of use in musical analysis can only be formulated if we remember firstly that the abstract exists only in degrees, and secondly that the idea of 'musical abstraction' is not independent of historical conditions. In its relation to the concrete intervals E–F (upper line) and Bb–A (lower line), the concept of the 'semitone', which specifies an interval but not its position, is an abstraction of the first degree, and the category of 'a second', which gives us the choice between semitone and whole tone, is a second-degree abstraction. Both these degrees of abstraction, hypothetical as the distinction may appear to be, play a role in the 'Diabelli' Variations.

At the same time, as stated, the concept of musical abstraction cannot be wholly divorced from historical circumstances. In tonal music, an intervallic structure without a specific harmonic context is abstract; in atonal music it counts as concrete. And there are passages in Variation 20 which seem to be on the borderline between these opposing possibilities.

Breaking bars 9–12 of the theme down into features which can be differentiated according to their degrees of abstraction is not supererogatory, to the extent that the individual particles and elements are able singly, independently of the others, to form the substratum which relates a variation to the theme. It is one of the peculiarities of Beethoven's late style that connections that appear to need to be inviolate, if the musical sense is to be preserved, can nevertheless be dissolved. Not that there is anything categorically unusual about breaking music down into parameters; but in Beethoven's late works it reaches an extreme that has scarcely been exceeded since, even in the New Music of the twentieth century.

In Variation 7 the motives E–F–A and F♯–G–B are firstly transposed to the bass-line, secondly harmonized differently from how they are in the theme, and thirdly extended, by the insertion of an extra note, to E–A–F–A and F♯–B–G–B (Ex. 13.4). The change of

Ex. 13.4

harmony means that the intervallic structure establishes the connection between theme and variation *in abstracto*, independently of the harmonic context of the notes. At the same time the interpolation of an extra note is so significant a change that we are only able to recognize it as a variant because we expect a connection with bars 9–12 of the theme, in whatsoever guise, in bars 9–12 of the variation.

In Variation 5, as in Variation 7, the sequence of notes from the theme (E–F–A) is 'amplified' by anticipation of the A, and it is divided between the lower and upper voices (Ex. 13.5). Furthermore,

Ex. 13.5

the major third (F–A) is replaced by the minor third (F♯–A), so that if we are to establish any kind of connection with the theme at all, we must assume a second-degree abstraction: that is, in addition to the

change of harmony, an enlargement of the interval 'major third' to
the interval class 'third' in general.

In Variation 1 the melodic and harmonic realizations of the theme's
sequence are different: in the two outer voices the melodic sequence
is at the second, the harmonic at the fourth. That is, the sequential
principle is broken down into separate parts, which we become aware
of because their original cohesion is dissolved. In the sequential
model the bass and the inner voice of the chords are thematic; the
sequential working affects the top line, which is not thematic, and in
the bass the semitone is replaced by a whole tone: that is, the concrete
interval is replaced by the abstract category of 'the interval of the
second'.

In Variation 20, the most problematic of the whole cycle, only the
structure of the repetition in bars 9–12 is retained, not that of the
sequence; nevertheless, the syntactic position means that the
relationship to the theme is undeniable (Ex. 13.6). The abstraction

Ex. 13.6

has been driven to an extreme. The model (bars 9–10) does indeed
contain contrary-motion semitone steps, but they are not those of the
theme: the intervallic localization is as much changed as the tonal
context. Also, the sequential structure has been dissolved. Even so,
we can relate bars 9–10 to D minor, and bars 11–12 to E minor, so
that a whole-tone interval comes to light between the implied
tonalities, which parallels the sequence of the theme, alluding to F
major and G major. Admittedly, features like a 'contrary-motion
semitone step' or a 'whole-tone interval between implied tonalities'
are so abstract that it is hard at first to be convinced that the
categories have any musical relevance beyond the purely
hypothetical. But if we do not want to abandon the idea of the
connection between variation and theme—which is, after all, the
criterion of what is and what is not musically real—we are forced to
grant the aesthetic reality even of the most extreme degrees of
abstraction, as being what Beethoven intended. The exchange of the
diatonic for the chromatic semitone reduces the connection to the
semitone *in abstracto*—an 'atonal' category, to some extent—but we
cannot deny the force of the logic.

4. 'The Magic of Association'

In the first movement of the B flat major Quartet, Op. 130, the second subject is related to the first by means of 'contrasting derivation' (Ex. 13.7). The semiquaver figure originates in the

Ex. 13.7

sotto voce

'allegro' of the first subject (bar 15), and the start of the cantilena corresponds to notes 4–7 of the 'adagio' melody which combines with the 'allegro' material to form the first subject (Ex. 13.8). In the

Ex. 13.8

Adagio ma non troppo

recapitulation the second subject is varied by means of a counterpoint in the form of a chromatic fourth-progression, which can be interpreted as an extension of the chromatic third-progression at the start of the first subject (Ex. 13.9). This fourth-progression replaces

Ex. 13.9

the counterpoint in the second violin part which forms a two-part cantilena with the first-violin melody in the exposition, and is, no less than the fourth-progression, 'thematic'—albeit in a way that reaches beyond the frontiers of the B flat major Quartet: it belongs in the context of a four-note figure that is a common feature of the four late works, Opp. 132, 130, 133, and 131. It is not overstating things at this juncture to appropriate a term that Thomas Mann coined for Wagner's use of leitmotiv: *Beziehungszauber*—the magic of association.

A fundamental form of this four-note figure does not exist, but it is found in a number of variants, one of them providing the opening of the fugal subject of the *Große Fuge*, Op. 133. The counterpoint to the second subject in the B flat major Quartet derives from that version of the figure, if we accept that Beethoven made use of retrograde inversion (Ex. 13.10). To justify the assumption that the

Ex. 13.10

retrograde inversion was intentional—and not a construction dreamt up by the analyst—we can refer to the motivic associations in the C sharp minor Quartet, Op. 131. Underlying the Finale of that work is a theme containing two versions of the four-note figure, in the second of which notes 3 and 4 appear in reverse order, in the manner of a motivic response (Ex. 13.11). The assumption that it is a matter of

Ex. 13.11

reversing the order of the notes is justified, in so far as it makes it possible to take the middle segment of the first subject (bars 22–3), and firstly, relate it to the start (bars 4–5) as inversion or retrograde (the two forms are identical), and thereby, secondly, include it in the overall context the four-note figure creates through its variants (Ex. 13.12). The recapitulation of the first subject differs from the

Ex. 13.12

exposition in that, in the bars corresponding to bars 6–9 (bars 169–72), a counterpoint is substituted which can be read as the retrograde of the first version (bars 2–3) of the four-note figure (Ex. 13.13). The

Ex. 13.13

prominence retrograde motion enjoys in the Finale justifies us in making an association that—similar to the case of the B flat major Quartet—stretches beyond this one work: the theme of the Finale of

the C sharp minor Quartet can be interpreted as the retrograde of the
first subject of the A minor Quartet, Op. 132 (Ex. 13.14). In other
Ex. 13.14

words, the A minor subject is identical with the countersubject in the
recapitulation of the C sharp minor Finale, and that means that the
connection between the quartets is brought to light, to some extent,
by the counterpoint, which is a secondary variant in the narrower
context of the C sharp minor Finale.

If we compare the A minor subject with the two versions of the
four-note figure that appear at the start of the *Große Fuge* (bars 1–13
and 14–16), we can speak of three versions that differ from one
another by transpositions of the first and second notes (Ex. 13.15).
Ex. 13.15

(In the A minor Quartet the first of these versions, rather than the
'thematic' third, forms the start of the development, so that once
again a secondary variant within the narrower context creates an
association within the larger.) The second version does not loom
large in the *Große Fuge*, but is to be found in one of the sketches
published by Nottebohm; furthermore, if the order of the third and
fourth notes is reversed, the continuation of the fugal subject can be
seen to derive from it (Ex. 13.16). Thus, in addition to inversion
Ex. 13.16

and retrograde, Beethoven's manipulative techniques include
transposition and permutation of individual notes. The only way, in
fact, to fit the fugal subject from the C sharp minor Quartet—which
irresistibly creates the impression of being a derivative of the four-
note figure—into the overall context described here, is to accept that
the notes it has in common with the subjects of the C sharp minor
Finale and the first movement of the A minor Quartet constitute

Ex. 13.17

sufficient agreement (Ex. 13.17). But if the aesthetic evidence of the connection compels us to accept the common stock of notes as adequate criterion, then we also have no reason for excluding the retrograde inversion that the second-subject counterpoint in the exposition of the B flat major Quartet turns out to be. We might even consider whether the chromatic third-progression with which the B flat major Quartet begins should not also be included, in so far as its notes are also notes 5–8 of the subject of the *Große Fuge*. There is a risk that we could carry on the reconstruction of motivic relationships to the crack of doom, but there is the fact that, in the recapitulation of the B flat major Quartet, the retrograde inversion of the first four notes of the fugal subject of the *Große Fuge* is replaced, as counterpoint to the second subject, by this same chromatic third-progression. This creates a formal-cum-functional connection between the motives, which at the very least speaks in favour of assuming a substantive association, however indirect and remote it may be, and notwithstanding the exceptional length of the trail that leads to it.

5. *Ambiguity*

The sonata-rondo, first defined in 1845, in the third volume of Adolf Bernhard Marx's *Lehre von der musikalischen Komposition*, is not an intermediate form, as some theorists insist, but an ambiguous one, whose dual meaning is part of its aesthetic point. The separate sections fulfil two different functions simultaneously, and while it is sometimes correct to describe one of these functions as primary and the other as secondary, it is not invariably so.

The sonata-rondo differs from true sonata form by inserting a ritornello between the exposition and the development, and turning the coda into a closing ritornello:

1st subject	Ritornello
Transition, 2nd subject, concluding group	Episode
1st subject	Ritornello
Development	Episode
1st subject	Ritornello
Transition, 2nd subject, concluding group	Episode
1st subject	Ritornello

The episodes reflect the norms of sonata form: the first and third consist of transition, second subject, and concluding group, the second comprises the development.

Beethoven's late quartets honour the spirit, rather than the substance, of the sonata-rondo. In the Finale of the E flat major Quartet, Op. 127, the closed syntax of the first subject resists a sonata-form development, and leads us to expect a rondo or a sonata-rondo: after a four-bar introduction, the theme is made up of two periods, the first 8 + 8 bars, the second 4 + 4, which are repeated immediately, giving a perfectly regular 32-bar construction. Expectation is disappointed at first, however. The development (bar 97) does indeed begin by repeating bars 1–4, but they are merely an introduction, albeit one that contains a latent anticipation of the theme (Ex. 13.18). The ritornello, instead of coming between

Ex. 13.18

exposition and development, does not appear until part-way through the development (bars 145–76), and is then in the subdominant, not the tonic. But in spite of the tonal and formal irregularity, there remains no doubt that this is a ritornello, and not one of the thematic quotations customary in a development, because the 32-bar passage is repeated in its entirety. Explanation is not difficult, if we start from the fact that it is in the nature of the sonata-rondo thoroughly to 'con-fuse' attributes of the rondo and sonata form. The *fausse reprise*—the pretence of recapitulation in an alien key in the middle of the development—is one of the features of Haydn's sonata form, on which Beethoven built; if we assume, furthermore, that he knew some of the examples by Bach of late baroque concerto form—which is simply a rondo with ritornellos in transposition—then we can think of the subdominant ritornello in the E flat major Quartet as the fruit of the startling idea of pairing the *fausse reprise* of sonata form with the transposed ritornello of the 'rondo-become-concerto' form. (The concluding ritornello in the home key even appears in bars 277–85, midway through a coda which represents a second development.)

A similar formal idea underlies the Finale of the C sharp minor Quartet. The first subject takes a simple, ternary, song form (bars 2–52), so that, as with the E flat major Quartet, we are led to expect a rondo or sonata-rondo movement: themes in closed forms correlate to the rondo, those in open forms to sonata form.

However, the simplicity of the syntactic outline bears a paradoxical relationship to the elaborate nature of the motivic associations between the separate sections of the first-subject group (Ex. 13.19).

Ex. 13.19

Both the opening of the first subject (bars 2–5) and the motive found in the middle section (bars 22–3) are derivatives of the four-note figure which connects the A minor, B flat major, and C sharp minor quartets, leading some commentators to speak of a cycle. But the use of the four-note figure to link the opening and the middle section of the first subject is an example of contrasting derivation, and suggests that the movement will evolve in accordance with sonata-form conventions. Thus the syntactic outline and the motivic technique create antithetical expectations. In other words, the opening of this movement anticipates the ambiguity of a sonata-rondo.

The second subject (bar 56) serves as the first episode of the sonata-rondo, the development (bar 94) as the second. The ritornello between the exposition and the development (bar 78) is, however, in the key of the subdominant, not the tonic, suggesting, as with the Finale of the E flat major Quartet, a modification of rondo form by reference to the baroque concerto. On the other hand, the transposition serves to link the ritornello more closely to the development, thus emphasizing the affinity to sonata form.

The recapitulation (bar 160) is partly a continuation of the development, following the precedent of Haydn's movements in sonata form. This developmental leavening of the recapitulation is an extreme instance of the dynamism of sonata form, which is the antithesis of the 'architectural' nature of the rondo. The main section of the development (bar 94) is a double fugato based on two phrases from the first subject, bars 14–17 on the one hand, and an augmented form of bar 24 on the other (Ex. 13.20). The fugato recurs in a

Ex. 13.20

modified version in the recapitulation (bar 170), where the semibreve subject is now a variant of the four-note figure which made the relationship between the sections of the first-subject group one of contrasting derivation (Ex. 13.21). The fact that in the recapitulation

Ex. 13.21

the second subject (the third episode) appears first in D major (bar 216), and then in C sharp major (bar 242), is wholly regular in a rondo, where the episodes are subject to no tonal rules; in sonata form, the other aspect of the sonata-rondo, however, the transposition breaks a rule and signifies, like the recurrence of the fugato in the first-subject group, that the development continues in the recapitulation.

Thus the recapitulation is drawn into the dynamic process of sonata form, and that can be regarded as the justification, according to the rules of sonata form, for the recurrence of the first-subject group after the recapitulation, which is required by the rules of rondo form (bar 264). In the alliance of rondo and sonata form, the 'second recapitulation' required as part of the basic formal scheme of a rondo needs a reason in terms of the other partner as well.

The form of the movement as a whole is thus seen to be a process in the course of which the twofold expectation aroused at the start, that it will be a rondo and that it will be in sonata form, is satisfied by the very fact that the sonata-rondo—ambiguous in any case— appears here in an irregular form. The juxtaposition of song form and contrasting derivation in the first-subject group, the transposition of the ritornello between the exposition and the development, and the modulation of the second subject in the recapitulation, all have a double meaning, and prove to be extreme manifestations of the ambiguity of the sonata-rondo, which has to be understood as rondo and sonata form, simultaneously and in one. If the dual nature of sonata-rondo form is to some extent only a postulate, the particular features of the Finale of the C sharp minor Quartet represent its realization. And it is one of the peculiarities of the late works that Beethoven was challenged by a form, the point of which lies in ambiguity, to undertake experiments that led him to extreme consequences.

6. Lyricism and Motivic Working

Lyricism and motivic working would seem to be mutually exclusive. Even the time structures they favour are fundamentally different. Motivic working, starting with a theme and unfolding its implications, seems to be the paradigm of the goal-directed processuality which has always been regarded as characteristic of Beethoven's style: a processuality to which the music is to some extent predisposed. Sequence, which is inherently capable of going on indefinitely, is one of the most frequently used syntactic methods of motivic working; and the harmonic process typical of Beethovenian development was described as 'roving' by Schoenberg: directed towards a goal, indeed, but not related to a centre.

If the time structure of thematic-motivic working is teleological, that of lyrical periods is 'rhythm over the large span', not so much furthering a process as establishing a balance. The metaphor of music as 'architecture in sound' stands for the idea of suspension of time, allowing the musical process to be visible for a moment as a 'Gestalt' as understood in Schillerian aesthetics. The principle of correspondence underlying classical syntax balances the components—beats, bars, phrases, periods—because there is always a successor to balance the first such. And the realization of this principle in steadily expanding dimensions means that the passage of time does not leave the past behind it, nor is it orientated towards the future; rather, quite the contrary, it serves to make the aesthetic present, experienced by the listener as 'architecture in sound', extend ever further. The musical time of 'rhythm over the large span' is a present time that expands with the dimensions of the correspondence, not a progress from a beginning, which is falling behind, towards an end, which beckons from ahead.

The Cavatina, Adagio molto espressivo, from the B flat major Quartet, Op. 130, is on the one hand a paradigm of the 'speaking principle' (C. P. E. Bach), which is manifested equally in the lyricism and in the recitative episode of the middle section; on the other hand it is also a dense mesh of motivic associations, with a degree of complication that merits the term labyrinthine. The movement can be interpreted as a solution to the problem of mediating between the two divergent principles.

The first subject (bars 2–9) is an eight-bar 'period', the simplicity and regularity of which is unaffected by a one-bar introduction and the repetition of the last bar. In the second subject (bars 23–9) the eight-bar components, each 'periodic' in themselves, relate to one another like antecedent and consequent, so that the correspondence is realized in no fewer than four orders of magnitude: 1 + 1, 2 + 2, 4 + 4, and 8 + 8. Even the recitative (bars 42–8) can be interpreted as a period, for the harmony justifies our looking on bar 45 as the overlapping of the fourth bar of one phrase with the first of the next.

The framework, in which the first-subject recapitulation (bars 50–7) should be included, consists of syntactically regular forms, therefore, but it contains irregular sections—the well-differentiated continuations of the first subject in the exposition (bars 11–22) and the recapitulation (bars 58–66)—in which motivic working, the contrary principle to lyricism, breaks out to produce some quite remote ramifications.

The motive from the one-bar introduction is used in the first subject to bridge caesuras, but it comes into its own in the continuation—in the recapitulation as well as in the exposition—as the substratum to a succession of sequences. The manifest motivic working, which is along traditional lines, is less important, however, than the process of making associations that remain half latent.

The recapitulation is a summary of the entire movement, in so far as the opening of the recitativo middle section from bar 42 appears in place of the repetition of the first subject (bars 58–9; Ex. 13.22). This

Ex. 13.22

lyrical version of the recitativo phrase, however, not only mediates between the differing styles that coexist in the movement, but also is integrated into the recapitulation in so far as it calls bars 53–4 to mind, which can be said to be 'answered' in bars 58–9. Thus bars 58–9 create a connection between phrases that were originally heterogeneous and unrelated (Ex. 13.23). A similar process underlies

Ex. 13.23

the first-subject continuation in the exposition (bars 17–21; Ex. 13.24). In spite of the inversion in bar 18 and the rhythmic

Ex. 13.24

modifications in bars 18 and 20, we can regard the bar-group as the sequential working of a down-beat iambic third-motive in a descending cycle of fifths (an interpretation supported by the counterpoint, originating from bar 1, which remains constant). Bars 20-1 on the one hand are a variant of bars 17-18, but on the other hand call bars 5-6 to mind: they share the rhythm of one, the intervallic structure of the other, and the melodic shape of both (Ex. 13.25). Again, exactly as in the recapitulation, heterogeneous phrases

Ex. 13.25

(which originally did not bear the least resemblance to each other) have become related retroactively because a later motive combines attributes taken from them both. Thus the motivic working does not start from a theme, and draw consequences that veer off in different directions, but has the effect of forging unexpected associations between things that were originally disparate. Multiplicity does not issue from a primary unity—a theme, a source-shape—but is drawn together at a secondary stage to create unity.

The fact that the connections on which the inner, 'thematic' coherence of the movement is based are established only when heterogeneous elements have been drawn together has the consequence, for the temporal structure of the movement, that the unity of the whole relies above all on the power of memory. Of course, in the case of developing variation of a theme, it is necessary for the listener to have the original theme in mind; but attention focuses primarily on each new consequence as it is drawn from the theme: that is, it is directed towards the future. On the other hand, when it is recognized that a motive has created a retroactive connection between two originally heterogeneous phrases, the backward look is the decisive element, giving insight into the associations in what has already passed. Only when we reach the outcome do we see the integrity, the previously hidden inner unity of the process leading to it.

When the unifying factor in a process of motivic transformation proves to be the combination of elements, building a final goal—instead of a theme from which everything begins—that process has, after all, a temporal structure reminiscent of that of 'rhythm over the large span'. The common factor is that the form does not evolve from a statement presented at the start, but consists of elements that are seen to make an integrated whole when surveyed in retrospect from the end. We can say without the suspicion of wilfulness that the specific type of motivic working characteristic of the Cavatina reveals a temporal structure similar to that of the 'rhythm over the large span' that underlies the movement. At the aesthetic heart of the music, the lyricism and the motivic working that seemed at first to be mutually exclusive prove to be in complete agreement.

Bibliography

ADLER, GUIDO, *Beethovens Charakter* (Regensburg, 1927).
Adler emphasizes the tension between extreme antitheses as an important trait in Beethoven's character, and avoids both the Scylla of 'mythologizing' and the Charybdis of facile psychologizing.

ANDERSON, EMILY (trans.), *The Letters of Beethoven* (3 vols.; London, 1961).
Until the Beethoven-Haus edition, currently in preparation, begins to appear, the English edition of the composer's letters is the most comprehensive and the most reliable that we have.

ARNOLD, DENIS, and FORTUNE, NIGEL, *The Beethoven Companion* (London, 1971).
This compilation seeks to strike a balance between scholarship and a popular style of presentation. The majority of the essays discuss Beethoven's works by genre.

BECKING, GUSTAV, *Studien zu Beethovens Personalstil: Das Scherzothema* (Leipzig, 1921).
The effect of Beethoven's 'scherzo', which must be distinguished from that of the 'scherzando', rests, according to Becking, on the 'pervasive contrast of parallel parts' and the 'imbalance of answering parts'.

BEETHOVEN, LUDWIG VAN, *Sämtliche Briefe und Aufzeichnungen*, ed. F. Prelinger (Vienna and Leipzig, 1907–9).

Beethoven-Jahrbuch, ed. Theodor von Frimmel (2 vols.; Munich and Leipzig, 1908–9).
Some of the contributions, such as that by Hermann Rietsch on the variations written on Diabelli's theme by other composers, are still of value.

Beethoven-Jahrbuch, ed. Joseph Schmidt-Görg; later vols., ed. Hans Schmidt and Martin Staehelin (Bonn, 1953–).
In spite of the steady growth of Beethoven studies, the *Beethoven-Jahrbuch* has failed so far to rival the Bach and Mozart Jahrbücher in regularity of publication.

Beethoven-Symposion Wien 1970, ed. Erich Schenk (Vienna, 1971).
An unusually wide range of subjects are covered in the fourteen contributions to this volume, from the concept of classicism to theories of syntax, and from the painting to the philosophy of Beethoven's time.

BEKKER, PAUL, *Beethoven* (Berlin and Leipzig, 1911).

The book is celebrated for the subtlety of the language Bekker uses in the attempt to put into words the expressive character of musical themes and motives.

Bericht über den Internationalen Beethoven-Kongreß 10–12. Dezember 1970 in Berlin, ed. Heinz Alfred Brockhaus and Konrad Niemann (Berlin, 1971).

The majority of the seventy-three papers presented at the congress are concerned with issues in the history of interpretation and influence.

Bericht über den Internationalen Beethoven-Kongreß Berlin 1977, ed. Harry Goldschmidt et al. (Leipzig, 1978).

Certain topics stand out from the wide range of things discussed at the congress as the central themes: study of the sketches, Anton Schindler's falsifications in the conversation books (often affecting the most frequently quoted passages), and the relationship between works and biographical studies.

Bericht über den Internationalen Kongreß der Gesellschaft für Musikforschung, Bonn 1970, ed. Carl Dahlhaus et al. (Kassel, n.d.).

A majority of the papers at this congress were devoted to Beethoven; issues discussed include rhythm and metre, methods of researching the sketches, Beethoven's relationship to Haydn, and to Eastern Europe.

BOETTCHER, HANS, *Beethoven als Liederkomponist* (Augsburg, 1928).

Boettcher begins with a typology of Lied forms, and explores issues of structure, with special reference to settings of the same texts by Beethoven and other composers.

COOPER, MARTIN, *Beethoven: The Last Decade, 1817–1827* (London, 1970).

There are complementary biographical and analytical sections, but the biography is not used to explain the music, and the biography is not coloured by conclusions drawn from the interpretation of the works.

DORMÜLLER, KURT (ed.), *Beiträge zur Beethoven-Bibliographie: Studien und Materialien zum Werkverzeichnis von Kinsky-Halm* (Munich, 1978).

In addition to essays on watermarks and the locations of autographs and first editions, the volume contains primarily addenda and corrigenda to the Kinsky-Halm catalogue.

EGGEBRECHT, HANS HEINRICH, *Zur Geschichte der Beethoven-Rezeption* (Wiesbaden, 1972).

The persistence with which certain general statements recur in the Beethoven literature leads Eggbrecht to conclusions about their validity.

FINSCHER, LUDWIG (ed.), *Ludwig van Beethoven* (Wege der Forschung, 428; Darmstadt, 1983).

Some of the central issues in Beethoven studies—such as the relationship between analysis and hermeneutics, the interpretation of the sketches, the relationship to romanticism—are discussed in essays which sometimes represent opposing viewpoints.

FISCHER, KURT VON, *Die Beziehung von Form und Motiv in Beethovens Instrumentalwerken* (Strasbourg and Zurich, 1948).

The author emphasizes the importance of the 'developmental motives', which frequently have a decisive importance for the inner dynamic of the form, without being thematic themselves.

FORBES, ELLIOT, *Thayer's Life of Beethoven* (Princeton, 1964).
The book has become a standard work because of its factual reliability. Thayer's text is reproduced with clearly marked interpolations which supplement and correct the original. What Forbes calls the 'Urtext' is, admittedly, in part a reconstruction: when Thayer died in 1897, he had completed his text only to 1817; the material he left covering the remaining decade was subsequently lost, and in the German edition by Deiters and Riemann takes a form different from that it has in the English edition by Krehbiel.

FORTE, ALLEN, *The Compositional Matrix* (New York, 1961).
Forte's discussion of the E major Sonata, Op. 109, is the first attempt to combine a Schenkerian structural analysis with a study of selected sketches.

FRIMMEL, THEODOR VON, *Beethoven-Handbuch* (2 vols; Leipzig, 1926).
This is an alphabetical lexicon, containing information about people, places, works and groups of works, character traits and biographical data.

GOLDSCHMIDT, HARRY (ed.), *Zu Beethoven* (Berlin, 1979).
The main themes of the Beethoven congress held in Berlin in 1977 are discussed in more detail in this compilation.

GROVE, GEORGE, *Beethoven and his Nine Symphonies* (London, 1896).
Grove's monograph may be out of date from the academic point of view, but the blend of technical analysis, historical and musicological commentary, and anecdotal excursus makes it an invaluable document of an aesthetic humanism which allows different points of view to coexist, although Grove would have deplored it if any of them had been codified as dogma.

GÜLKE, PETER, 'Zum Verhältnis zwischen Intention und Realisierung bei Beethoven', in *Bericht über den Internationalen Beethoven-Kongreß 10.– 12. Dezember 1970 in Berlin*, 517–32.
In Beethoven, realization stands in a relationship of 'creative tension with the work, in so far as the manner, and the degree, in which what is intended can be transformed into sound are themselves part of the composition'.

—— 'Zur Bestimmung des Sinfonischen bei Beethoven', *Deutsches Jahrbuch der Musikwissenschaft*, 1970, 67–95.
It is erroneous to refer to Beethoven's symphonies as 'orchestral sonatas', as the term fudges the essential formal factor of the genre; the orchestra is more than a vehicle, it is a 'partner in the dialectics of the musical form', and co-determines the structure of the movements.

HALM, AUGUST, *Von zwei Kulturen der Musik* (Munich, 1913; repr. Stuttgart, ³1947).
Halm compares fugue, in which the form acts as a function of the theme, to the sonata, in which, vice versa, the theme, however rudimentary, is a function of the form.

—— *Beethoven* (Berlin, 1926).

The book centres on the concept of form, which Halm understands as the 'principle and simultaneously the outcome of formal ordering'. Two chapters are devoted to a detailed analysis of the 'Diabelli' Variations.

HESS, WILLY, *Beethovens Oper Fidelio und ihrer drei Fassungen* (Zurich, 1953).

Hess compares the different versions of individual numbers, in the light of a view of musical form which goes back to the theories of Alfred Lorenz. An appendix contains the synoptic texts of the librettos of 1805 and 1806.

JOHNSON, DOUGLAS, TYSON, ALAN and WINTER, ROBERT, *The Beethoven Sketchbooks* (Berkeley and Los Angeles, 1985).

The handbook provides a firm foundation for study of the sketchbooks. It gives, for each one, a history of the provenance, a date with the evidence to support it, a description of the content, and a reconstruction of the original appearance.

KAISER, JOACHIM, *Beethovens 32 Klaviersonaten und ihre Interpretation* (Frankfurt am Main, 1975).

Kaiser describes interpretations of the piano sonatas by distinguished pianists, with an exactitude that is rare in music criticism. He does not measure the interpretations against a predetermined opinion, but, on the contrary, uses them as the basis for conclusions about musical coherence and meaning that emerge only gradually.

KERMAN, JOSEPH, *The Beethoven Quartets* (New York, 1967).

This is one of the fundamental texts in the literature on Beethoven. It rests on the belief that the interpretation of the work represents the centre on which musicology, the study of style, structural analysis, and aesthetic reflections all converge.

KERST, FRIEDRICH, *Die Erinnerungen an Beethoven* (Stuttgart, 1913; repr. [2]1925).

Kerst assembles the contemporary memoirs of Beethoven, without distinguishing between the essential and the inessential, the probable and the improbable. Attempts at historical criticism are few and far between.

KINSKY, GEORG, and HALM, HANS, *Das Werk Beethovens: Thematisch-bibliographisches Verzeichnis seiner sämtlichen vollendeten Kompositionen* (Munich and Duisburg, 1955).

The catalogue, begun by Kinsky and completed by Halm, is the standard bibliographical work, comprehensive without being unmanageable. Addenda and corrigenda were compiled by Kurt Dorfmüller (see above).

KIRKENDALE, WARREN, 'The "Great Fugue" Op. 133: Beethoven's "Art of Fugue"', *Acta Musicologica*, 34 (1963), 14–24.

When working on the *Große Fuge*, Beethoven appears to have been responding to the challenge presented by Albrechtsberger's assertion that it was rarely possible to encompass the entire repertory of 'graces and skills' (*Zierlichkeiten und Künste*) in a single fugue.

—— 'Beethovens Missa solemnis und die rhetorische Tradition', in *Beethoven-Symposion Wien 1970*, 121–58.

Kirkendale investigates the origins and history of traditional musical formulas that Beethoven adopted and modifed for use in the *Missa solemnis.*

KNEPLER, GEORG, 'Zu Beethovens Wahl von Werkgattungen', *Beiträge zur Musikwissenschaft,* 1970, 308–21.
Knepler proposes that there is an explanation in social history for the mediation between genres of different stylistic aspirations that he observes in Beethoven's work.

KÖHLER, KARL-HEINZ, and HERRE, GRITA (eds.), *Ludwig van Beethovens Konversationshefte* (Leipzig, 1972 ff.).
This, the third edition of Beethoven's conversation books to be started, following the failed enterprises of Walter Nohl and Georg Schunemann, is almost a diplomatic facsimile. Tears in the paper, meaningless dashes in the margin, are treated with the same conscientiousness.

KOLISCH, RUDOLF, 'Tempo and Character in Beethoven's Music', *Musical Quarterly,* 29 (1943), 169–87 and 291–312.
Kolisch does not trust 'musical common sense', and convincingly demonstrates that following Beethoven's directions more literally than is usually done has excellent results.

KRAMER, RICHARD, 'Notes to Beethoven's Education', *Journal of the American Musicological Society,* 28 (1975), 72–101.
A meticulous survey of the scanty material surviving from Beethoven's composition studies in Bonn enables Kramer to point to the evidence of the influence of Johann Philipp Kirnberger and Johann Mattheson.

KROPFINGER, KLAUS, *Wagner und Beethoven* (Regensburg, 1975).
Wagner's response to Beethoven is not only significant in respect of Wagner himself, but also lies behind certain aspects of posterity's image of Beethoven, even to the present day.

LANDON, H. C. ROBBINS, *Beethoven: A Documentary Study* (London, 1970).
Landon provides a commentary to this selection of contemporary documentation. This includes 256 illustrations, which make the volume a standard work of Beethoven iconography.

LANG, PAUL HENRY (ed.), *The Creative World of Beethoven* (New York, 1971).
This symposium originated as an issue of *Musical Quarterly*. It comprises fifteen essays, covering a wide range of subject matter, from study of the sketches to the history of ideas, and from interpretation to theories of musical syntax.

LENZ, WILHELM VON, *Beethoven et ses trois styles* (St Petersburg, 1852–3).
The custom of dividing Beethoven's work into three stylistic periods was first suggested by Johann Aloys Schlosser in 1828, but Lenz's book led to its becoming generally accepted.

LOCKWOOD, LEWIS, 'The Autograph of the first movement of Beethoven's Sonata for violoncello and piano, Op. 69', *Music Forum,* 2 (1970), 1–109.
Investigations of the sketches and analysis of the finished work come together in Lockwood's paper, to give a paradigmatic demonstration of how to avoid isolating the study of sketches.

—— 'On Beethoven's Sketches and Autographs: Some Problems of Definition and Interpretation', *Acta Musicologica*, 42 (1970), 32–47.
Lockwood shows that starting to score by no means marked the final stage for Beethoven, who often broke off and returned to do further work on his sketches. In this he differed from a composer like Wagner, who was relatively systematic in working through the composition process in separate stages.

MANN, ALFRED, 'Beethoven's Contrapuntal Studies with Haydn', *Musical Quarterly*, 56 (1970), 711–26.
Mann revises Nottebohm's condemnation of Haydn's teaching methods in respect of the charge of a lack of consistency, although he admits there are signs of cursoriness.

MARX, ADOLPH BERNHARD, *Ludwig van Beethoven: Leben und Schaffen* (2 vols; Berlin, 1859).
Marx interprets the works as 'pictures of the soul', which can be related to the story of Beethoven's life in cases where there is documentary evidence to support it. The interpretations serve to supplement the formal analyses which constitute a substantial part of Marx's study.

MIES, PAUL, *Die Bedeutung der Skizzen Beethovens zur Erkenntnis seines Stiles* (Leipzig, 1925).
Mies notes the types of changes between the sketches published by Nottebohm and the completed works: these include the elimination of suspensions, the bridging-over of caesuras, and the reduction of overt motivic relationships between first and second subjects to more latent associations.

MISCH, LUDWIG, *Beethoven-Studien* (Berlin, 1950).
—— *Neue Beethoven-Studien und andere Themen* (Munich and Duisburg, 1967).
Misch concerns himself primarily, though not exclusively, with questions of musical form.
—— *Die Faktoren der Einheit in der Mehrsätzigkeit der Werke Beethovens* (Munich and Duisburg, 1958).
Misch discovers stylistic traits that can constitute the basis of the inner association between the movements of a cyclic work in all the parameters of the composition: melodic turns and rhythmic figures are as effective in establishing aesthetic unity as features of instrumentation or prominently recurring chordal structures.

Neues Beethoven-Jahrbuch, ed. Adolf Sandberger (10 vols. 1924–42).
A balance is maintained between biographical studies and interpretation of the works. Contains regular reviews of new publications.

NEWMAN, WILLIAM S., *Performance Practices in Beethoven's Piano Sonatas* (New York, 1971).
In spite of its sound historical footing, this is an extremely concise introduction to the essential issues of tempo, articulation, dynamics, and ornamentation.

NOTTEBOHM, GUSTAV, *Beethoveniana* (Leipzig and Winterthur, 1872).
—— *Zweite Beethoveniana* (Leipzig, 1887).

As a rule, Nottebohm first published the results of his study of Beethoven's manuscripts and sketches in various periodicals, but they were later collected in these volumes. One exception is the substantial treatise in which he proves that Seyfried's book about Beethoven's studies is 'a work of forgery'.

RÉTI, RUDOLPH, *The Thematic Process in Music* (London, ³1961).

—— *Thematic Patterns in Sonatas of Beethoven* (London, 1967).

Réti adopts a method of demonstrating the inner unity of musical works which involves tracing essential themes and motives back to intervallic 'cells' of no more than two or three notes, without reference to rhythm.

RIEMANN, HUGO, *L. van Beethovens sämtliche Klavier-Sonaten* (3 vols; Berlin, 1918–19).

Riemann devoted a substantial part of his immense scholarly output to Beethoven—not merely the analyses in the edition of Thayer's biography, but also the *System der musikalischen Rhythmik*, and the *Große Kompositionslehres*. His book on the piano sonatas gives priority to issues of phrasing, metre and harmony; he uses analysis more to prove the validity of general theories by reference to examples in Beethoven's work than to seek out the individual character of separate works.

RIEZLER, WALTER *Beethoven* (Berlin and Zurich, 1936).

Fifty years on, Riezler's book is still the most thoughtful and reliable monograph on Beethoven in the German language. The first part is a brief life, the second outlines an aesthetic theory of absolute music, and the third contains an overview of the works. An appendix gives a detailed analysis of the first movement of the 'Eroica' Symphony.

RINGER, ALEXANDER L., 'Beethoven and the London Pianoforte School', *Musical Quarterly*, 56 (1970), 742–58.

The works of the composers who may be described as a 'London Pianoforte School'—Clementi, Dussek, Cramer, Field, and Pinto—constitute an important part of the historical context to which Beethoven's piano works needs to be related.

ROLLAND, ROMAIN, *Beethoven: Les grandes époques créatrices* (2 vols; Paris, 1927; repr. 1966).

Rolland was a polymath, but above all a great story-teller, as the biographical parts of this book demonstrate. The interpretations of the works are imaginary biographical and psychological reconstructions.

ROSEN, CHARLES, *The Classical Style: Haydn, Mozart, Beethoven* (New York, 1971).

Rosen's learned essay vindicates his mixing of various styles of writing that might have been thought incompatible. A large section of his Beethoven chapter is devoted to the interval of the third in the 'Hammerklavier' Sonata.

SANDBERGER, ADOLF, *Ausgewählte Aufsätze zur Musikgeschichte, ii: Studien und Kritiken zu Beethoven und zur Beethovenliteratur* (Munich, 1924).

In addition to some smaller items, the volume contains a history of the literature on Beethoven up to 1922, and an important essay on the background of the 'Pastoral' Symphony in the context of the histories of music and ideas.

SCHENK, ERICH (ed.), *Beethoven-Studien* (Vienna, 1970).
The fourteen studies in this volume centre on three subjects: biography, the music-history tradition, and analysis of the works.

SCHENKER, HEINRICH, *Beethovens Neunte Symphonie* (Vienna and Leipzig, 1912).
Schenker's earliest published work on Beethoven predates the development of reduction technique. It combines harmonic and motivic analysis with remarks on performance and a frequently polemical survey of the literature.

—— *Die letzten Sonaten von Beethoven: kritische Ausgabe mit Einführung und Erläuterung* (Vienna, 1913–20).
The analysis of Op. 109, based on the autograph, is intended first and foremost to lay the foundations for adequate performance. In the cases of Opp. 110 and 111, Schenker refers to the sketches as well as the autographs. The construction of *Urlinien* in the analysis of Op. 101 is new.

—— *Beethovens V. Symphonie* (Vienna, 1925).
A feature of this volume that is not present in the book on the Ninth Symphony is the construction of *Urlinien*, though they do not yet represent Schenkerian method at its final stage of development. The polemic against the 'dismal, deplorable, debased state' of the literature is even more acerbic.

SCHERING, ARNOLD, *Beethoven und die Dichtung* (Berlin, 1936).
Schering argues that Beethoven based his instrumental works on 'programmes' drawn from major works of literature. He tests his hypothesis against works from different genres, and expounds its historical and aesthetic justification in a wide-ranging introduction.

SCHIEDERMAIR, LUDWIG, *Der junge Beethoven* (Leipzig, 1925).
This account of Beethoven's early life in Bonn combines biography with analysis of early works and excursuses in the field of the history of ideas.

SCHINDLER, ANTON, *Biographie von Ludwig van Beethoven* (Munster, 1840).
Schindler's biography is more a collection of clumsily linked raw material than a coherent narrative, and it is both indispensable and exasperating: indispensable, as the testimony of incidents and oral utterances of which there is no other record; exasperating, on account of an unreliability that owes less to failing memory than to the vanity of the 'ami de Beethoven'.

SCHMIDT, HANS, 'Verzeichnis der Skizzen Beethovens', *Beethoven-Jahrbuch*, 1965–8, 7–128.
This necessarily provisional catalogue, in conjunction with the handbook by Johnson, Tyson, and Winters, is the foundation-stone of all research on the sketches.

—— 'Die Beethovenhandschriften des Beethovenhauses in Bonn', *Beethoven-Jahrbuch* 1969–70.
The holdings of the Beethovenhaus and Beethoven-Archiv in Bonn

amount to hundreds of thousands of original manuscripts and copies. Publication is a wellnigh unending task.

SCHMIDT-GÖRG, JOSEPH, *Beethoven: die Geschichte seiner Familie* (Munich, 1964).
The book assembles a large amount of the source material on Beethoven's genealogy.

SCHMITZ, ARNOLD, *Beethovens 'Zwei Prinzipe'* (Berlin and Bonn, 1923).
The fundamental importance of 'contrasting derivation' in Beethoven's instrumental works is not undermined by the subsequent discovery that the actual expression 'two principles' is an invention of Schindler's. The interpretation of the 'two principles' as 'contrasting derivation' was not well-founded in itself.

—— *Das romantische Beethovenbild* (Berlin and Bonn, 1927).
The digressions—on Beethoven's religious attitudes, on the influence of French Revolutionary music on the 'heroic style', and on songlike and picturesque elements in the romantic symphony—are more significant than the treatment of the central theme of the book, which rests on a simplistic conception of romanticism.

—— (ed.) *Beethoven und die Gegenwart* (Berlin and Bonn, 1937).
The volume, a Festschrift for Ludwig Schiedermair, contains seven essays: on German and French perceptions of Beethoven, his family tree, the 'word and tone' problem, his view of nature, the influence of the baroque tradition, and his philosophy of life.

SCHRADE, LEO, *Beethoven in France* (New Haven, Conn., 1942).
The thesis of the book is that Beethoven is, 'of his nature, an idea' in France. The ground covered ranges from Cambini and Stendhal, through Berlioz, to Rolland, Péguy, and Suarès.

SOLOMON, MAYNARD, *Beethoven* (New York, 1977).
The psychoanalytical orientation of the book is innovative and original. This is made especially clear in the treatment of subjects like the attempt to query his year of birth, his attitude to Paris and his feelings about Napoleon, the 'immortal beloved' (identified with Antonie von Brentano), and Beethoven's relationship with his nephew.

STADLEN, PETER, 'Beethoven and the Metronome', *Soundings*, 9 (1982), 38 ff.
Stadlen's astute survey combines a large number of different aspects, and leads to the conclusion that Beethoven's metronome markings deserve more respect than they are generally given, even if falsifications cannot be completely ruled out.

STEPHAN, RUDOLF, 'Zu Beethovens letzten Quartetten', *Die Musikforschung*, 28 (1970), 245–56.
The paper can be regarded as a chapter from a theory of musical form. It is concerned primarily with the difference between 'sonata-rondo' and 'rondo-sonata'—one of those small distinctions that have large aesthetic consequences.

STERBA, EDITH and RICHARD, *Beethoven and his Nephew* (New York, 1954).
A sensation when it was new, this charges Beethoven with latent homosexuality. By its open hostility towards the composer it discredits the psychoanalytical method, which is always problematical when applied to historical figures.

TELLENBACH, MARIE-ELISABETH, *Beethoven und seine 'unsterbliche Geliebte' Josephine Brunswick* (Zurich, 1983).
Even though the external evidence remains hypothetical, internal evidence makes it probable that Josephine Brunswick was the intended recipient of the letter to the 'immortal beloved'.

THAYER, ALEXANDER WHEELOCK, *Ludwig van Beethovens Leben*; i–iii ed. and trans. Hermann Deiters (Berlin 1866–79); iv–v prepared by Deiters on the basis of notes left by Thayer, completed after Deiters's death by Hugo Riemann (Leipzig, 1907–8). Vol. i, ²1901, ³1917; ii–iii, ²1910–11. (English edns. by Henry Krehbiel, New York, 1921, and Elliot Forbes (Princeton, 1964, ²1967).
Thayer's ambition to tell the story of Beethoven's life, without musical commentary, and using only material borne out by documentary evidence, leads to a manner of presentation which is in stark contrast to the rhetoric of the popular literature on Beethoven; to that extent its positively lapidary sobriety is a style, rather than a lack of style. Both as a collection of sources and a critical commentary on them, Thayer's *Life* is still indispensable. Riemann's interpolated remarks on the music are descriptive rather than analytical, and were omitted by Krehbiel and Forbes from the English editions using Thayer's original text. Forbes's editions incorporate addenda and corrigenda.

TOVEY, DONALD, *Beethoven* (London, 1944).
This book was incomplete on Tovey's death, but it serves to supplement the interpretations of Beethoven's works in the *Essays in Musical Analysis* and *A Companion to Beethoven's Pianoforte Sonatas*, in so far as it is more systematic in the treatment of aspects such as tonality, rhythm, and tempo.

TREITLER, LEO, 'History, Criticism, and Beethoven's Ninth Symphony', *Nineteenth Century Music*, 3 (1980), 193–210.
Starting with the problems that attend interpretation of the Ninth Symphony—he distinguishes between interpretations that do justice to the individual character of a work and those that serve to prove a theory—Treitler takes issue with Schenker, and then reflects on theories of history from Droysen and Dilthey to Eliot and Collingwood.

TYSON, ALAN (ed.), *Beethoven Studies* (3 vols.: i–ii, London, 1973–7; iii, Cambridge, 1982).
Study of the sketches and structural analysis—in combination or separately—form the centres of gravity in recent Beethoven studies, as reflected in these volumes.

UHDE, JÜRGEN, *Beethovens Klaviermusik* (3 vols; Stuttgart, 1968–74).
Although the preface refers enthusiastically to the technique of 'social decipherment', the book itself consists exclusively of structural analyses.

WEGELER, FRANZ GERHARD, and RIES, FERDINAND, *Biographische Notizen über Ludwig van Beethoven* (Koblenz, 1838).
Wegeler, a friend of Beethoven's youth, and Ries, a pupil, do not provide coherent narratives, but string together memories, which are sometimes quite inconsequential but also comprise some of the essential source material for Beethoven's life.

WESTPHAL, KURT, *Vom Einfall zur Symphonie* (Berlin, 1965).
Westphal takes the Second Symphony as the example in a description of the composition process, from the first sketches to the definitive version, which eschews psychological interpretation.

Index

Index of Beethoven's Works

(Note: WoO indicates 'works without opus numbers', as listed in G. Kinsky and H. Halm, *Das Werk Beethovens*, Duisburg 1955).